The
QUIET REVOLUTION
of
CAROLINE
HERSCHEL

The
QUIET REVOLUTION
of
CAROLINE
HERSCHEL

The Lost Heroine
of Astronomy

EMILY WINTERBURN

For my quiet, clever family and for
Austin & Paul, and the quiet, clever
families they left behind.

First published 2017

The History Press
The Mill, Brimscombe Port
Stroud, Gloucestershire, GL5 2QG
www.thehistorypress.co.uk

British Library Cataloguing in Publication Data.
A catalogue record for this book is available from the British Library.

ISBN 978 0 7509 8067 8

Typesetting and origination by The History Press
Printed and bound in Great Britain by TJ International Ltd

CONTENTS

PREFACE

This book has been a long time in the making but is, I think, the better for it. I was first 'introduced' to the Herschels back in around 1999 when the curator of astronomy at the Royal Observatory, Greenwich, Maria Blyzinsky, showed me around the stores, talking me through the collections I was soon to take over. Piled up, I remember, in the middle of the floor in the basement to Flamsteed House (in the cellars of the former hunting lodge on which the observatory was subsequently built) were a number of acid-free conservation grade cardboard boxes. Inside those boxes – treasure!

The boxes contained the contents of two cabinets that had once belonged to the Herschel family. Three generations had used them as a set of handy drawers, depositing parts of half-finished experiments, lenses, mirrors, coloured glass, a pin cushion, a pair of small scissors. The boxes contained all manner of bits and bobs, invitingly hinting at this family's peculiar mix of domestic and scientific life; providing questions, if not yet answers, about how science and family life might have once coexisted side by side down the generations.

The Herschel family, I knew, were famous. They had achieved many great things, but what those were, or which of the plethora of Herschels had achieved what, I was not quite sure. And so I set about finding out – and from that learning process eventually grew a PhD and, later still, this book.

Where research for my PhD ended and the research for this book began is a grey area, but all of it has been fascinating. I have been to some amazing places. I have talked to people all over the world – at conferences, but also in conversation, the moment anyone has shown the slightest bit of interest in the Herschels. I have investigated numerous archives, often to be found in beautiful libraries. I even met the Herschels' modern-day descendants, who very kindly put me up for a week and allowed me to nose around their private family archive uncovering all kinds of material that previous generations of historians, archivists and collectors had left behind.

From this mass of material – from all the letters, diaries, artefacts and other ephemera – stories emerged that seemed to not quite tally with the existing accounts I had by this stage already read. Perhaps my background in physics made me see things differently. All that time spent studying physics and always being one of the only girls; feeling that my voice was quieter, less confident, less certain than my male peers – perhaps that gave me a different perspective. Certainly the picture of Caroline Herschel these sources painted was very different to what I had read in biographies and articles on this pioneering woman of science.

Caroline Herschel wrote a lot about her life. She kept diaries, accounts and an observing book. She also wrote extensively about her life, especially her early life, in two autobiographies written for relatives in old age, and supplemented these with anecdotes in her letters. Much of the time this was in response to direct questions: people wanted to know how she had become an astronomer when so few women were visible in that field; they wanted to know about her and her background – and she wanted to tell them a good story.

In her letters, and especially in her autobiographies, Caroline was very careful to present herself in a particular way. When she put her mind to it, the image she presented of her life and her path to success was that of an innocent, wide-eyed, but put-upon heroine. She was a passive but grateful recipient of good fortune. These accounts were, after all, written in the years when the Grimm brothers were collecting and recording their fairy tales. Heroines in those stories were kind and gentle, willing participants complicit in their own subjugation. Caroline, as ever, was quick to pick up on the prevailing mood and to weave those images into her own accounts of her life. At one point in those stories, she even referred to herself as the Cinderella or '*Ashenbröthe* of the Family (being the only girl)'.[1]

To an extent, those fairy stories and the portrayal Caroline adopted from them reflected the real-life experiences of women, and especially low-status women, in eighteenth-century Europe. Women were expected to fit in with men, to have access to education only if they had a male relative who chose to allow it. They were expected to stay at home, cook, clean and raise children while their brothers, fathers and husbands went out into the world. They were expected to accept their fate quietly, their only hope of escape to be found in meeting a prince or, at the very least, a wealthy man, and to marry him.

Caroline grew up in the part of the world from which the Brothers Grimm collected most of their stories. Those stories came out of a folk tradition with which Caroline would have been familiar and so her adoption of some of the caricatures in her accounts of herself and her life is understandable. What has always seemed stranger to me is that historians have also often adopted these fairy-tale caricatures when talking about Caroline's life. She is very often, even now, described as 'astronomy's Cinderella'. Her mother, meanwhile, is cast with annoying regularity as the wicked stepmother, while William gets to be her saviour prince.

Perhaps Caroline's mother is often presented in such damning terms because her story otherwise lacks any real tangible enemy. Although Caroline was very much a woman of her time, faced with all the barriers to education and scientific institutions and public debate which that entailed, she was never victim to any direct attacks, as some women were. Her story contains no 'Big Bad Wolf'. Overall, most of her fellow astronomers and the many other scientific individuals she came across were welcoming and encouraging. In a sense, her enemy was more abstract. While no one individual insisted that she stay quiet or be kept down, just simply by virtue of being a woman, fellow prac- titioners of science and the wider world were less ready to believe in her abilities and accept her claims. That she found ways around this obstacle is very much to her credit, and an essential although often overlooked part of her story.

Accounts of Caroline to date tend to have taken her fairy-tale depic- tion of herself and her family at face value. They have overlooked her struggles for recognition in the absence of any overt force putting her down. Most puzzling of all, though, is the uncritical acceptance of her ten missing years. The years 1788 to 1797 are entirely absent in Caroline's accounts of herself. They are gone – deliberately destroyed – and yet they were, in many ways, her most significant years in terms of work. The missing period dates from the year her brother William married to the year she moved out of her brother's home – and they are *completely* gone; we know nothing of them.

At some point in her later life Caroline destroyed this decade of journal entries. What is striking, however, is that coincidentally these were the ten most astronomically productive years of her life. While we have a detailed record of her Cinderella-like childhood, cooking and cleaning for her family, and almost as much detail of her bitter old age, praised from afar by philosophers, mathematicians and astronomers, while surrounded by ignorant and conceited relatives, much less has been written about her middle years. Her most productive period is glossed over, reeled off simply as a list of achievements rather than a time spent generating great science.

It has always been said that she destroyed her diaries because they contained all her mean and bitter thoughts towards her new sister-in- law, and the timing does add up to an extent. These were the ten years that followed her brother William's marriage to the widow Mary Pitt (née Baldwin). However, they were also the years in which she made discoveries, wrote and generally became celebrated for her work as a lady in science. It always seemed odd to me that she would destroy that record.

During those missing years, Caroline was not hiding in her room writing mean things about the woman who would later become her friend. These were the years in which she did her most important work, in which she became a 'comet huntress', a 'lady astronomer' and a 'priestess of the heavens', all the things we now celebrate about her today. This was the same decade she came to the attention of the core of Europe's scientific elite – Astronomer Royal Nevil Maskelyne, Jérôme de Lalande and Joseph Banks – and won them over. Why would she destroy her personal thoughts on these key professional breakthroughs? This was also the period in which her nephew, John Herschel, was born. Why would she not want a record of her reaction to the birth of the child on whom she doted and who, in return, came to confide in her as he grew up and made his own way in the scientific world?

The current portrayal of Caroline Herschel, told in many potted biographies celebrating 'women in science', leaves us with a picture of Caroline broken by her brother's marriage, while astronomical break-throughs seem simply to have happened to her. The coincidence of the timing is never mentioned (though it is occasionally acknowledged that her comet discoveries tended to take place when her brother was out). This book sets out with a different purpose. It focuses on just those ten tumultuous years, when family life was turned upside down while Caroline's astronomical career was blossoming. By piecing together – from letters, reminiscences and sometimes museum objects – a detailed account of that time, we get to see a new side to Caroline. Perhaps she was not just snidely complaining about her brother and his marriage the whole time. Perhaps she had other reasons to destroy her diaries, ones that offer a less socially acceptable side to this woman than simple jealousy over a man.

When it comes to women in the history of science, only a very few have managed to capture the public imagination. Marie Curie might be a household name, but few others have managed that level of recognition. Even after decades of trying to find heroic but forgotten women in the history of science, we struggle to find anyone who can capture the public imagination quite so well as Curie. We do not even expect our male heroes of science to be quite as brilliant as the two-time Nobel Prize winner. Yet, somehow, we expect women who do not reach that mark to hold some responsibility for their historical invisibility.

Caroline Herschel, in many ways, is a more typical woman in science than Marie Curie, and that is part of her charm. She was, as so many were, a scientific partner to a male relative and many of her achievements came out of that partnership. She had less education than her brother and less access to scientific societies. She took on typically female roles within that partnership: she organised, recorded and wrote out their collaborative work. She also, however, made discoveries, and this is what she is best known for today – in total, Caroline Herschel discovered eight comets.

Caroline lived through a period of tremendous political and social change. Equality was being fought for with vigour, even if there was some disagreement about the interpretation of the term. Philosophers of the Enlightenment had begun questioning the natural order of things, asking what it is to be human, how we learn and what is innate about human nature. It no longer followed that the aristocracy and the Church should run everything while the rest of the population remained obediently happy with their lot. The American, French and British industrial revolutions all took place within Caroline's lifetime. These were dramatic upheavals of the status quo. And alongside this, other movements were emerging, also arguing for equality. Anti-slavery campaigns were just beginning, and women were starting to map out logical arguments against their own treatment compared to that of powerful white men.

As all these political arguments raged, Caroline got on, in her own small quiet way, with putting those arguments into practice. As Mary Wollstonecraft and other early campaigners were arguing in favour of women's potential, Caroline was quietly fulfilling it. In just one decade,

Caroline destroyed centuries-old arguments about what women were capable of. She showed, simply by doing, that women could observe and catalogue, discover and study, and even write papers good enough to read to the Royal Society. In doing so, Caroline began to transform astronomy from a very masculine branch of the physical sciences, into something much more feminine. Thanks to her, future generations of women began to look to astronomy as a subject in which they, too, might be able to succeed.

Caroline's story, pieced together here from letters, memoirs and publications, is one of quiet determination. She has fascinated scientists and historians of science for generations. She does not easily lend herself to the heroic stories of discovery we are used to hearing about, but that to me is what makes her story so interesting. It is what makes her story resonate with many of the problems women in science still face today. Even now, girls are rarely encouraged to see themselves as heroes and innovators; instead, we tend to see ourselves as conscientious and dedicated, helpful and hardworking. This difference comes out in the ways we talk about ourselves and our work.

Caroline's story teaches us to look past our differences and to celebrate the work of women in science – however they present themselves.

1787

I

FOUNDATIONS

In early 1787, Caroline Herschel, a middle-aged economic refugee, waited expectantly for her first ever scientific article to be published. As a woman, she had not been allowed to announce her discovery in person to the gentlemen and natural philosophers of the Royal Society of London. Instead, she had written a letter which her brother William had read on her behalf at a meeting on 9 November 1786.

The letter had told the assembled guests, in very polite and modest terms, how, in the course of 'sweeping' the heavens, she had happened across a new comet. She did not want to make any presumptions, but thought that for science, and for the sake of her brother and his astronomical friends, she should pass on this information:

In consequence of the Friendship which I know to exist between you and my Brother I venture to trouble you in his absence with the following imperfect account of a comet.

Her paper ended with a request to Charles Blagden (secretary to the Royal Society, to whom the letter was addressed) asking if he would 'do me the favour of communicating these observations to my brother's astronomical friends'.

Caroline's paper was the very first written by a woman to be read to the Royal Society. It was uncharted territory. To the end of her paper, William had added a few remarks, mainly to confirm that he agreed with his sister on what she claimed to have seen. The following week, the society met again and William delivered a paper of his own, to the effect that he had seen Caroline's comet too, when he returned from Germany, adding his own small description. It was almost as though he were trying to reassure the society members that the observations of a woman could be trusted.

A month later, their friend Reverend Francis Wollaston waded in too, with a paper declaring that he had seen Caroline's comet, though adding very little beyond that, in terms of new scientific insight. Perhaps assurance from Caroline's own brother was not considered convincing enough …

Caroline's paper makes interesting reading today, when women often still struggle to be heard, and are still inclined towards language that can seem out of place in the sometimes aggressively competitive culture of the scientific world. Her casual remark that her account is 'imperfect', though without stating what it might lack, her apologetic opening, 'I venture to trouble you', and her need to justify why it is her and not her brother making the announcement all seem decidedly feminine. In a modern piece, she would be criticised for her lack of assertiveness, with the responsibility for her lack of voice placed squarely on her own shoulders. And yet, the curious thing about Caroline Herschel is that it was precisely because she used this very feminine style, with its exaggerated good manners and self-depreciation, that she managed to gain attention and, in time, respect and admiration. She made people listen by essentially being very, very polite.

The publication of her paper in 1787 was a great moment for Caroline Herschel, and for women in science everywhere, but it was slow in coming and arrived only after many years of hard work. She was by no means a scientific ingénue waiting for her chance to shine. There was little in her early years that later biographers could point to as evidence that this would eventually and undoubtedly become her fate. Rather, her early years give a glimpse of how hard life was for women of very little wealth in the eighteenth century and how extraordinary it would be for a woman from such a background to even imagine entering the prestigious world of Royal Society science.

Nothing about Caroline's early life suggested she would grow up to become a pioneering female astronomer. She was the younger of two surviving daughters in a large Germanic family from Hanover. Their father, Isaac, was a self-taught army musician (his father had been a gardener), her mother was illiterate and without regular work (besides looking after her large family), although she would sometimes take on piecemeal work such as sewing. Caroline, the youngest daughter, was expected – as was typical in poor Hanoverian households in the eighteenth century – to help her mother look after her home and family. She was taught to cook, clean, spin and make clothes, and was required to look after younger children as well as take care of her older brothers and ageing parents. While her brothers were trained by their father to follow him into careers as musicians, Caroline and her older sister Sophia were trained to run a household and to be useful and agreeable to her family. Sophia got married (to another musician) and left home when Caroline was just 5 years old, leaving her and her mother to look after the rest of the family.

Hanover was an area of Lower Saxony and part of Prussia in the eighteenth century. Since 1714 the region had had a special connection with Britain when the ruling Elector of Hanover became Britain's King George I. For women like Caroline Herschel, this region within a pre-industrial Germanic state was much like any other. The connections made by the nobility with another country had little impact on the day-to-day running of her life. Instead, she, like other women in her situation, was brought up with very few options. She was trained to look after her family and could look forward to looking after her parents in their old age, and then hopefully being taken in by one of her siblings in later life. Alternatively, she might get married or become a maid. If she was especially enterprising, she might find a means of earning her own living sewing or spinning while still living at home (to do so independently was frowned upon) or find a loophole that allowed her to work for a guild – most guilds explicitly prohibited the employment of women, but a few left their rules open to interpretation.

Prospects were bleak for women in Caroline's position but, academically at least, things were beginning to show signs of improvement. The Protestant Reformation had begun around 200 years before Caroline was born, but its effects were still being felt and the new Protestant movement was promoting a strong emphasis on personal understanding of the Bible. It was no longer enough, as it had been under Catholicism, to hear the stories of the Bible in sermons, or see them in stained-glass windows, via the priest and the Church. Protestants were expected to read, interpret and understand the Bible for themselves and with that came a need for mass literacy. All children, not just the very rich, were required for the first time in Europe to learn to read.

Desiring mass literacy, even being religiously motivated to teach everyone to read, was one thing, but making it happen in practice was quite another. Slowly, however, a system of mass education began to emerge and within Europe it happened first in the Germanic states. For the Herschels, they were helped by their father's position as an army musician within the Hanoverian Guards since that made him part of the Prussian Army.

The Prussian Army had begun to set up garrison schools from the early eighteenth century onwards, aiming to provide elementary education for all the children (girls *and* boys) of its personnel, excluding those at the very top. All the Herschel children went to the school, though there is some disagreement among historians as to exactly what they were taught. Reading, writing and religion seem to have been taught to all, mathematics and Latin may have been taught only to boys. The system, as was typical for the time and place, was to encourage the best of the older pupils to help teach the younger children alongside employed teachers.

Throughout her childhood, Caroline was kept very busy going to school with her brothers, and after school helping her mother to cook, clean and look after her family. As she learned to read and write, those skills were immediately put to good use and she was called upon to read and write for her mother and the other illiterate women in their neighbourhood, allowing them to correspond with their husbands when they were away on military service. Sometimes Caroline would even go to additional classes after school to learn extra domestic skills. Her job was to be as useful as she possibly could, and to use her education to learn skills that might be useful to her loved ones – and she recognised early on that this was her key to survival.

As Caroline grew up, cooking, cleaning and writing letters on behalf of her mother and other local, illiterate women, she could see her brothers receiving quite a different education. Her four brothers, three older (Jacob, William and Alexander), one younger (Dietrich), were all being trained to follow their father into his profession. Their father was an army musician, but his aspiration was to teach his sons to rise higher than he had ever managed himself, perhaps even finding work at the royal court. To this end, they were trained intensively, with hours of practice every evening. Caroline was occasionally permitted to join in, but never had quite enough time. Her time was precious and needed to make her brothers' home life comfortable, so her musical education was never a priority.

Caroline did her best, in many accounts of her early life, to try to come across as selfless and nurturing and accommodating. Now and then, however (and this is one of the reasons she is such a joy to research), she would let her anger show through. She could see the unfairness of it all, though it would take her many years to work out how to redress the balance. When writing, for example, of her rare chances to learn some music, she wrote as evenly as she could that she 'felt very unhappy that no time at all was left for improving myself in music'. On another occasion, when her cousin came to stay and followed her around presumably trying to be friendly, Caroline complained:

This young woman, full of good nature and ignorance, grew unfortunately so fond of me that she was for ever at my side, and by that means I lost that little interval of leisure I might then have had for reading, practising the violin, etc.

Although she took her responsibilities to her family very seriously, worrying for example how her work would get done if she got sick, growing up with four brothers, all musicians and all starting to find their way in the world, had a profound effect. She had no reason to expect to be able to join them, but she could still envy them just a little.

Then, in 1757, war broke out near where the Herschels lived. Ostensibly this was part of a larger battle (the Seven Years War) between Britain and Prussia on one side and France and its allies on the other. It was about land, colonies and power and was ultimately won by the British side as Britain rose to become the world's dominant empire. The battle that took place in 1757 at Hastenbeck, however, was less successful for the British/Prussian/Hanoverian armies. The French won and occupied Hanover for several months. The Herschels had soldiers living in their building.

For the battle itself, Isaac had to go to play in the army band on the battlefield. His two eldest sons, Jacob and William, should have gone too. At 14 they had both auditioned and joined the Hanoverian Guards like their father, in their first jobs as professional musicians and Jacob was now 23 and William 19. The life of an army musician in wartime, however, was one of extreme danger, playing unarmed on the front line, and Isaac and Anna were not going risk their sons' lives if they could help it. Quietly and in secret, they made plans. Caroline helped her mother work into the night, preparing clothing and food for the journey. Then, one night the boys were off, sent to England to seek their fortune as musicians.

England was well known for its opportunities for German and Italian musicians, who were considered to be the best in Europe. Famous contemporary composers – people such as Bach, Vivaldi and Haydn – came disproportionately from those two areas of Europe, and for that reason every fashionable household in England wanted a German or Italian music teacher.

England had another reason for attracting musicians – there was simply more work for them in England than elsewhere in Europe. While in many places, including the Herschels' home town, musicians had to compete for the small number of positions at court, in England there was a growing market for musicians who could play at the newly established public concert venues and chapels, and in the country homes of the emergent trade and merchant class. Added to that, Isaac had contacts in London whom the boys could call upon. Hanover's supposed 'special relationship' with England at the time also suggested the boys should be fine.

Caroline was 7 years old when her brothers left. Jacob came back soon after when a job at court came up, while William stayed and would, in time, make England his home for the rest of his life. That left Caroline at home with her two remaining brothers, Alexander and Dietrich. She adored Alexander. He was five years older than her and was always happy to spend time with his little sister. They would chat of an evening as their mother spun, Caroline sewed and Alexander tinkered away experimenting with constructing his own telescope or clock.

As a family, they were always busy, the women with endless house-work, the men with professional engagements, practice and relaxing with arts and crafts of an evening – and all this in addition to school-work. Alexander's childhood attempts at building scientific instruments was a popular eighteenth-century hobby. Many boys would look back on childhoods spent trying to build clocks, telescopes and globes, although only those who later made it a profession would regard that early play as significant. Alexander was particularly keen, but William also built a globe or two during his fireside evenings as a child. Dietrich, meanwhile, generally preferred to draw or collect, being more drawn to natural history than the mechanics favoured by his brothers.

Over in England, after several years of struggle piecing together a precarious existence as a jobbing musician, travelling around the country and working where he could, William finally found a steady post as organist in a new chapel in Bath. Once settled and established, he sent word to his family in Hanover, and one by one, his brothers came over to try their luck. Jacob went first, staying only for 'the season' and then coming home. Alexander, however, liked it very much and decided to stay.

As the boys ventured forth, travelling abroad, mixing in high society (albeit as musicians there only to entertain and occasionally to teach), Caroline continued dutifully to cook, clean, mend and sew, and care for her home and family. However, she began to imagine a future in which the services of a domestically versatile sister might not be needed. When her father died in 1767, the realisation dawned on her that her job caring dutifully for her ageing parents would not last forever, either:

> I began to feel great anxiety about my future destination, for I saw that all my exertions would not save me from becoming a burden to my brothers, and I had by this time imbibed too much pride for submitting to take a place as a Ladiesmaid, and for a Governess I was not qualified for want of knowledge in languages.

Her father's warning that since she was 'neither handsom nor rich it was not likely that anyone would make me an offer, till perhaps, when far advanced in life, some old man might take me for my good qualities' came back to haunt her. As marriage was then unlikely, her role was to be indispensable to her family so that they might keep her instead. There were very few options open to working-class women and Caroline had already dismissed almost all of them.

Luckily for her, Alexander was still thinking of her even as he set about building a new life for himself in Bath with William. He thought back to the long walks to school they had shared as children, to their evenings spent diligently working side by side, and to the memory of her embracing every opportunity she was given to snatch a music lesson from her father or hide away and practise when she thought no one could hear or might need her. He persuaded William that their little sister might, with a bit of training, make a good singer to perform at his concerts. They put this to their mother and older brother Jacob, neither of whom was entirely convinced.

Anna was unhappy about any of her children moving away and was not unknown to blame education for giving them the tools with which to leave. Jacob, on the other hand, had simply grown accustomed to having his little sister wait on him and did not like any change that had the potential to inconvenience him. Caroline, however, was delighted and determined to make it work. She now threw herself into even more housework, ensuring the family were well stocked up with clothes before she set off for her two-year trial in England.

William did what he could to alleviate at least Jacob's concerns. He agreed to pay for a maid to take over some of Caroline's duties in Hanover so the family would not suffer from her absence too much. Anna, with her ill-expressed grief at the break-up of her family, was overruled, and William came to collect his sister.

Caroline was 22 years old when she arrived in England. She had never left her country before, and had only ventured beyond Hanover very occasionally (there had been her cousin's wedding, and she would sometimes visit her older, married sister, Sophia, a few towns away). It was quite the culture shock.

The journey itself was horrendous, which did not get her off to a good start. They travelled for twelve days in all, crossing the Low Countries then taking a boat from Utrecht to Yarmouth. The crossing was stormy and, rather alarmingly, the boat lost its mast. From Yarmouth, they continued by horse-drawn cart which again took a rather eventful turn when the horse bolted and the cart was overturned in a ditch. During their brief stop in London, William dragged his physically and emotionally exhausted sister around opticians looking for ideas (he had plans to make telescopes). When they finally arrived in Bath, Caroline had a quick meal and then went to bed, sleeping well into the next day. Travel, she decided, was not for her.

Caroline's recuperation time from her traumatic journey was very short. The 'season' would soon be upon them, and William wanted to get started on her lessons. On her second morning in Bath, her brother asked her to meet him for breakfast at 7 a.m. ('much too early for me,' she wrote), to begin her lessons. William taught her

English, mathematics (so she could do his accounts) and singing. His housekeeper taught her English cooking. As her English improved she was sent alone (or so she thought) to the market to buy food and haggle with stallholders. Alexander would secretly follow her on those first few trips to ensure she was not taken advantage of as she bought the family's groceries. As time went on, William brought in extra tutors to teach her how to hold herself on stage and the appropriate ways to act as an English lady. And as she mastered each skill, more and more of William's day-to-day work – keeping household accounts, training the choir, dealing with staff – was passed onto her.

For William, Caroline and Alexander's arrival was a terrific boon. With Alexander's interest and ability in mechanics and Caroline's apparent willingness to take on more and more of his time-consuming duties, William now found he had the time and skills to take up a hobby that had interested him for a while. He had for some years been reading up on philosophy, natural philosophy (an all-encompassing term, roughly equating to today's 'science') and astronomy.

With his musical reputation now well established, and his siblings around to help out, William began to build his own telescopes with the aim of trying to see some of the astronomical objects he had been reading about. He found a local amateur, who sold him tools and lessons, he bought books that gave him further instruction, and he got started. The house, to Caroline's dismay, was transformed:

> It was to my sorrow that I saw almost every room turned into a workshop. A cabinet maker making a tube and stands of all descriptions in a handsome furnished drawing-room. Alex putting up a huge turning machine ... in a bedroom for turning patterns, grinding glasses and turning eye-pieces &c ... I was to amuse myself with making the tube of pasteboard against the glasses arrived from London.

This was back in 1773, and it took the siblings several years to work out the perfect design for the telescopes, and longer still to establish a programme of observing that worked for them – in their case, scanning the sky with a telescope section by section, looking for new objects. In that time, their collaboration was successful because each gradually fell into a different, complimentary but equally essential role.

William was in charge, with the big vision and his pick of activities. Alexander was their technical expert; he designed and made the detailed metalwork, the micrometers (for measuring across the eyepiece) and the eyepieces themselves. Caroline, meanwhile, with some help from her brothers, was left with the menial, often unpleasant work. She would, for example, make the mirror moulds 'from horse dung of which an immense quantity was to be pounded in a morter [*sic*] and sifted through a fine seaf [sieve]; it was an endless piece of work and served me for many hours' exercise'. She was also their interpreter, listening and understanding each brother so that she could explain to the other what was needed. With such dramatically different ways of looking at the world – William concerning himself with the very big, Alexander with the very small and detailed – Caroline's role was invaluable.

Eight years of practice later, all that work paid off, and in a way they could never possibly have predicted. On 13 March 1781 William spotted what he thought was a new and previously undiscovered comet. He sent word to his new friends (friends of a friend in Bath) at the Royal Society. Hasty discussions then followed, there and across the Channel in France, until it was established beyond doubt that this 'comet' was in fact something far more impressive. William had discovered a planet.

To put this into context, no one had discovered a planet ever before in the history of the world. The known planets – Mercury, Venus, Mars, Jupiter and Saturn – were all visible to the naked eye and known to all ancient cultures. Along with the Sun and Moon, they were named as gods and form the basis for the names of our days of the week. Telescopes had been around for nearly 200 years when William made his discovery with his small 7ft reflector set up in his back garden in Bath – after 200 years of telescopes, his was the first to unequivocally show us a new planet!

The establishment of this new discovery transformed the Herschels' lives. William was encouraged to flatter the king as a way of securing royal patronage and so named his new planet *Georgium Sidus* ('George's Star'), after George III. His friends in London campaigned for him to get a court position so he could give up music and devote himself full time to astronomy.

Eventually, a deal was struck and a new post was established, that of 'Royal Astronomer' (differentiating it from the 'Astronomer Royal' at the Royal Observatory, Greenwich, and the 'King's Astronomer' at the king's private observatory in Kew). The pay was not huge – £200 per year, less than the Astronomer Royal and less than he was currently earning as a musician, but still considerably more than a school teacher or clerk – but then very little was required of him for that money. He was expected to move nearer to the king's main residence, Windsor Castle, and to occasionally bring his telescopes to the palace to entertain royal guests, but that was it.

In the summer of 1782, William and Caroline moved down to a village called Datchet, near Windsor, leaving Alexander behind in Bath to continue his life as a musician. The house they moved into was a wreck. It had been an old hunting lodge and had not been lived in for years. It was falling apart and the grounds were very overgrown. Alexander – down to help them unpack – nearly fell down a well, it was so completely hidden by overgrown weeds.

Getting by on their new reduced income also proved something of a challenge. When William told his good friend William Watson about the deal struck over his salary, Watson exclaimed, 'Never bought Monarch honour so cheap!' After that, if anyone asked, he would be extremely vague about the exact figure and only say, 'the King had provided for him'. Embarrassed as he was, however, it was mostly down to Caroline to work out the details of how in practice they were going to be able to live on less. They did not have a servant in their first few months there, not out of choice but because the lady they had employed at a distance had been imprisoned for theft by the time they arrived and they were unable to find anyone else.

Like all newcomers to London and the Home Counties, then as now, Caroline was shocked to discover everything was much dearer than in her old home. In her autobiographies, she went into some detail about the exact differences in price, even down to the cost of a plate of eggs and bacon – their plans for living cheaply in the country were going to need some refining.

While the cost of living and the state of the house preyed on Caroline's mind, William was busy hatching other plans for his sister. She wrote:

> I found I was to be trained for an assistant Astronomer, and by way of encouragement a Telescope adapted for sweeping consisting of a Tube with two glasses such as are commonly used in a finder, I was to sweep for comets.

It was not something she took to immediately but, like all opportunities with which she found herself presented, she made the best of it. It took several months of regular practice 'before I felt the least encouragement for spending the starlight nights on a grass-plot covered by dew or hoar frost without a human being near enough to be within call'. Gradually, however, as she got used to the cold and, more importantly, became familiar with the night sky, she actually began to enjoy herself. She felt useful, and she saw the potential she had for slowly developing enough understanding to be able to take part in her brother's astronomical projects.

By this time, William had begun working on a very specific project. He was attempting to create a catalogue of all the nebulae, star clusters and double stars he could see with his telescopes. Nebulae, as we understand them today, are the regions of space in which the matter needed to form stars is found but has yet to form into, or is only just beginning to form into stars. They are sometimes, rather nicely, described as the birthplace of stars and are sometimes formed out of the material expelled from a dying star as it becomes supernova and explodes. In the Herschels' time, a nebula (Latin for 'cloud') was simply any blurred bit of the night sky that was not easily resolved into a single point of light or star.

Not many people were that interested in nebulae. Most eighteenth-century astronomers concerned themselves almost exclusively with the inside of our solar system. They thought of the star beyond as fixed, unchanging, uninteresting. As telescopes became more powerful, it was assumed by those who gave the matter any thought that eventually nebulae would no longer exist. If nebulae were the unexplained blurs in the night sky, presumably very powerful telescopes could resolve those blurs into individual stars. It might be that they were groups of stars (star clusters) or pairs (double stars). The idea that some might continue to appear as blurs, however much they were magnified, was not yet a defined theory – and no one at this stage had ever heard of a 'galaxy'. William's plan was to systematically scan the sky with his powerful telescopes, looking at the blurs and trying to resolve them, identifying which were star clusters, which were double stars and which still appeared as blurs or nebulae even with the increased magnification his telescopes offered.

William's telescopes had been established – thanks to considerable testing, after his discovery of Uranus – as being among the most powerful in the world. This put him in an excellent position to create a catalogue of such objects. Catalogues of this type had been produced before – Charles Messier had created one a few years earlier – but their purpose was different. Nebulae, star clusters and double stars were not very well understood in the eighteenth century, since to the naked eye most just look like single stars. Look at them through a powerful enough telescope, however, and they might still look blurry, but you may be able to pick out individual stars in a pair, for example. To eighteenth-century astronomers, these objects were regarded simply as a hindrance to comet hunters. No one really cared what they were – astronomers in the eighteenth century were mostly concerned with our solar system, how it moved, distances between bodies, what predictions and laws might be deduced; the 'fixed stars' beyond were of little interest, but they did need to know where they were, so that they were not mistaken for comets, which often looked very similar. So, Messier produced a catalogue of objects not to be confused with comets. By the 1780s, Messier had catalogued around eighty nebulae and star clusters – William was on track to catalogue around 2,000.

Caroline began observing in August 1782. As early as February 1783 she had found her first nebulae, which she gave to William for his catalogue. William footnoted his catalogue to acknowledge her contribution. By the end of the same year, she complained of only having found fourteen nebulae, attributing this apparently small number to the many times her sweeping was interrupted 'by being employed with writing down my Brother's observations with the large 20-feet'. This was how her training as an astronomer progressed. On the one hand, she was being trained to help her brother observe; on the other, she kept herself busy making her own observations whenever time would allow.

To catalogue a star, you must take measurements or observations of two co-ordinates: you need to know the angular height of your star (its height in degrees above the horizon), and the exact time of your observation (since the Earth turns, making a different part of the sky visible at different times). William was, by this time, using very large, unwieldy telescopes. He had progressed from his 7ft reflector (with which he had single-handedly discovered Uranus) onto a 10ft and then a 20ft telescope. The latter required several workmen to manoeuvre and a communication system for relaying observations to Caroline, who was stationed in a small hut on the ground. William needed a workman to help him move his 20ft telescope tube to the position he wanted to observe, and he needed to sit high up on a platform to see into the eyepiece. All this meant that he needed an assistant. He would shout down his observation, and Caroline, from a small shed, her clock and notebook lit by candlelight in front of her, would note down his observation and the time.

In Hanover, Caroline had always kept herself busy, making use of every free moment to try to learn music or seek out training in all sorts of domestic and decorative skills. Now an astronomer, she did the same, prioritising her work serving her family – this time as her brother's astronomical assistant – but, at the same time, filling her spare time with self-improvement. What seems extraordinary is that, while William needed large telescopes, an assistant and workmen to discover his nebulae, Caroline was able to add some herself after only a few months of interrupted study and practice, observing on her own and with a much smaller instrument.

After just a few years of living in their house in Datchet, the Herschels decided to move. The house was near a river, and the cold, damp nights were making William ill. The house they moved to, called 'Clay Hall', was owned by 'a litigious woman who told him [William] he must expect to have the rent raised every year according to the improvements he was making on the premises'. Unsurprisingly, they moved again soon after, on 3 April 1786, to a house in Slough. This was to become known as 'Observatory House' and was to be home to the Herschel family for the next two centuries.

In the nearly fourteen years that Caroline had been living in England, learning to be first a musician then an astronomer, the world around her had changed dramatically. Throughout the 1770s, tensions had been growing and revolution was brewing. Britain seemed fairly stable in comparison to the rest of the world, although it was, in many cases, responsible for the instabilities elsewhere. But there was a sense, certainly within intellectual circles, that these political protests could have some future meaning for Britain. If a change in power – so that the 'middling sort' rather than the current ruling aristocracy had some say in how the country was run – could work elsewhere, why not in Britain? Many, including several scientifically minded friends of the Herschels, were watching with keen interest.

Over in America, the Boston Tea Party took place in 1773. Demonstrators stole onto British East India Company ships and threw huge boxes of tea overboard in protest against new British tax policies. This was the start of the American Revolution. America was officially declared independent of British rule in 1783.

In France, teenagers Louis XVI and Marie Antoinette became king and queen in 1774, inheriting huge debts. Their attempts at reform mostly failed (the Edict of Tolerance, which overturned many legal inequalities between people of different faiths, was an exception). The population, meanwhile, was starving after a series of poor harvests, and absolute monarchy, it was felt more and more, was no way to run a country.

Back in England, rulers appeared to be doing a lot better. Despite the loss of America, the British Empire was growing. In the 1770s, Captain James Cook had been sent on a series of expeditions to discover and claim new lands. The first had been presented as a scientific mission, to view the transit of Venus and make observations that astronomers could analyse and use to calculate the size of the solar system. It was only in secret that he had been instructed also to go further, and try to seek out (and claim for the British) the mysterious Southern Continent.

The second and third expeditions were more explicitly voyages of geographical discovery. On the second, Cook returned to New Zealand and Australia, mapping coastlines and travelling still further south, almost to Antarctica. Cook's third voyage set out to find the Northwest Passage, a route thought to link the Atlantic and Pacific oceans which might allow British merchants to trade more easily and more directly with Asia. It was on this trip that Cook landed on Hawaii, upset the locals and was stabbed and killed.

Accompanying Cook on his first voyage was a young botanist called Joseph Banks. Banks was from a wealthy Lincolnshire family. He was educated at Harrow, Eton and then Oxford University. He left without a degree; but the same year he inherited a large fortune and used it to finance his new career as a botanical explorer. At 23, he joined Captain Phipps on the HMS *Niger* as his botanist, documenting and collecting natural history from Newfoundland and Labrador. Two years later, he was appointed botanist on Cook's voyage, returning home in 1771 to immediate fame.

Not only were Cook's voyages themselves newsworthy, but Banks had himself attracted attention, bringing to England fascinating descriptions of exotic flora and fauna. Just a few years later, Banks was elected president of the prestigious Royal Society of London, and remained in post for forty-one years, bringing together practitioners and patrons and promoting science in Britain.

By 1786 the Herschels could confidently describe Sir Joseph Banks (he was knighted in 1781) as one of their friends. He had been among the first to hear of William's discovery of Uranus back in 1781 and was instrumental in ensuring that William received the king's patronage. From time to time after that, Banks would write to William, introducing him to an up-and-coming young astronomer, or getting the Herschels to check out a possible discovery. While Banks specialised in natural history, William was often the person he turned to on astronomical matters.

Back in Slough, the Herschels' new home, Observatory House, was taking shape. Originally called 'The Grove', it had been owned by a local lady, Elizabeth Baldwin, whose daughter and son-in-law, Mary and John Pitt, lived nearby. It was a comfortable house with four bedrooms, loft space for servants and a converted stable in which Caroline made her home. Another outbuilding was made their writing room, and its flat roof used to house Caroline's telescope. The house was perfect, but the many moves and the construction of ever larger telescopes were eating into their savings. Their £200 per year was not enough to live on and so, following the king's advice (he was perhaps feeling guilty at paying his Royal Astronomer so little), William, with help from his siblings, began to make telescopes to sell.

There was certainly a market for William's telescopes. Everyone had heard of them and their quality, thanks to his discovery of Uranus, and many fashionable homes felt they would rather like an example of their own. It could be a talking piece, if not necessarily a piece of well-used or even well-understood scientific apparatus. Despite building his reputation on the quality of his telescopes, William had never actually built the whole thing himself. Instrument makers did not – it was not expected. To be the named maker of an instrument simply meant you took charge of the overall design and, generally speaking, made the most prestigious element of the instrument. In reflector telescopes, that part was the primary mirror, and William certainly took charge of that process – the rest he contracted out. He employed a brass workman, a cabinetmaker for the wooden frames, a joiner and a smith. He put together price lists, and Caroline wrote out neat instructions on how to assemble and use each telescope. Here was yet another job Caroline was landed with, taking her away from her independent study and observing, but, as ever, she was happy to help.

Alongside building telescopes for others, William began to make plans for a more ambitious telescope of his own. His reputation had been built on making better telescopes than anyone before him, building telescopes that were more powerful and could see further than ever before. He now had the 7ft reflector, with which he had discovered Uranus. Added to this he had a 10ft telescope, and now a 20ft tube, but with a little help he felt he could do better still.

His ambition was to build a 40ft telescope, the biggest the world had ever seen. The proposed telescope would have a primary mirror a metre in diameter, made – as all his telescope mirrors were – of a specially designed metal compound called speculum. This was before the days of silvered glass mirrors. Instead, mirrors were made of a metal alloy and polished regularly because they tarnished easily (especially when left outside, as William's very large telescopes inevitably were).

The telescope would take a huge amount of thought, technical skill, imagination and money. In September 1785, the king gave the Herschels a one-off, final payment of £2,000 with which to build the telescope. To that end, they employed a team of some forty workmen, whom Caroline often supervised, to start cutting down trees, laying the telescope's foundations, and converting the washhouse into a forge (for the mirror and metalwork).

In the meantime, the Herschels were busy with their observing projects and commercial telescope business. The 7ft reflector, as the telescope that had discovered Uranus, was a big seller. Examples can still be found in museums around the world, evidence that the market for these souvenirs was international. Bigger scopes were also in demand, although more expensive and therefore for a more limited audience.

In the summer of 1786 William and Alexander went to Göttingen to deliver one of the larger telescopes to the university there. They were away for nearly two months, leaving Caroline to supervise the continuing work on the 40ft telescope and run the house in their absence. She also had to deal with visitors. Since William discovered Uranus in 1781, Herschel had become a household name, and articles were written throughout Europe in the popular as well as the scientific press about this curious musician turned astronomer and his amazing telescopes. As a result, the Herschel home had become a popular tourist destination for rich sightseers and natural philosophers alike. Caroline was never too keen on company, but understood this as a necessary duty – part of her role running her brother's house.

In addition to the 40ft telescope, the house and visitors, Caroline was also busy preparing their catalogue of nebulae and star clusters for publication. This task included not only writing up the work neatly and structuring it in such a way as to make it easy to use, it also meant calculation – turning raw data into useable information. All of that might sound like enough to keep anyone busy and occupied, but Caroline always liked to use her time as efficiently as possible and was acutely aware of how little time she ordinarily had to herself. The two months with her brothers away and the house to herself offered her a fantastic opportunity that she was not about to throw away.

Her days were spent supervising workmen, dealing with visitors, and calculating data for their catalogue. Her nights, meanwhile, were spent on the writing room roof with her very own small telescope. Each night was carefully documented in her observing book:

1st August: I have calculated 100 nebulae today, and this evening I saw an object which I believe will prove to-morrow to be a comet. 2nd August: To-day I calculated 150 nebulae. I fear it will not be clear to-night, it has been raining throughout the whole day, but seems now to clear up a little. 1 o'clock; the object of last night is a Comet. I did not go to rest till I had wrote to Dr Blagden and Mr Aubert to announce the comet.

2

THE FIRST 'LADY'S COMET'

S ettled in their new home, with the foundations of their large 40ft reflector already laid and a scientific reputation that was steadily growing for both siblings, the Herschels' fortunes were most definitely on the rise from the outset of 1787. William had been a household name since word had spread of his discovery of a planet through first the scientific and then the popular press back in 1781. And after the announcement of her new comet, curiosity about Caroline was also growing. In January, the pair began their observations on two new moons of Uranus. Then there were the many nebulae, star clusters and double stars that the pair added regularly to their catalogues. In just that one year, Caroline wrote up six papers for her brother to submit to the Royal Society. This kept her busy, exactly as she liked to be, and kept her mind off the publication of her own paper by that same institution.

Even before publication, word had spread of the extraordinary discovery by this extraordinary woman. Fanny Burney, the author and diarist, wrote of a visit to the palace: William had been summoned as part of his duties as Royal Astronomer to show collected guests his sister's comet. Burney remarked that she was 'very desirous to see it'. Although it was small and 'had nothing grand or striking in its appearance', she wanted very much to see it because 'it is the first lady's comet'. And that was reason enough.

Astronomer friends were even more enthusiastic. The amateur astronomer and family friend Alexander Aubert wrote gushingly to Caroline after hearing of and then seeing the comet for himself. 'I wish you joy most sincerely for the discovery,' he wrote. 'I am more pleased than you can well conceive that you have made it and I think I see your wonderfully clever and wonderfully amiable Brother, upon the news of it, shed a tear of joy.'[1]

A few months later, Fanny visited the Herschels with her father and met Caroline for the first time. 'She is very little,' Fanny remarked, 'very gentle, very modest, very ingenuous; and her manners are those of a person unhackneyed and unawed by the world, yet desirous to meet and return its smiles.'

A neighbour of the Herschels, Mrs Papendiek, made similar observations on Caroline's character, though she was more generous in describing her talents. According to her, 'Miss Caroline Herschel was by no means prepossessing, but a most excellent, kind-hearted creature, and though not a young woman of brilliant talents, yet one of unremitting perseverance, and of natural cleverness.'[2] It was this appearance of gentle modesty and apparent desire to please that helped Caroline become the first (named) woman to discover a comet and the first to have her paper read to and published by the Royal Society in the oldest and longest-running scientific journal in the world.

William and Alexander had both been away when Caroline made her discovery. Etiquette dictated that had they been around, they would have been expected to speak for her, to have announced her discovery to their scientific friends on her behalf, simply because they were men. Men's voices carried authority on scientific matters; women's did not. Even after Caroline made her announcement in her own words, William felt obliged to add his own a few days later, when he got back, to add weight to her claim. Women were not expected to participate in science in the way that Caroline did; she had to be very careful about her wording and her presentation, and she needed allies.

It would be completely wrong to say that women have not participated much in science historically or that Caroline was among the first. A
much truer claim would be to say that women have always participated
in science but that their contributions have, for centuries, been unac-
knowledged, trivialised or simply labelled anything other than science.
In early modern chemistry-heavy industries like brewing, for example,
women often dominated up until the seventeenth century, when men
began to take over. As a female-dominated industry, brewing tended to
be regarded as a part of cooking; once men became involved, it came
to be regarded as a more scientific and industrial process. In medicine,
similarly, where women dominated, practices tended to be labelled as
domestic, part of the overall process of caring; male involvement in
medicine, meanwhile, was regarded as professional and analytical.

In later periods too, women were often involved in scientific
practice, but convention dictated that only very few participants in
that process received credit. Robert Boyle, for example, known to
schoolchildren everywhere for Boyle's Law (describing the relationship
between pressure, volume and temperature in a gas), carried out grand
experiments in his home. He wrote them up, describing his work as
though he was the only one there, yet he had a team of assistants and
technicians helping him. Just as servants were invisible to people of
Boyle's class, so too were the multitude of scientific helpers that made
their work possible.

The help of servants, assistants, technicians, wives, sisters and daughters was very much taken for granted in science right up until the
late nineteenth century. History has only recently begun to grudg-
ingly acknowledge that these men could only have achieved what
they did by virtue of the team of predominantly female relatives and
servants keeping them clean and fed, helping them in the laboratory
and tending to their social networks. Looking more closely at these
women and the work they performed, the line between domestic help
and scientific help gets increasingly blurred.

It would have been perfectly in keeping with conventions of the
time for William to have claimed all Caroline's nebulae discoveries as

his own. He was the male figurehead of the family's scientific enterprise and therefore he was the official discoverer of everything they found, the maker of all their telescopes and the creator of all their theoretical work. The work of his siblings and the many servants and workmen was not generally considered important enough to the enterprise to receive credit. Today, scientific papers often have long lists of authors, discoveries are often claimed by teams rather than individuals, whereas in the past, history seems to have been made by only a handful of white men. Boyle, by this logic, carried out his experiments single-handed and Darwin alone collected, catalogued and interpreted his specimens.

Very occasionally, female partners' contributions have been acknowledged in portraits (Elisabeth Hevelius, or Marie-Anne Lavoisier,[3] for example) but it was extremely rare for it to happen in print. In fact, science was *always* a team effort, but historically large swathes of people – women, servants, the lower classes – were seen as invisible and unimportant to knowledge creation. What makes the Herschels – not just Caroline, but the whole family – different is their disregard for this convention, at least as it applied to women.

William had already broken with convention, naming Caroline as the discoverer of several nebulae in his catalogue. Now it was Caroline's turn. Her years training as a society musician would not go to waste. These were what taught her how to win over a sceptical crowd. She had once been warned by a well-meaning woman in rehearsals for a concert in Bath not to be 'her own trumpeter'. It was not seemly – for a woman especially – to be too self-congratulatory; much better to be self-depreciating, to present an image of exaggerated modesty and allow others to recognise and celebrate your talent. It was this lesson that Caroline now applied to science.

'In consequence of the Friendship I know to exist between you and my brother I venture to trouble you in his absence with the following imperfect account of a comet.' This is how Caroline began her letter to Royal Society secretary Charles Blagden, a letter that would form the basis of her published article. Today, claiming that your account of a scientific observation was imperfect might seem a little shoddy and unprofessional, but for Caroline it was essential to being taken seriously. It allowed the men within the Royal Society to accept this paper by a woman without immediately dismissing her and her work as over-confident and arrogant. She ventures to trouble him, again putting him and other readers off guard, forcing them to politely assure her it was no trouble rather than offending them by demanding attention. She explains it is because of 'his absence' that she is writing, again assuring her reader that it is only because there was no alternative that it is she and not a man who is writing. In just that one opening sentence, Caroline, using her lessons in society manners and perfor-mance, managed to completely neutralise any possible opposition she, as a woman, might have expected to encounter.

Her paper continued, carefully, diligently neutralising all and any opposition that might arise. Her brother helped too, stepping in at the end with his assurance that he too had seen what his sister claimed, and could vouch for her abilities. Another friend also assisted, offering his own observations in a paper read a little later and published in the same volume of *Philosophical Transactions*, the journal of the Royal Society.

Caroline's caution regarding her dealings with the Royal Society seems, historically at least, to have been extremely wise. While she may not have been aware of the details, she was almost certainly aware of the frosty reception the Royal Society tended to give women. Generally speaking, most eighteenth-century public and professional institutions were unwelcoming to women. Women would no more expect entry to the Royal Society than to a university or the Houses of Parliament.

There had been women at the Royal Society in the 120 years of its existence before Caroline, but none had received the welcome – such as it was – that Caroline enjoyed. Margaret Cavendish, for example, the Duchess of Newcastle-upon-Tyne no less, was the first woman to attend a meeting at the Royal Society, a year after it was founded. Cavendish was openly ambitious and wrote unapologetically on natural philosophy (writing in total six books on the subject) at a time when women writers rarely published anything under their own names. Her presence, however, made the fellows uncomfortable. Some of the more unkind members began referring to her as 'mad Madge'. They were rude, not just about her ideas, but about her clothes, her stance, everything about her. Just to make sure this sort of thing did not happen again, women were barred from attending meetings for another two centuries.

Several decades later, Margaret Flamsteed, a woman in a position more similar to Caroline's, had a run-in of her own with England's all-male scientific elite. As the wife of the first Astronomer Royal, she had often assisted her husband with his observing and calculating at the Royal Observatory in Greenwich. She had been his eyes when his sight deteriorated with age. She offered continuity too, as observatory assistants came and went, rarely staying long due to the long, solitary hours and the bad pay. When her husband died, Margaret naturally saw it as her job to complete his work, bring it together and have his catalogue – the first catalogue of northern hemisphere stars made with a telescope – published. (An earlier incomplete version had been published before, through some devious goings on between Edmund Halley and Isaac Newton, but John, Margaret's husband, had been furious about this and had them all destroyed, bar a very small number he had been unable to track down.) Margaret assumed she would be the one to carry out her husband's wishes to publish his improved version of the catalogue. Yet her assumptions about her abilities and the logical sense in having those most familiar with the material work with it to completion appeared only to antagonise her male peers. Eventually she achieved what she set out to do, but not before dealing with a huge amount of condescension and obstruction.

Even before her article on her comet, news had spread about Caroline's discovery; after her publication in the prestigious *Philosophical Transactions* she became a household name. Scientific journals in the eighteenth century were not quite what they are today. *Philosophical Transactions of the Royal Society* was one of only a very small number of scientific journals in the world. It covered most science, or natural philosophy as it was then known, and was read by the entire Royal Society membership, which included both practitioners of science and gentlemen interested enough to pay the fees and of a high enough social ranking to be elected.

The journal was also read by a growing and disparate group of interested amateurs: people such as the Herschels before they gained their royal patronage. These interested amateurs, not quite proficient enough, or of high enough social status to become members of the society themselves, would borrow copies from philanthropic neighbours or from travelling libraries. These men and women – often nominally scientific through their occupations as teachers or naval men (or not at all in the case of leisured country gentlemen) – called themselves 'philomaths' in the eighteenth century. They were interested in philosophy and mathematics (hence the name) but as consumers rather than producers of new knowledge. They read second-hand copies of *Philosophical Tranactions* or, more often, watered-down versions of the same works in journals especially designed for them, such as *The Ladies' Diary*. There were also, for the even less committed or for those starting out, more populist journals such as *The European Magazine*, which would often publish discussions on Royal Society papers for their non-specialist readers. All of this meant that certain ideas, when they caught the imagination of readers and journalists, could travel quickly. A female comet hunter was an eye-catching story.

While Caroline's comet paper was big news, and an important moment in the creation and development of her independent reputation, it was by no means the only astronomical achievement for her that year. As she had been doing for the past five years, Caroline continued to assist her brother in his observations. In January 1787, William and Caroline first recorded seeing two new satellites, or moons, of Uranus. Since Galileo first spotted four moons around Jupiter in 1610, other moons around other planets had been discovered, although not many. Today, we know of around 200 moons (or natural satellites) orbiting planets and dwarf planets in our solar system. By 1787, however, only Galileo's four moons and another five around Saturn were known. Two new satellites around Uranus was therefore a significant discovery, if not quite as huge as William's earlier discovery of the planet itself.

In February, the pair oversaw further work on the 40ft telescope. The tube was now finished and one of the mirrors that had been cast in London to William's own specifications and brought down the river to Slough was placed in the tube for the first time. The telescope was still a long way from being complete, but it was significant progress. Then, in April the Herschels had a visitor.

By 1787 the Herschels were used to having a lot of guests. By the summer, they were getting visitors to see not only the famous astronomer and instrument maker William Herschel, and his planet Uranus and its satellites but also the discoverer of the first lady's comet. These visitors were mainly aristocrats, people with titles but no real interest in science, who came to see what all the talk was about. Caroline found these people rather tiresome. She saw their reception as a duty, a professional obligation, but took no real pleasure in their company. Occasionally they were visited by a philosopher or mathematician, an artist or poet and these visits were more welcome, although they still took Caroline away from the practical, self-improving solitude which was her main pleasure.

Their April visitor, however, was quite different to their regular evening guests. Between April and October, William and Caroline's older brother Jacob came over from Hanover to stay. Ordinarily Caroline was very family orientated. She loved solitude and her family in almost equal measure and would happily shun all society to be with and to look after her loved ones. However, she disliked Jacob, sixteen years her senior, intensely.

Her autobiographies are peppered with remarks on how irritating she found his behaviour, and at times even his very existence. He embodied everything she disapproved of. That he had inherited the role of head of the household after their father died, giving him authority in all decisions about her life and future back in Hanover, did not help. She also noted her brother's profligate spending, alongside his disdain for earning a living. Rather caustically, she observed that he always saw himself above teaching and would never sell his compositions as no printer ever offered enough. She also felt he had been spoilt by being overindulged by his family. He was, she felt, 'too much admired for his musical and other promising abilities ... to deny him any gratification'.

Back in Hanover, his attempts (as Caroline saw them) to mix in high society would frequently have a negative impact on Caroline's already busy and thankless life. He would often have friends over, she would complain, and Caroline was expected to serve them drinks, on top of her already onerous domestic workload. At one point, he felt his station demanded a servant – except they did not have a room for one, and so Caroline was expected to share hers. Even when Caroline had the chance to leave and come to England, it was Jacob, according to Caroline, who was the greatest obstacle to her gaining permission.

Like all the Herschel brothers from the time William had settled in Bath as a musician, Jacob had made frequent visits to England to stay. This would be his first visit since they had moved to Slough, and the first in which he did not have the ready excuse of coming to join them as a fellow professional musician. Jacob's stay is left remarkably undocumented in the Herschels' extant papers. Caroline simply and curtly states in her autobiography that, 'My brother Jacob was with us from April till October when he returned to Hanover again.' She adds that Alexander came over from Bath briefly during that time, but not for long, as his wife – who had kept Caroline company the summer before, when William and Alexander had been in Göttingen – was very ill. Given her desire always to come across as obliging (at least when she thought about it), this suggests that perhaps Caroline did not say anything about this visit because if you have nothing nice to say, you should not say anything at all.

It seems likely that Jacob visited his nephews, sons of their older sister Sophia, while he was in England. Sophia was the eldest of the Herschel children. In 1755, when Caroline was just 5, she had left home to marry Heinrich Griesbach, a musician in the same military band as her father and brothers. Their first son, George, was born two years later, followed soon after by Charles (born 1760), Henry (1762), Frederick (1769) and William (1772). Not long after George was born, Heinrich left the military and became a town musician in Coppenbrügge. The pay was not fantastic, but at least it meant he could see his family. To supplement their income, Heinrich would take on private engagements, playing at weddings and parties, and sometimes copied music to earn some extra money. Sophia, when she was not busy with her own young children, took a post teaching at a local girls' school for a while.

Like the Herschel children, the Griesbach children went to the local school and were taught music intensively at home. By the time George was 5 he could play a few tunes on the violin, and by the time he was a teenager he could play much more, and on a range of instruments. His brothers were much the same. In 1759, they had been joined by their uncle, Sophia's brother Alexander, who came to live with them as Heinrich's apprentice. Again, like the Herschels, this was a very busy, musically ambitious household where money was always tight, but where it could generally be found through a musical engagement or two.

In 1773, when George was just 15, their father Heinrich died and his post as town musician was passed down to his eldest son, giving him his first experience of professional employment. A few years later, George's godfather, his Uncle Jacob, came across an opportunity that would transform the family's fortunes. Jacob had heard on one of his visits to England that George III was sending a scout to Hanover to look for musicians for the royal court. He pointed his eldest nephew in his direction.

George was successful, and although worried for her young son leaving her to live so far away, Sophia was comforted by the fact that three of her siblings were already settled in England and would keep an eye on him. She let him go. From that day in 1777 until the mid-nineteenth century, the Griesbach family dominated music at the English royal court. Very much like William, George settled in England and then gradually called over his brothers, one by one, as opportunities for them arose. The Griesbach brothers would surely have given Jacob a warm reception, even if Caroline had been a little frosty.

Ordinarily Caroline would have gone to great lengths and huge personal cost to make her visiting family comfortable. When the baby of the family, Dietrich (five years her junior), came to visit in 1782, she gave up everything to look after him. Dietrich had run away from Hanover, but not planned his trip well. He was deserted by his travelling companion and had sent a very distressed letter on his arrival in England, telling William and Caroline that he was ill and staying in Wapping. They had asked a friend to help him get to Bath and, once there, Caroline nursed him back to health, barely leaving his side in over a fortnight.

Jacob, however, was perfectly healthy and could look after himself. To ensure she did not have the kind of spare time she knew her brother had a habit of exploiting, Caroline looked around for astronomical work that might need doing. 'I had always in hand,' she wrote, 'some kind of work with which I could proceed without troubling him [William] with questions.' And so it was that she began the 'Temporary Index' in June 1787.

Caroline's 'Temporary Index' was an organising, transcribing and improving project that would help make William's cataloguing work much easier to carry out. William was at the time cataloguing the sky, section by section, using his large telescopes, which were renowned for their exceptional magnifying power. To do this, or at least to make sure that what he listed was genuinely new to astronomers, he and Caroline had to cross reference each new point of light in the night sky against previous catalogues. Their main source was Flamsteed's catalogue, the first survey of the night sky made with a telescope, which had been produced nearly a century earlier from Greenwich. They also consulted Charles Messier's catalogue of nebulae and star clusters. There may have been others.

All the catalogues, however, had one flaw: they were ordered according to constellation. This was very much how European astronomers worked at the time. The sky was divided up into constellations, some Greek, some invented more recently by explorers, and the stars were listed according to which constellation they were said to belong to. Constellations, however, fill the sky in a rather haphazard way; they overlap, vary in size and bend around one another. The Herschels' survey, on the other hand, was methodical, structured and took a section of the sky at a time. They would scan one vertical strip of sky and each strip would typically include a few stars from a number of different constellations. There was no order to it, and so it was that Caroline decided to impose her own order.

To begin with, Caroline set about creating a cross-referencing system, an index that would allow the siblings to more easily incorporate the information from published catalogues into their own work. This was her 'Index' – 'Temporary' because she considered it to be a temporary stopgap, a tool to assist rather than the finished product. This kept her busy in the daytime during the summer they had their elder brother to stay. It helped her to become more familiar with the night sky, what had been found before and how those discoveries had previously been described. However, it had one other valuable contribution to make to Caroline's well-being: it gave her a project that was all her own. It gave her a sense of control and even, within the confines of her domestic arrangements, independence.

The summer of 1787 was turning into an exceptionally busy one, even for the Herschels. Her indexing project aside, Caroline barely had time to worry about Jacob, or indeed much else besides astronomy and the development of the instruments. William's expensive and ambitious 40ft telescope was starting to take shape and she was increasingly involved in the future plans for it.

William had become famous in astronomy when he discovered the new planet Uranus in 1781, but it was on the quality of his telescope that he had built his reputation. After he announced his discovery, astronomers in London and Paris had quickly checked the observations and soon confirmed it as a new planet. What they were less convinced by were the claims he made about his telescopes and their magnifying power. They were so far beyond anything then known, it just seemed to them too unlikely.

William tried to explain his telescopes with a musical analogy. The magnification, he claimed, was possible through practice; it was a combination of magnifying power and getting your eyes used to seeing. 'You must not expect to be able to see at sight or *a livre ouvert*,' he told a friend. However, the astronomers at the Royal Society needed more to convince them. They ordered him to bring his telescopes to Greenwich so they could see for themselves. To their astonishment, his claims were entirely accurate.

With his reputation as an instrument maker secured, he set about building on it, designing bigger and bigger telescopes until he came up with his plan for the biggest telescope in the world. In 1785 William, with the help of some friends, had successfully petitioned the king to get funding for the 40ft telescope. By 1787, the money had all been spent and the telescope was still a long way from completion.

George III prided himself on being a patron of science. He had had his own observatory built at Kew, near London, and supported the Royal Society and many scientific expeditions. For centuries, art and science had been largely funded in this way, practised either by rich individuals who could fund themselves or by those who could persuade rich individuals to become their patrons. Galileo had named the moons of Jupiter the 'Medician Stars' because this was a good way to flatter and gain funding and patronage from the Medici family. Johanne Kepler dedicated an essay to the Archduke Ferdinand in order to win his support. William had done the same when he originally named his planet Georgium Sidus. He now hoped he could flatter the king enough for his support to continue.

In July, imagining the king would still be enthusiastic about the project, William wrote asking for more money. The king, however, was not as keen as William had hoped. He expected the original grant to have been enough and was not happy about being asked for more money. Before he answered the request, he decided to go and see what progress had been made. He brought with him a large party, including the Archbishop of Canterbury.

However annoyed the king might have been, the sight of the partially built telescope, including the huge 40ft tube lying on the ground, obviously delighted him. It put him in a good mood. He saw its potential and realised that such a statement structure might help cement his image as a scientifically enlightened monarch. Leading the archbishop through the tube (on the Herschels' invitation – it was their current party trick), he quipped, 'Come, my Lord Bishop, I will show you the way to Heaven.'[4]

A few days later, William received word from the palace. The king would provide further funds. William now had to provide a reasonable estimate of what those additional costs might be to have the telescope up and running. He made his calculations: another £1,000 for construction, plus £200 a year in running costs. He had an additional suggestion, however, and it concerned his sister.

For all her public claims to family devotion and her assertions about wanting nothing more than to serve her family, Caroline had clearly shown her brother another side to her feelings. She had been offered independence as a musician, back in 1778 when she had been asked to leave her family for a post in Birmingham. She had turned it down because the thought of working completely separately and far away from her siblings had seemed too big a step. It had obviously sparked something in her, however, because a few years later William had helped her set up her own millinery business with some friends, using skills she had gained from a course she had attended a few years earlier in Hanover. Unfortunately the business failed.

The Herschels blamed staff, partners and location for this, but it did show both William and Caroline that she had a desire for independence and was happy to work hard for it. Since then, the siblings had moved to Slough, and Caroline had been trained in astronomy as William's assistant. Her old desire for some kind of independence, however, was never completely lost, and so when it came to asking for more money for the 40ft telescope, these disparate ideas and desires that had been floating about for a while came together. The 40ft telescope might just offer the siblings a new way to help Caroline achieve her ambition to be financially secure, free at last from becoming a burden on her family.

William set about making his case. Caroline, William argued to the king, was now highly trained and an invaluable assistant to him in his work. To train a replacement would be costly and time consuming. And of course, to employ a man to do the same job would cost the king twice as much. Caroline was good at what she did, and she was a bargain! Perhaps, as discoverer of the first lady's comet, she could receive her pension from the queen, woman to woman? Unpalatable as they might seem in the modern era (and yet at the same time, wearily familiar), William's arguments worked. Caroline was to receive her own salary – or, to be more technically accurate, pension – for her work in science.

'Firsts' in history are always popular, and always problematic. Was Caroline the first woman, or at least the first woman in England to be paid for her science? Well, no. For centuries women had worked in industries, arts and crafts that today would all plausibly be labelled as scientific. Wise women, female apothecaries and early modern female brewers, for example, were all practitioners of sciences of sorts. Before the mid-1600s and the formation of the Royal Society, there were no strict boundaries about what did and did not count as natural philosophy or, as we call it today, science. Lots of work, however, involved processes that we would now consider to be scientific. Chemistry, for example, was practised by people making medicines, dying fabric and brewing beer – and some of those people were women, and some of them were even paid. Astronomy similarly was used in understanding and planning agricultural timetables and in astrology, and many women were paid for work in those fields.

Even if we look at higher-status roles in science, Caroline was not the first woman to be paid. Laura Bassi is generally ascribed that honour, as the first female professor at Bologna University in Italy in 1732. In England, however, Caroline could be said to be the first high-status woman paid for her science, and almost certainly the first to receive royal patronage. Let us give her that at least.

Caroline received £12 10s, the first of the quarterly instalments of her annual pension, in October 1787. It was to give her the kind of financial independence she had never imagined would be hers.

1788

3

WILLIAM AND MARY

From the moment the first instalment of her pension arrived, Caroline began to write her own accounts, taking pride in an activity that she had only ever been able to do before for other people. She would keep track of her spending and live properly and within her means. She was no longer a dependant, no longer a potential burden to her family. Indeed, she would soon find others depending on her, as relatives back in Hanover, upon hearing of her good fortune, came to her with stories of need. Later in life she would become quite critical of these, accusing her relatives then, as in childhood, of reckless extravagance. At the same time, it was nice to be in a position to help and refreshing to be the one with the power of the purse strings for once.

Caroline's delight at her new-found independence was, however, soon tempered by some troubling news from her older brother. William had become engaged. This should have been happy news, a chance for celebration, as he found himself starting out on a new, more grown-up life. He was 50 years old and had never married, and now settled in Slough, he had found a local widow he wanted to spend the rest of his life with. From Caroline's point of view, though, it had worrisome repercussions. His new life would undoubtedly mean a new life imposed upon her and she was not quite sure what to make of that. While, on the one hand, she was happy that her brother might have found happiness, she was worried for her future and where his decisions might leave her. She may no longer have been financially dependent on her family but there were other ways in which she still relied on her brother and these, she felt, were now in danger.

Mary Pitt,[1] the local widow who was to be William's future bride, was a local businesswoman and property owner. She had money from her family and first husband and she had local roots; her family had lived and worked in the area for generations. Her mother, Elizabeth Baldwin, owned property, including the house the Herschels were living in. Mary's father, Adee Baldwin, had been a merchant in the City. Her great-great-grandfather had been the local vicar. Most of the generations in between had included lawyers, clerics and businessmen. They were a well-established upper-middle-class family.

Very much like the Herschels, Mary's mother was barely literate while Mary herself was reasonably well educated, though not in the sciences particularly. Her books suggest that her main interests were religion (like many of her contemporaries, she had a number of collections of sermons within her library) and poetry. Her son, Paul Adee, like many local boys of their class, went to Eton College where he made friends with the sons and brothers of Mary's friends, many of whom were associated with the royal court.

When William and Caroline first met Mary Pitt, she was happily married to John Pitt, a well-educated businessman, and living in a house a short walk away in Upton. William and John Pitt got on well. They were about the same age and they both had an interest in learning, science and books. John Pitt has been described as having accumulated a 'well-chosen library', which he was generous enough to share with those he found to have similar interests and a desire to learn. John Pitt was already sick when the Herschels moved in. He was unable to go out much, making the Herschels' visits – William would generally walk over accompanied by Caroline – all the more welcome.

While the Pitts may have been favourites with the Herschels, they were not the only family the Herschels got to know in their new surroundings. Being near to the royal court and London with its Royal Society, there was already a well-developed intellectual community around Windsor, in which the Herschels felt very comfortable. Some were direct employees of the royal court; others were simply drawn to the area, perhaps attracted by the enthusiasm and encouragement offered by the current monarch for the arts and the sciences.

George III tends to be best known today for his porphyria, a condition which caused him to have periodic bouts of mental confusion or, as the play and film title have it, 'madness'. In his periods of mental clarity, however, he was a strong supporter and investor in the cultural life of Britain. Museums such as the Royal Collection and the Science Museum are filled with artefacts demonstrating this commitment to the arts and the sciences. The George III Collection at the Science Museum, in particular, originating in the teaching collection used by George III's tutor, Stephen Demainbray, to teach him science, and added to by George as an adult, shows the extent to which the king was aware and supportive of the scientific instrument trade in Britain at the time. It also shows the breadth of scientific disciplines in which he was tutored, giving him the broad overview which he used to identify and find value in the work of natural philosophers like William Herschel.

George III was also very supportive of the arts, and gave royal status to the newly founded Academy of Arts and Society of Arts as well as offering patronage to individual artists. He had an observatory established in Kew initially to observe the transit of Venus, and he invented a new astronomical post for William Herschel. More than that, he also encouraged scientific investigation and enquiry in those around him, including those who did not need his financial support, and so did his wife, Queen Charlotte.

The queen was a keen amateur botanist and very supportive of the early development of Kew Botanical Gardens. She was very active in championing women and children, helping to found orphanages, a hospital for expectant mothers and schools to encourage the education of young girls. It was in keeping with her support of both science and educated women that she came to be Caroline's patron. She was also keen to fill her home with intelligent rather than simply obedient and obsequious staff.

One of Queen Charlotte's 'readers', who was also a neighbour and good friend of the Herschels, was Jean-André de Luc. While his court position gave him an income and status, his reputation beyond was built on his interest in natural philosophy, and geology in particular. He was a fellow of the Royal Society, he invented meteorological measuring instruments to use on geological expeditions and is even credited with coining the term 'geology'.

Another court associate (though never in any official post), supported and encouraged in his interests by the palace, was the Herschels' neighbour, Dr James Lind. Lind (not to be confused with his cousin James Lind, who discovered how to prevent scurvy) was a doctor and botanist who had travelled with Sir Joseph Banks on one of his voyages of discovery. Like de Luc and Herschel, Lind was a fellow of the Royal Society and after many years' voyaging had settled in Windsor where he mixed with the Herschels and other intellectual local families. To keep himself solvent he offered science tutoring to Eton College boys, including, in the early 1800s, the poet Percy Bysshe Shelley.

One other family that the Herschels got to know, this time very definitely through the Pitts rather than independently as local residents, was the Papendieks. Charlotte Papendiek was a lady-in-waiting, assistant and reader to Queen Charlotte. Her granddaughter published her diaries after her death. Ostensibly, these were accounts showing a behind-the-scenes view of the royal court and the life of a queen. In reality, they were filled with gossipy stories of local residents.

Caroline never liked Charlotte Papendiek. On hearing of her death in 1840, Caroline wrote to her nephew, 'I could not help thanking God loudly for ridding the world of such a deceitful being.'[2] Caroline and Charlotte were never friends but Mary and Charlotte went back a long way. Whether they liked it or not, and Caroline most certainly did not, the Papendieks were intimately connected with the Herschels in the new lives they were trying to build for themselves. Charlotte's father had been the former resident of their new house, making her rather pointedly critical of every alteration they made to it. Charlotte's brother and Mary Pitt's son were also friends together at Eton, and according to Charlotte's accounts, she and her family were so close to the Pitts they were practically confidants; they also considered themselves central characters on the local social circuit. They had parties to which all the important local families were invited, and expected invitations to the parties of others. Charlotte Papendiek embodied all that Caroline disliked about society women: they were gossipy, opinionated and judgemental. That William was about to marry one of Charlotte's friends did not bode well.

After a long illness, John Pitt had sadly passed away in late 1786. Mary's friends and neighbours had rallied round to support her at this difficult time. Mr and Mrs Papendiek were, according to Charlotte Papendiek, constantly with Mrs Pitt at Upton:

> … enjoying the homely fare of cake or bread with wine, in the dear brick-floored parlour. She, poor woman, complained much of the dullness of her life, and we did our best to cheer her, as did also Dr Herschel, who often walked over to her house with his sister of an evening, and as often induced her to join his snug dinner at Slough.[3]

In time, this friendly concern between neighbours developed into something more. William began to look upon Mary as more than simply his widowed neighbour and to think that perhaps she was beginning to see him differently, too. In the summer of 1787 William proposed and Mary said yes.

Soon, however, it began to dawn on Mary that she had not thought the offer through properly. She began to have and voice doubts. Their lives were very different. They needed to be very clear as to how they would make their two lifestyles work together. She was a local matriarch, a fixture in the social scene of their town; he, on the other hand, was a man of science whose work took place mostly at night and whose place of work was rooted to a single spot. Where would they live? How, if at all, would her prospective husband's working arrangements change, and if they didn't, when would she ever see him?

William had assumed that they would keep both the house in Upton and the one in Slough. They would live together in Upton, while giving full charge of the house at Slough to Caroline. Slough would remain the Herschels' place of business, so William would continue to work there, just not live there any more. They could not very well move the telescopes and Caroline was now his official astronomical assistant – to him, this arrangement made perfect sense. Mary, however, began to see some major flaws in such a plan.

Mary's concerns were essentially ones of power, appearance and position. She was the lady of the house. As William Herschel's wife, she would expect to be in charge of their shared household. Yet, if he continued to work (which he intended to do) at what was to become Caroline's home, where did that leave her? Mary did not like the idea of being left, as she saw it, on the sideline, to be visited occasionally while her husband's main life, in the house where he spent the majority of his time and where he continued to work and welcome visitors, was elsewhere. Having thoroughly thought through the situation, she decided to turn him down after all.

William was not discouraged. If continuing as they were but handing over the house at Slough to Caroline did not suit Mary, he would think of something else. By the autumn, they had come up with a new plan, one which met with Mary's, if not Caroline's, approval. Mary and William would live in *both* houses and Mary would be mistress of both. They would have accommodation and two maid servants at each residence, and one footman would move between the two and have a place to stay in both houses. Caroline would have an apartment over the workshop so she and William could continue to work together on the large telescopes. As a plan, this one seemed neatly to have addressed all of Mary's concerns.

For Caroline, this second plan was a huge blow. Initially, it had seemed as though she would have charge of her own home, and have work collaborating with her brother on astronomical projects. Now, in this new, revised arrangement, she was put, as she felt it, very firmly back in her place. With her apartments above the workshops, her new position was only marginally better than the maid servants they were employing for each house. She was now the paid help with living space provided; no longer an integral and authoritative part of the family with the additional status of astronomical assistant.

Stoically, Caroline tried not to make a fuss. Or at least, she tried not to leave any evidence of any upset she may have felt. Several pages from her diary from this period are missing; ripped out for fear that readers might judge her harshly for her reaction to the supposedly happy news of her brother's impending marriage.

However, if Caroline was tempted to dwell on the step back her journey to independence had taken, she was not given the opportunity. In November, the Herschel household opened its doors to a group of French astronomers and mathematicians who had come over to meet them and see their now famous telescopes. The group, comprising Messrs Cassini, Méchain and Legendre, came to visit and observe with William and Caroline through the 20ft telescope on 26 and 27 November 1787.

In fact, the group were in England for other scientific reasons beyond just visiting the Herschels. They were part of the 'Anglo-French Survey', measuring very accurately the distance between the Paris Observatory and the Royal Observatory in Greenwich using trigonometry. The British side of the project was run by William Roy, who went on to establish Britain's very first Ordnance Survey (on which Herschel's 40ft telescope featured as a landmark).[4] The project itself was initiated by Jean-Dominique, Comte de Cassini, with the aim of better determining the latitude and longitude of each place and improving the accuracy of mapping and navigation. Cassini was the astronomer – the French equivalent of the Astronomer Royal – at the Paris Observatory. He had grown up at the observatory, his father having been astronomer there before him. At the time, major observatories were mainly concerned with mapping stars to aid nautical navigation, so the connection with the survey made sense. Pierre Méchain and Adrien-Marie Legendre were already known to the Herschels through correspondence, although this was their first meeting in person.

Like the Herschels, Méchain was interested in what we today term 'deep-sky objects', that is, stars, or, more precisely, objects that at first glance look like stars, but on closer inspection turn out to be nebulae or star clusters. Like William, he had discovered and catalogued quite a number of objects, though his motives were quite different. His interest was in finding comets. He catalogued deep-sky objects like his colleague Charles Messier, not because he was interested in what they were but to ensure that he and his fellow comet hunters did not mistake them for comets. His cataloguing meant that Caroline knew of his work and her comet discovery meant he knew her through hers.

Adrien-Marie Legendre, known to mathematics students everywhere for his Legendre Polynomials and his Legendre Transformation, had also been a correspondent of the Herschels. Legendre was not only a mathematician but also a surveyor. He had come to England on this occasion because of his surveying interests but, like Méchain, he was already known to the Herschels for his other works. When William discovered Uranus in 1781 and sent his observations to the Astronomer Royal, Nevil Maskelyne, Maskelyne immediately sent word to his colleagues in France, Méchain and Legendre among them, to do some calculations.

Eighteenth-century mathematics had developed differently according to geography. When Isaac Newton and Gottfried Wilhelm Leibniz both claimed to have discovered calculus at the same time, mathematicians took sides. Cambridge and, to an extent, other English mathematicians followed Newton; elsewhere, Leibniz was considered more popular. For nearly a century there developed two distinct traditions of mathematics, each one moving further and further away from the other. Both created useful mathematical tools, though which was better depended on what you wanted to use the mathematics for. Getting in the way of any neutral assessment of usefulness was the political environment, which meant there was a certain nationalistic pride in following the mathematics of one's particular country. Maskelyne was one of a handful of mathematically minded English natural philosophers to see past such nationalistic divides. To him, his French colleagues were the best equipped to make calculations on the movement of Uranus and establish a good understanding of its orbit. Knowing this, he sent William's observations to them, introducing both Herschel and his work to astronomers and mathematicians across the Channel.

By the time of their visit, William and Caroline knew of a great number of French mathematicians and philosophers, and had come to deeply admire their work. William had exchanged a few letters with colleagues of this group of mathematical astronomers, and even responded to their interest in his sister and her discovery. However, this was the Herschels' first meeting with these men.

William was very impressed. He recognised in their mathematics a set of skills that would be very useful to him and his work, yet it was slightly beyond his comprehension. He wished he could understand their work better. He admired what they were able to do, and they, in turn, were very impressed with the Herschels, their telescopes and instrument-making skills, and the astronomical achievements of both William and his sister. For Caroline, the visit offered a welcome relief. She could be the celebrated astronomer sister once more, an impressive collaborator and discoverer, who could demurely play down her pride in the name of feminine good manners.

After they left, Caroline's thoughts turned again to the downgrade in her status represented by her brother's impending nuptials. Staving off the inevitable, she threw herself into her work, helping William get his second catalogue of nebulae, star clusters and double stars ready for publication (the first had been published in 1786).

Then, in February 1788 came sad news for which Caroline could legitimately grieve. While William's forthcoming marriage was upsetting, leaving Caroline uncertain of her standing within the new family group and unhappy about her apparent drop in status, this news, from her brother Alexander, was genuinely and selflessly upsetting. Alexander's wife Margaret, after months of illness, had died.

On hearing the news, William wrote to his brother to send their condolences:

> This morning [Thursday, 7 February] I received your sad informa-
> tion of your loss, which occasioned a very sincere grief. Having
> been up all night Carolina was still in bed when your letter came.
> Poor Girl, she has hardly had a dry eye to-day … Carolina is not
> well enough to write to-day but will either to-morrow or next day
> endeavour to take up the pen.[5]

Caroline, it would seem, was so overcome with grief that she could not even write. Possibly she was already upset about many things when Margaret died, and her brother's sad news gave her an outlet for that frustration and grief. She was grieving, not only the loss of a sister but also her old life.

Up until that moment, there was nothing in her written records to suggest a close bond between the two women. Alexander had married shortly after William and Caroline had moved to Slough, leaving him (at his own choice) alone in Bath. Margaret Smith, as she then was, was a widow when they married. Little more is known of her except for the few impressions left by Caroline, her sister-in-law. William and Caroline did not attend the wedding; indeed, it has been suggested they were not invited, which is odd. Hints were made by Caroline in her personal papers that her brother had married poorly. As a family, they could be rather disapproving at times.

Some years earlier, Caroline described Alexander as being saved by his family from another woman. This was in Bath in the 1770s, and the woman in question – a Miss Coleman – was a friend of William's housekeeper, Mrs Bulman. Alexander even went as far as to get engaged to this woman, but after seeing her 'walking and talking' with a previous boyfriend, he had been encouraged to break it off. Perhaps Alexander had poor taste in women. Perhaps his family was overprotective of him. Perhaps no one would have been good enough.

Whatever differences they had, the family seemed to have patched things up by the summer of 1786, and accepted Alexander's decision to marry Margaret Smith, even if they did not wholeheartedly approve. When, that summer, William and Alexander travelled to Göttingen to deliver a telescope, Margaret came down to Slough to keep Caroline company while the boys were away. True to form, Caroline found this intrusion on her personal space and time trying, especially as it was imposed upon her by her brothers. Her main criticism was that she considered Margaret to be a gossip, one of the worst characteristics imaginable for Caroline. In that busy summer when Caroline was supervising workmen building the 40ft telescope, making calculations and discovering a comet, she found it annoying that she was forced to lose an hour here and there listening to Margaret's gossip.

Nevertheless, when this woman, who had been ill since at least Easter the previous year, died in February 1788, Caroline was grief-stricken. The changes taking place all around her, within the close-knit family group she had been a part of since coming to England in 1772 were too much for her. She had always feared that her brothers would one day marry and have wives to take care of them and their homes, leaving her without a role. She had just about come to terms with Alexander's wife, had even learned to tolerate her company, and now she was dead.

Alexander was now alone and nearly 100 miles away from his closest family. Caroline worried for him. He was not like William, outgoing and showman-like; Alexander was much more withdrawn. He liked to make things, study and keep to himself. He felt most comfortable with family, yet when William and Caroline moved to Slough neither they nor their brother Jacob in Hanover could persuade Alexander to leave the life he had made for himself in Bath and come to live with them. He did not like change, yet now he had had change imposed upon him and Caroline was worried about him.

Caroline's concern for her brother was at least a little coloured by concern she could not admit for herself. She, too, disliked change, and a very big one was now on the immediate horizon. Looking back, Caroline wrote of May 1788:

And the 8th of that month being fixed on for my Brother's marriage it may easily be supposed that I must have been fully employed (besides minding the heavens) to prepare everything as well as I could, against the time I was to give up the place of a Housekeeper, which was the 8th May 1788.[6]

Always taking care not to appear too bitter or ungrateful, Caroline destroyed her diaries from this period, leaving only this rather curt statement. It was recorded in the autobiography written in the 1820s for her brother Dietrich. Her simple remark that she had to prepare to 'give up' her post, though with no indication of what she was then to do, is filled with sadness. Her position within the family home that she had spent so many years cultivating – learning English and accounting, as well as English cooking and social etiquette – was all gone. Her paid position as William's astronomical assistant had felt like a royal appointment, a prestigious post, but now she was not sure that it did not simply compound the idea that she was the paid help. She did not doubt her brother's feelings for his fiancée, and she had no reason to personally dislike her; she was just unhappy and uncertain about her position in the newly arranged household.

Caroline had very personal reasons for finding her brother's marriage troubling, but she was not the only one questioning its repercussions. Others in the local area were more condescending in their light-hearted disapproval. Mary, as a local landowner and widow of a successful businessman, was much wealthier than the Herschels. Indeed, her mother owned their house. More than one local resident noticed this disparity in their wealth. 'Astronomers,' Fanny Burney noted at a tea party held by Mrs de Luc, 'are as able as other men to discern that gold can glitter as well as the stars.' Mary Pitt was wealthy and the Herschels were struggling. Therefore, local gossip concluded, William was marrying for money.

William may well have been marrying for money. Certainly their lives were far more comfortable after he married than before, when they were struggling to live on their royal pensions and supplementing their income making and selling telescopes. The sale of telescopes, however, continued after William married, so perhaps not.

The Herschels tended to be quite coy about romantic entanglements earlier in their lives; given the circles in which they moved, it seems entirely possible that had William wanted to marry for money he might have had plenty of opportunity to do so earlier. Certainly there were rumours while he was living in Bath, but nothing definite. Caroline never took much notice of the rumours, but then she had a very low opinion of gossip generally.

While Mary's wealth was an understandable advantage, it seems likely that William was attracted by more than just that. He was 50 years old and had been fiercely ambitious all his life. He had studied tirelessly as a child; in England, he had worked long hours building a reputation and a large network of pupils and employers, rising in status and income. After leaving music for astronomy, he had then had to work again developing a name for himself, proving his worth all over again. Now he had finally arrived, and made a home for himself. He was settled, able to make friends rather than simply colleagues. He had found, in the Pitts, people with whom he could relax and spend time away from music, astronomy and professional reputations. When John Pitt died, he lost a friend, but he was also given an opportunity to become part of a new family, just as Mary and her son Paul Adee would become part of his.

Had Caroline been able to think straight she may have felt happy for her brother. She was, however, far too preoccupied with fears for her future. She had felt like this once before, when she was 22 and in Hanover. Then William and Alexander had helped her out, bringing her over to England to start a new life. Now, once again, her family seemed to have outgrown her, but this time she was 38 and it did not seem that there were any other relatives on the horizon ready to help. She was on her own.

4

JÉRÔME DE LALANDE

The months following William's wedding were hard for Caroline as she tried to adjust and put a brave face on her new situation. How much she let on to her family about her worries is unclear. When, back in Hanover at the age of 22, she had found herself in a similar situation, again worried that her family was changing and needing her less and less, she had kept it to herself. Here, in astronomy at least, she was still very much needed, which must have been a comfort. On the domestic front, she seems to have been cross at her fall in status as much as worried for her future. But once again, not wanting to seem ungrateful or to appear too demanding, she kept her head down and made the best of things.

Caroline and Alexander were the witnesses at their brother's marriage at Upton church. If she held a grudge, she did so very quietly and without inconveniencing anyone. Mary's brother, John Baldwin, gave her away and following the ceremony the happy couple returned to their Slough home for their honeymoon. Six weeks later they moved into their Upton home, where they received visitors offering congratulations. Traditionally, a 'honeymoon' was simply the period post-wedding when a married couple would be left alone; it was not until the nineteenth century that it involved a holiday. In the case of William and Mary, the beginning and end of their honeymoon period was marked by where they chose to live. It seems a little tactless that they should have chosen Slough, Caroline's home, to spend their honeymoon, but it is possible they did so for her benefit, so she might have company and get to know her new sister-in-law away from the glaring eyes of society.

William and Mary's honeymoon period took them to roughly the end of June, the beginning of the English summer. For astronomers, the summer can often be their least productive time since the skies are lighter and towards midsummer, in England at least, it never gets fully dark. The Herschels never let this worry them unduly. Several of Caroline's comets were discovered in the summer, showing that she continued to observe whenever she got the chance, regardless of the season. Mostly, however, the summer was a time for taking trips and entertaining visitors.

William clearly did not completely remove himself from the world during his honeymoon. About halfway through, on 24 May, William seems to have found time to take a trip into London to read a paper to the Royal Society. The paper was on his planet (still called the Georgian Planet – the German name of Uranus having not yet found universal currency) and the moons or satellites he had discovered orbiting it. Finishing off this paper could explain why William was so keen to have his honeymoon in Slough, where he could continue to work on and off with his sister. It is not recorded what Mary thought of this arrangement, although perhaps she used this time to get reacquainted with the house her mother owned, and in which William and Caroline had been living for the past three years.

Caroline found she was still adjusting. She was coming to terms with her new position within the household, and too preoccupied by that to give much consideration to the character of William's new wife. William's friends, however, were full of praise for Mary and her plans to improve her husband. Initially, according to William's Bath friend, William Watson, there had been concern within the astronomical community that a wife might take William's attention away from his work to the detriment of astronomy as a whole. When this proved unlikely, they warmed to her at once.

In fact, the only change she brought on that front was to encourage annual breaks from work, holidays in the summer when the skies were brighter and the stars harder to see. As well as being generally good for his health and mental well-being, breaks allowed William to visit friends across the country and see the rapidly changing British landscape. They may even have helped his work, allowing him to refresh his mind and develop social networks with scientific men and women across the country. For Caroline, the trips gave her some freedom. While her brother and his wife were away, she was left in charge of the house to do as she wished. She could observe, study or write as she pleased. Those holidays were some of her most productive times.

However, in this first summer of their married life together, William and Mary did not go away but instead made themselves and their home ready for an important guest. The French astronomer and mathematician, Joseph-Jérôme le Français de Lalande was planning to visit England. Lalande and William had been correspondents for a long time, ever since 1782 when Lalande had first written to William with information calculated about his planet. Since then they had been exchanging papers, observations, questions and calculations with increasing regularity. When Caroline discovered her first comet in 1786, Lalande was among the first to offer his congratulations. By the time he eventually came to stay in August 1788, they were all old friends.

Jérôme de Lalande was roughly the same age as William and well established in his career as an astronomer when they began to correspond in the early 1780s. Astronomy was a profession that few in the eighteenth century considered outright, and Lalande was no different. He had not gone straight into it, but rather had started his adult life thinking he wanted to join the Jesuit Church and began training accordingly. His parents persuaded him to consider law instead, and he left his Jesuit college in Lyon and went to live and study in Paris. There he discovered astronomy through his landlord, Joseph-Nicolas Delisle. He attended Delisle's astronomy lectures at the Collège Royale and others on mathematical physics. Even with all these distractions, he still managed to pass his law degree and had planned to go back home to use it, when he was offered a job by his mathematical physics lecturer, Pierre Lemonnier. The job involved him going to the Cape of Good Hope (now Cape Town in South Africa) to take observations of the Moon and Mars that would then be compared to other observations taken at other points around the world. The point of this co-ordinated effort was to compare the results, apply some trigonometry and work out the distances between the Earth, the Moon and Mars, and ultimately to extrapolate back from those observations to calculate the size of the whole solar system. It was all part of the eighteenth-century obsession with measuring every aspect of our solar system very, very accurately.

For Lalande, the value of the experience came not so much from the answers it provided to questions raised in astronomy, but from the position it put him in. From this one project, he was invited to join several prestigious societies, had his work published and found he could now talk about astronomy with people as well established and admired in intellectual circles as Voltaire and Maupertuis. And he did all of this by the age of 21 …

From his Cape Town project, Lalande was then invited to join another. Where his first project had involved using observation, measurement and mathematics to measure the size of the solar system, the next required him to study historical observations and measurements, then apply mathematics to that raw data to calculate very accurately the orbit of Halley's Comet. From these calculations Lalande, together with Alexis Clairaut and Madame Nicole-Reine Lepaute,[1] correctly predicted the details of the path of the comet's return in 1758–59. Theirs was a more precise update on calculations made earlier in the century by Edmund Halley, taking into account the affect passing by Jupiter and Saturn would have on the comet's trajectory. It meant astronomers would now have more accurate information about when and where to look for the comet's return.

Following these two successful projects, there came many offers of work. Lalande became editor of the prestigious *Connaissance des Temps*, the major French astronomical almanac, in 1760 remaining until the post was passed to the astronomer Edme Jeaurat in 1775 and then on to one of Lalande's students, Pierre Méchain in 1788. *Connaissance des Temps* was an annual publication (the longest running of its kind in the world) listing astronomical data derived from the Paris Observatory in a form that made the information useful primarily to mariners.

Two years later, Lalande also took over from his former teacher, Delisle, as Professor of Astronomy at the Collège Royale, a post he held until his death in 1807. Besides holding some very prestigious posts, Lalande also survived the French Revolution unscathed, a not inconsequential achievement. Several men of science were guillotined (the most famous was the chemist Antoine Lavoisier) after the abolition of the Royal Academy of Science, and several more died in prison. Lalande, however, continued as he always had. His only concession was to discreetly change his name from the aristocratic sounding 'de la Lande' to 'Lalande'.

Of all his achievements over his long and eventful life, however, he is perhaps best known for his writing and his championing of women in science. In 1764, Lalande published the first two volumes of his most famous book, *Traité d'astronomie*. The line between academic and popular writing was somewhat blurry in the eighteenth century, with a big grey area in the middle – and this book fell very much within that blurry grey area. The *Traité* introduced many new readers to astronomy, and Lalande wrote about all the latest developments in a way that would appeal to both the novice and the seasoned observer. The book went into several editions, each one updated to include the latest discoveries and new theories on the subject. After Lalande got to know the Herschels, he made sure they were included in this work, along with their 40ft reflector telescope once it was finished.

Twenty years later, in 1785 Lalande published *Astronomie des Dames*, celebrating the history of women in astronomy and adding new information in each later edition – those published in 1795 and 1806 – so that all but the first included mention of Caroline Herschel and her comets. His book tried to celebrate all the major women in astronomy from the ancient Greek Hypatia right through to the women he knew and in some cases had collaborated with, such as Madame Lepaute and Madame Dupiery. His support of women astronomers was not, however, limited to celebrating women's achievements in print. In 1791, when he became head of the Collège Royale, he changed the rules and among his many improvements and updates allowed women to attend as students for the first time.

In telling stories about women in science and the terrible inequalities they have had to overcome to make any headway in their chosen subject, we sometimes forget to give proper thought to the men who helped them. Of course, there were men who actively hindered the progress of women, and many more who indirectly got in the way by supporting, or at least not resisting, rules that kept women from participating in science. However, there were also men like Lalande who saw a problem and tried to use their authority as a man of science to make a difference.

When Lalande was put in charge of first *Connaissance des Temps* in 1760 and then the *Éphémérides des Mouvements Célestes* in 1763, he took over what was already a large and complex organisation. Tables such as those contained in these publications took a lot of work to produce. Astronomers would do the basic observing, and then needed a team of people who would use a string of mathematical processes to turn that raw data into useable tables. This calculating, recalculating and checking work tended to be done piecemeal by workers in their own homes. These workers were known as 'computers'. Each computer would be sent several books to help with their calculations, a set of instructions and a set of raw data. A university degree was not needed for this work, but the computers did need to be competent mathematicians. It is from these human computers that we get the term 'computer' that we use today. Occasionally the computers happened to be women, and this explains some of Lalande's sympathy for and support of scientific women. He knew at first hand that women could be just as capable as men in scientific and mathematical work, given the opportunity. He had worked with Madame Lepaute on calculating the orbit of Halley's Comet, and had since provided work for several women as homeworker computers. He had, by the time of writing *Astronomie des Dames* and meeting Caroline Herschel, worked with some very talented women whose expertise he had encouraged and made use of in his work.

Lalande was both a teacher and a compiler of tables and he blended the two roles so that many of his best students were given their first jobs working for him as computers. Among the best known of those students were Jean-Baptiste Delambre, Pierre Méchain (who had just visited the Herschels) and Lalande's nephew, Michel Lefrançois de Lalande. Lesser known students also followed this route, including several women, among whom were Lalande's illegitimate daughter, Amelie Harley, and the mathematical astronomer-turned-chemist, Madame Marie Louise Elisabeth Félicité Dupiery.

Madame Dupiery (sometimes written Madame du Pierry, or du Piery) went to work with Lalande as a computer (it is not exactly clear how this came about) around the time that she was widowed in 1780. She was already a competent mathematician, thanks to some familiarity with bookkeeping garnered from her father and husband, who both worked as tax collectors. She lived half an hour's walk from Lalande's apartments at the Collège Royale, moving right next door to the college in 1793. In 1779, shortly before her husband died, she began to learn astronomical calculus from Lalande. By 1782, her astronomical tables and accompanying explanations were being published with her name attached.

By the mid-1780s she was described as one of Lalande's 'expert' computers, with duties including checking the work of other student computers, supervising them in Lalande's absence and proofreading Lalande's work before it went to print. In November 1786, in writing his congratulations to Caroline on her comet discovery, Lalande wrote:

[translation] Madame du Piery ... is a philosopher who tries to follow in the footsteps of Miss Caroline Herschel, but has not discovered a comet; she asks her happy rival to receive her admiration, and I ask the same grace.

In reply, William wrote on Caroline's behalf that she, in turn, admired her happy rival, and her ability to do calculus, something she could not do herself but had begged her brother to teach her. It was a very polite exchange of mutual admiration and respect.

Madame Dupiery went on to work in chemistry, dropping out of science for a while when money was tight to work as a tutor and governess, before returning to teach her own course in astronomy designed for women. In keeping with convention, she took great care, in the publicity for her course, not to appear too ambitious or thorough. The course, she reassured the public, 'is in no way a *Savante* attempting to teach a thorough course in astronomy', as she 'knows how important still it is for people of her gender to avoid the ridicule of claiming to be able to do so'.[2] Given that the course seemed to have taught everything from Kepler and Newton's laws on the movement of the planets, right through to the more recent philosophical theories such as the Plurality of Worlds, it is hard to imagine the precise nature of the 'thoroughness' she was trying so purposefully to avoid.

Lalande had worked with Dupiery, taught her and given her opportunities and introductions. She worked extremely hard to build her reputation and produce work that deserved it, but she was also aware of the part Lalande had played in the process. He had helped her, as he had a number of other women, not out of any particular sense of duty or condescension but because his work and experience of working with women had shown him the irrationality of excluding them. When he came to learn about the Herschels, their brother-sister collaboration came as no surprise to him. Throughout his career he had worked on projects in partnership with a series of highly skilled women and saw nothing remarkable or untoward about William and Caroline forming a similar pairing. At the same time, he was aware that the scientific world did not treat men and women equally and saw it as his duty, and that of others, to redress this balance and offer encouragement wherever he could. From early on in his friendship with William, he took care wherever possible to include Caroline in his good wishes and support.

William Herschel and Jérôme de Lalande had begun writing to one another in May 1782. Lalande wrote the first letter, informing William about the calculations that he and other French mathematicians had relating to his planet. From these, he told William, they could describe the planet's orbit and predict when it would disappear and reappear from view on Earth (that is, when it would be on the opposite side of the Sun from us). Then he probed William for information. First, he wanted to know all about the telescope he had used to find his planet. Was this the same as the one he had written about recently in the *Philosophical Transactions of the Royal Society*, in relation to his observations of the spots on Jupiter? Then he asked about the man himself. Everyone in Paris, it seemed, wanted to know about this musician turned instrument maker turned discoverer. Where was he born? What brought him to England? How did he come to take up optics and astronomy? He wanted to know, he told William, not just out of curiosity, but for something he was writing. William, it seems, was to appear in the next edition of Lalande's *Traité D'astronomie*, or just *d'astronomie*, as it became known.

William was immensely flattered. Always keen to tell his story, he began, 'I was born in the city of Hannover Nov 15 1738 and brought up on Music; my leisure hours were generally devoted to Mathematics and other studies.'[3] His turn of phrase was important. He wanted to get across the facts – that he was a trained musician who took up mathematics and astronomy in his spare time – yet he also wanted to convey a certain image. He was keen to emphasise, some might say exaggerate, his early interest in mathematics. He presented this interest as one of 'leisure', implying that he was of a class that could utilise significant amounts of their time in such a way. Never mind that, when he and his siblings were children, all these different subjects were wrapped up together as self-improvement, a means of making themselves more marketable musicians, or that his early interest as an adult had a professional bent, giving him an edge over fellow musicians as one who could also converse fashionably on the latest philomathematical puzzles. To Lalande, and the world Lalande would be writing for, he was keen to present himself as a leisured man with curiosities, rather than a jobbing musician who found success. Women were not the only ones who had to hide their true intentions.

William told Lalande about his telescope and gushed in admiration of Lalande as a man of science and the writer of the great work on astronomy of which he had just bought the latest volume. After that, their correspondence settled down a little. In May 1783 William wrote to Lalande telling him that his latest paper was inspired by him. The paper was on the motion of the Sun and the solar system and William felt his work confirmed claims that Lalande had made in a much earlier piece. On other occasions, William would send Lalande papers before they were published to get his opinion and approval. Lalande, in turn, would send William calculations that he and other French mathematicians had made or news on discussions that had taken place in Paris on his work and legacy.

To Caroline, Lalande was always gracious and supportive, and his students were equally encouraging. Following Méchain's visit to Slough earlier in 1788, he wrote to William asking him to pass on his admiration for Caroline, whom he felt would be remembered and celebrated for centuries to come. A few years after his own visit, Lalande named his niece and god-daughter after her. Baby Caroline had a brother, also named by Lalande. He was called Isaac, after Isaac Newton – Lalande had put Caroline on a par with Isaac Newton. This gesture finally broke Caroline's resolve, encouraging her to write herself, rather than through her brother, to this illustrious man of science who offered her so much attention. She wrote:

> Our good friend, General Komarzewski [Polish nobleman involved in mining] will persuade me to believe that I am capable of giving you pleasure, by writing a few lines, but I am under an apprehension that he is overrating my abilities. You, my dear Sir, certainly overrate them.[4]

Caroline found it hard to take a compliment, but she was, despite her insistent modesty, rather pleased and wished the new baby good health and her parents and uncle great happiness and pleasure.

By the summer of 1788, when Lalande began to plan his trip to England, the Herschels could consider him a family friend. Lalande's trip was to take in a stay with the Herschels, of course, but also a visit to the royal palace, where he had been granted an audience with the king. He was also to go and visit Sir Joseph Banks at the Royal Society and Nevil Maskelyne at the Royal Observatory, Greenwich. Politically, relations between Britain and France were already becoming frosty, but these men of science, unlike a number of their peers, were open to ideas and the philosophers attached to them from across the Channel. There was already a theoretical belief among philosophical individuals that science transcended borders and was above politics but, as is so often the case, putting such ideals into practice was another matter. William Herschel with his direct patronage, and Joseph Banks and Nevil Maskelyne from their royal institutions, had to be careful, but if the king was willing to grant audience, who were they to argue?

Lalande's visit was a great success and he and the Herschels became much closer friends as a result. William even braved showing this renowned mathematician some of his own attempts at calculation, with mixed results. Lalande, having received William's letter, had looked over his calculations, as had their friend, fellow mathematician M. Delambre, and unfortunately found many errors. William, quite embarrassed, wrote back with thanks and excuses. He blustered:

> I have so little leisure for practice it would be no wonder, on account of the multiplicity of things that take up my time and continually disturb my thoughts, when I am calculating, if I had made many more blunders than I have made.[5]

Caroline made no such attempt to impress. She had no illusions about her mathematical ability. Indeed, she had already said as much to Lalande and Madame Dupiery in her comments on not having been taught calculus. What she did do well, however – and she knew it – was observe in her spare time with her small telescope on the roof. As the nights drew in and the summer visitors became fewer, and as she adjusted to her newly married brother and her new sister-in-law, Caroline got back to work.

On the night of 21 December 1788 her vigilant and careful observing again paid off. The next day, she wrote to Nevil Maskelyne, this time announcing confidently, 'I discovered a comet,' before giving details on its location and how it had moved between the early evening and that morning. Then, to soften the force of her rather abrupt announcement, she added, 'I beg the favour of you to take it under your protection.'[6] She then signed off, passing on compliments from her brothers and sister-in-law to Maskelyne and his wife.

Caroline's announcement of the second comet was far bolder than her first. Whereas in 1786 she had written timidly to Dr Blagden, apologising for being the one to announce it but explaining that her brother was away, this time she was far more upfront. Her request of a 'favour' and for the comet to be taken under Maskelyne's 'protection' shows she was trying to conform and still play the part of the grateful and unassuming woman, but this was much more of a token effort than before. Maskelyne was, by now, enough of a friend that she could announce her discovery to him without fear of being seen as overstepping any lines. To others within the scientific community she remained a little more cautious, letting her brother, as was traditional, speak for her.

Sir Henry Englefield, a baron and fellow of the Royal Society, had recently published some work on comets and so William told him about Caroline's new discovery. Englefield was very impressed, sending her his compliments and declaring, 'She will soon be the great Comet finder and bear away the Prize from Messieurs Messier and Méchain.' There was undoubtedly a touch of xenophobia, or at least anti-French sentiment, in that comment but it was a compliment to Caroline nonetheless, and she took it. Her findings were read to the Royal Society (on her behalf – as a woman she was still forbidden from attending meetings) and published in *Philosophical Transactions* the following year. Caroline was now officially a comet hunter.

Today we know Caroline's second comet as 35P/Herschel–Rigollet, after Caroline and Roger Rigollet, the man who rediscovered the comet 151 years later. Why is his name also attached to her comet? The reasoning here seems very unclear. It was not immediately identified as the same comet – that took a few days and some calculations by L.E. Cunningham – but that does not seem entirely satisfactory as an explanation. It seems unlikely that the same consideration would have been given had it been the other way around. How astronomical bodies, and comets in particular, have been named over history has been rather ambiguous. The International Astronomical Union (IAU) was established in 1922 with the aim of ironing out the many inconsistencies in astronomical nomenclature. Before the IAU existed, no one could agree, for example, how many constellations there were, or which bodies did and did not count as planets. Internationally agreed conventions on comet naming took a little longer and are, to some extent, still left to the discretion of the discoverer. Perhaps we should think of this comet's name as a historical inconsistency.

Caroline ended 1788 on a high. Her relegation to live-in astronomical assistant upon her brother's marriage, having previously been lady of the house, was a blow. However, some friendly visits by admiring French philosophers and her second comet discovery, followed by many flattering compliments regarding her abilities and importance, had started to make up for it. It was early days, but she may even have begun to like her new sister-in-law. Of course, she was still worried for her widowed brother Alexander, alone in Bath, but they were a close family despite the distances involved and he was always welcome in Slough. Indeed, he would be especially welcome in the coming year, with his technical skills and keen eye for mechanical detail. The Herschel household had some big changes ahead; they would need all the skills their family could provide and more besides.

1789

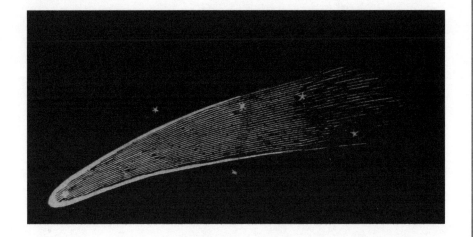

5

ASTRONOMY AND ENGINEERING

Having ended the year with another comet discovery, Caroline began 1789 feeling rather pleased with herself. She had her own income and was becoming known as a hunter of comets. Contrary to her initial fears, she was also needed around the home – the astronomical parts of it, at least – as much as ever before. The pace was picking up on a project that had been around for a while, and was in many ways the reason for them choosing to live in that house. The great 40ft reflector telescope was almost ready for use.

William had been building telescopes for sixteen years by this time. He began small, with his 7ft reflector, a telescope only slightly different from one he had read about in a book. This was the telescope he used to discover Uranus. By June 1776 he had built a 10ft reflector, which copied much of the same design as the 7ft but scaled up. Again, it had an octagonal wooden tube, with a rectangular wooden frame that could pivot on wheels and moved up and down with pulleys.

Next, he doubled the size of the tube and came up with two different versions of a 20ft telescope. Both telescopes had, as the name would imply, a tube 20ft (about 6m) in length. The first, which William was using by 1781, comprised an octagonal wooden tube mounted on a frame that was essentially a ladder. One end was fixed to a ratchet and wheel on the floor, allowing it to be moved side to side; the other, as before, was attached to a pulley and wheel system to allow the telescope to be moved up and down. This was the 'small' 20ft, referring to the size of the primary mirror. This first 20ft reflector had a primary mirror of 12in (about 30cm); the second had a primary mirror of 18.7in (nearly half a metre).

The job of any telescope is to make the things we see appear larger. There are two main ways of doing this: by using a lens (refractor) or a mirror (reflector). The larger the primary lens or mirror, the greater the magnifying power. Telescopes will often have other lenses and mirrors, to direct the light or magnified image into the eyepiece. These tend to be termed 'secondary' mirrors or lenses. This is why, when talking about the size of the main mirror or lens, it is important to emphasis the term 'primary', to demonstrate which lens or mirror we are talking about. Generally, the bigger the primary lens or mirror, the longer the telescope needs to be (depending on the curve on the mirror or lens) in order to produce an image that is in focus. The problem with making very big telescopes with big lenses or mirrors is that the large discs tend to become very heavy and sag in the middle. This is why mirror (or reflector) telescopes lend themselves more to this process of expansion than lens (or refractor) telescopes. You need to be able to see through a lens; a mirror, on the other hand, can be supported at the back.

The Herschels' second 20ft reflector was much bigger than the first. The tube was the same length, but its diameter was half as big again. This meant it needed a more substantial frame than the small 20ft. It also meant it was more cumbersome to use. William could not use this one on his own; he needed Caroline to assist him. This must have been a motivating factor in William's decision to train Caroline in astronomy.

The second 20ft telescope was first used in 1783, not long after Caroline had begun her training. For this telescope, the Herschels had built a large wooden frame, consisting essentially of two self-supporting ladders, one on each side of the tube. These were fixed onto a hexagonal frame on the floor, which itself was on coasters so the whole frame could be rotated. The bottom of the telescope was also fixed onto this frame. Across the top of the ladders was a beam from which a rope and pulley system was hung, allowing the telescope to be raised and lowered. Finally, a platform was hung across the ladders in such a way that it (and the observer, William) could be raised and lowered with the telescope. This was how he made his observations, sitting on the platform and looking into the tube.

Reflector telescopes come in many designs. The main ones available in the Herschels' day were the 'Newtonian' and the 'Gregorian' designs. The Newtonian reflector design, invented by Isaac Newton, uses a large concave primary mirror that collects the light at one end of the telescope, bringing it to a focus at the other, at which point the light is directed out of the side of the tube by a diagonal secondary mirror. This means the eyepiece of this type of telescope is on the side of the telescope, at the opposite end to the primary mirror. The other type was the Gregorian reflector. In this design, the primary mirror is concave again, but this time has a hole in the middle. Again, the primary mirror brings the light coming in to a focus at the other end of the tube, but this time the secondary mirror reflects it straight back down the tube, through the hole in the middle of the secondary mirror and into the eyepiece. In this design, the eyepiece is at the bottom of the telescope, at the same end as the primary mirror.

The Herschel telescopes were all broadly Newtonian, but William was never quite happy with that design. Eventually he came up with a design of his own. Initially, the large 20ft had been a Newtonian, with an eyepiece mounted at the top end, just off to one side. After several years of experimentation, however, trying out different options, William eventually came up with a new design, making this the first 'Herschelian' reflector. In this new design, there was no secondary mirror, partly because each time a beam of light is reflected some light is lost, so the fewer bounces it makes, the more light you can see and so the more stars become visible. But the other reason was that mirrors in the eighteenth century were made from a metal compound called speculum, which tarnished easily and needed regular polishing. Without a secondary mirror, the new design required less maintenance.

In Herschel's new design, the primary mirror is mounted at an angle. Light comes in, down the tube, and is then reflected and focused towards one edge of the tube. This means the observer is not in the way of incoming light, he can just hang from his platform with his eyepieces and observe near the edge of the tube, at the point at which the light reaches its focus.

By the late 1780s most of the design elements of the 40ft had been worked out and tested in the large 20ft. William now had a design for its frame, tube and configuration of mirrors and eyepieces. Having also secured sufficient funds from the king, the Herschels were now ready to assemble their giant telescope. The larger frame for the new 40ft telescope had been put up in 1786. A year later, the finished tube arrived. Alexander, together with some locally employed brassmen, was working on the eyepieces and micrometers (measuring tools to use with eyepieces).

The main problem, however, was the mirrors. Despite having come up with a design of telescope that only used one mirror, the Herschels still needed to have two cast because they tarnished easily and took a long time to polish. To have any chance of using the telescope regularly, they needed two, so that at any one time, there would be one in use and one being polished. No one had ever cast a mirror this big – the mirrors needed to be around a metre in diameter – so understandably there were issues. The first attempt was too thin at the centre and lost some of its shape when mounted in the tube. The second, more successful try was thicker but also much heavier. It weighed nearly 1,000kg, making each attempt to move it an event requiring several people and lots of equipment. Then there came the problem of polishing the mirrors. William had always polished his mirrors on his own. He had a technique which he had perfected over many years involving continuous movement so that his hand did not leave the mirror, and he would do this for hours at a time. Caroline would often keep him company in those long hours, feeding him and reading him stories.[1]

A mirror of the size needed for the 40ft, however, was too much for a single person, even one prepared to work on it for hours at a time. The mirror would need a team of polishers.

The first of the mirrors for the 40ft was polished by around twenty men, working in teams, under William or Caroline's supervision. They worked in teams of twelve and each man was given a number on their protective overalls that corresponded to the part of the mirror on which they were charged with working. It took a very long time and the results were uneven. It would not do.

Not happy with the finish, William began experimenting with tools to simplify the process. He needed a means of overcoming the inconsistencies between workers and providing continuity where there was division between workmen on different sections and different shifts. Eventually he came up with a polishing machine, which he tried out first on the mirror for the large 20ft in January 1789 and then, when he was happy with the results, on the second mirror, for the 40ft in March. The finished mirror here was much better. In fact, William was so pleased with the results he went on to make polishing machines for the mirrors of his smaller telescopes too. A team was still needed for the 40ft, but a much smaller one that worked faster, and the results were better. By August, the telescope was finally ready to test.

While a great deal of concentration in the Herschel household had been lavished on the 40ft, getting it all assembled and getting those mirrors just right, they cannot have been entirely unaware of the huge upheavals taking place in the world around them. Unrest was growing across the Channel. France was in a huge amount of debt, mainly racked up by their involvement in the American Revolution and the Seven Years War. People were starving and taxation was high for many but not paid at all by the highest echelons of society. Tensions were rising, as those at the bottom were beginning to resent their lack of say in how the country was run and how those taxes were spent.

Where England's medieval hierarchy had been shaken up a century before by the English Civil War, the French still had the three-tier system of 'estates' that had once been common across Europe. The first estate comprised the clergy, the second, the nobility and the third, the 'commoners', sometimes subdivided further into urban dwelling business types (bourgeoisie) and rural labourers.[2] In France, while the king had ultimate authority, he was advised by representatives from each of these estates. Each estate used to meet and make recommendations to the king based on the needs of those they represented. Although each estate would debate in separate assemblies, together they formed the Estates General. When the system ran smoothly, everyone felt they had a say and were being heard. However, by 1789 it was not going smoothly. The fact that a tax set by the king and levied only on the third estate (the first two estates were exempt) was increasing at a time when people could least afford it was causing considerable resentment. The lack of equality regarding jobs was also becoming an issue. The second estate had the monopoly over most high-powered jobs, meaning that major decisions were often made in their favour. Also, while the third estate represented around 98 per cent of the population, their voting power within the Estates General was only equal to the other estates.

On 5 May 1789, an Estates General meeting was convened to try to deal with the country's economic crisis. The third estate offered some radical reforms which they hoped would go some way to addressing some of the inequalities. The second estate, however, stopped them at every turn, ostensibly for reasons of protocol and procedure. This was the last straw. Fed up, the third estate set up their own meeting – the National Assembly, on 17 June. They invited the others along, but made clear they would proceed with or without them.

Gradually more and more people came around to the National Assembly's cause, including the press and even parts of the army. At first, it looked like this new National Assembly might be the answer. It was being listened to, it seemed. The Assembly managed to get some political prisoners pardoned by the king and things looked like they might be getting better. Then, on 11 July the king, on the recommendation of advisors from the second estate, sacked his finance minister, Jacques Necker, one of the few political advisors sympathetic to the third estate. Soldiers were brought in from neighbouring countries (by now the king did not trust his own soldiers) and they lined the streets of Paris. There were public demonstrations on 12 July, which ended in fighting. There were riots and looting. Then, on 14 July a crowd gathered outside the Bastille, a barely used prison that had become a symbol of the abuses of royal power and wasted public money. On that day it contained just seven prisoners.

The storming of the Bastille marked the beginning of the French Revolution. The crowds took control, the prisoners were released and the arms held inside became the property of the revolutionaries. Paris was now ruled by the Paris Commune. Across the country, smaller rebellions took place and the king reinstated his finance minister, Jacques Necker, in response. Many aristocrats took the opportunity to flee the country, but for many of their countrymen and women this was a victory.

Meanwhile, leaders and aristocrats across the rest of Europe looked on with some concern. To commentators like Fanny Burney, from the comfort and security of the Queen's Lodge in Windsor, the news from Paris was 'truly terrible and tremendous'. To her, and those around her in Windsor and at the palace (including many friends of the Herschels), it represented 'the demolition of this Great Nation, which rises up, all against itself, for its own ruin – perhaps annihilation'.[3] Could it happen in England? No one, at this stage, was quite sure.

Among the scientific men known by the Herschels, to start with, little appeared to have changed. *Connaissance des Temps* continued to produce its annual publications of astronomical tables for mariners and Pierre Méchain continued as its editor, as he had since his appointment the year before. The Collège Royale continued to run classes, and so Lalande also continued to work; books were still published and Madame Dupiery continued to teach her astronomy class to women. Scientific letters – for now – continued to circulate around Europe, keeping men and women up to date with all the latest news and developments. Scientifically, the world continued just as it had before; politically, however, these were uncertain times.

On a much less dramatic scale, the Herschels were causing a mini-revolution of their own at the Royal Society. In April, William's account of Caroline's second comet discovery was read to the Royal Society. Where her first comet had been announced by her – making it the first paper in that journal written by a woman – they went with a more conventional approach for her second. This time, William wrote on her behalf, announcing her discovery to the society. This was the more usual way in which women were expected to participate in public debate, although still unusual in the sense that it was discussed as her work and she was given full credit.

Then, in June, William read a paper on his own work, presenting to the society his second catalogue of star clusters, nebulae and double stars. In this catalogue, as in his first, William credited Caroline with the discovery of those nebulae which she had found entirely on her own. For the eighteenth century, this was an unusual move. Not only was the subject matter revolutionary – focusing on the 'fixed stars', rather than the movement of bodies within the solar system – but so too was the acknowledgement of the work as a collaboration. Ordinarily, the maker of the catalogue would simply compile the data collected at their observatory. Sometimes, such as at the Royal Observatory, notes were kept on who took which observation in case of mistakes or particular observers having a slower than average reaction speed, but these were not generally published. What makes William's crediting of Caroline all the more unusual was that she was both a relative *and* a woman. He could very easily have absorbed her work into his – he chose not to.

One more thing made William's paper on his second catalogue revolutionary: the paper was not just a catalogue. It was a call for a new kind of astronomy. In this paper, William suggested that perhaps it might be time for astronomers to stop worrying quite so much about measuring exactly every aspect of our solar system and start studying the stars beyond, in the manner of a natural historian. That is, he suggested that we might study the stars with a view to understanding better what they are and how they evolve.

This was revolutionary, but it was also timely. To study the stars in detail, it was important to look at them as closely as possible and this meant using increasingly more powerful telescopes. By the time this paper was published, William was very close to completing his building of the world's most powerful telescope, perfectly suited to just the kind of astronomical project he was advocating. He had very nearly finished his large and expensive 40ft telescope.

The 40ft telescope was ready to use a month[4] after William read the paper about his catalogue to the Royal Society. On 28 August 1789, he and Caroline took their first observation together. While William looked for celestial objects through the eyepiece of the telescope, Caroline sat below in one of the two specially constructed huts at the bottom, with her two very accurate timepieces. When William saw an object, he would call down to her through a special pipe. She would then note down both the height measurement given by William and the time measurement from the clocks in front of her. Both observations were needed to record an object with any degree of accuracy.

To plot an object on a map you need two co-ordinates. In the case of stars and other celestial bodies, the co-ordinates are a measurement of height – either above the horizon or below the zenith – and a measurement of time. The time component comes from the fact that the Earth turns at a regular rate, showing different parts of the sky as it turns. When the Herschels discovered an object with the 40ft or with one of William's smaller telescopes, they did it together. William would spot the object and measure the height as it related to other nearby landmark stars; Caroline would record the observation and measure the time. In this way, they were able to collect all the information they needed to plot each object on a celestial map.

With the 40ft telescope, because of its size, Caroline's participation was confined to the hut, recording William's observation and then taking and recording her own. To use this telescope, they also needed an extra workman to move the telescope each time they needed to observe a new 'zone', or section of the sky. The workman (the Herschels rarely recorded names) would be stationed in a second hut, and William would communicate with him from his observing platform through a second pipe. When they were using a smaller telescope – the 20ft, for example – Caroline would sometimes be expected to perform both these tasks.

Caroline records an incident back in 1784 when they were working in this way. The weather had been bad on the night of 31 December 1784, and so they had almost written off any hope of observing. (They evidently did not go in much for celebrating New Year's Eve.) When the sky cleared unexpectedly at about 10 p.m., they rushed out to the large 20ft reflector. William climbed up onto the observing platform and shouted down to Caroline to make various adjustments. At the mirror end of the telescope was some machinery that contained large hooks 'such as butchers use'. William was instructing her to move this, quite impatiently, according to her accounts. In her haste she tripped, and one of the hooks went right into her thigh. She cried out, obviously in a huge amount of pain, and William helped her inside and called for the wife of his workman to come and help. The workman's wife was not sure what to do, so Caroline did what she could with the medicines they had in the house.

A few days later, having heard about her injury, their neighbour Dr Lind visited with some ointment. As if to justify, or excuse, the fuss she felt she was making, she recorded that Dr Lind had told her it was very serious, so serious that had she been a soldier she would have been entitled to six weeks in hospital. Ever the martyr, Caroline wrote afterwards that she found comfort in knowing that the next few nights were cloudy, so her injury would not unduly inconvenience her brother.

On that very first night observing with the 40ft, Friday 28 August 1789, William recorded a discovery. He wrote to Joseph Banks the next day, 'As soon as I could get hold of Saturn it gave me convincing proof of its [the 40ft's] superior power by shewing me immediately a sixth satellite, which has till now escaped the vigilance of astronomers.'[5] A couple of months later, he wrote again of his success with his new telescope:

Perhaps I ought to make an apology for troubling you again with a letter on the same subject as my former one; but if satellites will come in the way of my 40 feet reflector, it is a little hard to resist discovering them.[6]

He had discovered a seventh moon around Saturn to go with the sixth he had discovered in August. It was almost as though he were doing it on purpose to prove the very expensive telescope was value for money after all! The telescope had caused Banks considerable trouble, as he had been the go-between who was continually being sent to ask the king for more money on William's behalf. Here, William was offering proof that it had all been worthwhile.

The two satellites turned out to be the only discoveries ever made with the 40ft reflector. By the end of October, William was already complaining about condensation on the mirror, and soon he would be complaining of how much work was involved in maintaining and using such a large telescope. It was cumbersome and complicated to move around, and this was especially problematic given the uncertain weather conditions in England, where every moment of clear sky counted. While it was pioneering, its time had not really come. It would be another fifty years before anyone attempted to build a telescope bigger than this one, by which time William's idea of studying the stars and star grouping had gained some currency.

The successor to the 40ft telescope was built by an aristocrat, Lord Rosse, who spent his own money to build his telescope in his castle grounds. Unlike the Herschel telescope, it was not quite so burdened with expectation. The mirrors were *expected* to tarnish, and workmen were employed accordingly. It had no need to prove its value for money to anyone but Lord Rosse.

As it happens, historians have been rather sceptical of William's claims about his sudden and fortuitous discoveries so soon after the 40ft reflector was completed. In a letter from William to Joseph Banks in September 1789, William did hint that he might possibly have already seen Saturn's sixth satellite with his 20ft reflector, back in 1787.

In it, he mentioned, 'My 20 feet instrument had already given strong suspicions of its existence',[7] but he stopped short of suggesting that he had, in fact, discovered it already. The seventh, similarly, it has been suggested, was spotted first with the 20ft (on 8 September 1789) and then confirmed with the 40ft, a few weeks later. Whatever the case, it proved useful to save any official announcement of such discoveries until he could say with certainty that he had seen the moons through the new 40ft reflector.

Putting those two discoveries together, William hurriedly produced a paper for the Royal Society, read on 12 November 1789 and published the following year. In it, he talked about the surprise astronomers might feel that these satellites had not been discovered sooner, given the frequency with which astronomers viewed Saturn. However, he goes on to say, they did not have his telescope. It was with careful crafting that he made the following statement:

It will be seen presently that the situation and size of the satellites, that we could hardly expect to discover them till a telescope of the dimensions and aperture of my forty-feet reflector should be constructed; and I need not observe how much we Members of this Society must feel ourselves obliged to our Royal Patron, for his encouragement of the sciences, when we perceive that the discovery of these satellites is intirely [*sic*] owing to the liberal support whereby our most benevolent King has enabled his humble astronomer to complete the arduous undertaking of constructing this instrument.[8]

William understood the rules. If he hoped to receive royal patronage and funding ever again, he had to be publicly very grateful.

Caroline, sensibly, did not get involved in this side of the project. She would happily work anywhere, in her little hut by the 40ft, nearby as her brother worked at the 20ft or on her own on the roof. She would record William's observations and her own, but left the selling of the results and the promotion of their telescope and observing programme to her brother. That was his strong point, hers was the diligent recording, organising and ordering of their observations. To suggest that one of those traits was more useful to science than the other would be to misunderstand the process of what science is and how it functions. Both were essential; the siblings worked well together, complementing each other's strengths, and that is what made them such a good team.

The 40ft reflector became a powerful symbol of its time. It may not have been wildly successful scientifically, it may have required too much maintenance and been rather too cumbersome for regular use, but it was timely nonetheless. Reaching completion just one month after the storming of the Bastille, it offered a powerful message about Britain, its royalty and science. The British king, it showed, was a friend to science. Indeed, without him how could this telescope ever have been built? It reinforced a particular image of British science as pioneering, innovative, practical and tangible. It placed British astronomy on the map. The Herschels, in their adoptive new home, had made British astronomy and engineering the envy of the world.

1790

6

TWO MORE COMETS

The year 1790 had barely begun when Caroline discovered her third comet. The year before had been a busy one for the family with all the work needed to finish the 40ft telescope and prove its worth. The completion, promotion and early observing with the 40ft had virtually filled the entire year, leaving Caroline almost no time at all to herself.

They were exciting times. It was an undeniably grand and inspiring project to be a part of, but by the time the year had finally come to a close, Caroline was glad to be back to her old routine. She had missed her times away from her family and visitors. People were exhausting. To Caroline, it could sometimes be much nicer, even in the bitter cold of a January night, to be alone up on her roof with her telescope and the stars. William's grand projects were all very well, and she was pleased to be a part of them, but sometimes it was nice to be left alone with no one to talk to, just a little time apart to recharge and to reconnect with the universe above.

On 7 January 1790, Caroline discovered Comet C/1790 A1 (Herschel). This comet was just too dim to be seen with the naked eye, with its 'apparent magnitude' of +7, and remained in the visible part of the night sky for just a few more days after her discovery, until around 21 January. All celestial objects can be described in terms of their apparent brightness or magnitude (m) – their brightness as it appears from Earth. How bright a star really is may be different from its *apparent* brightness because of its relative distance from the Earth. A very bright star that is far away may look the same brightness as a dull star that is nearby. Apparent brightness allows one to talk about the brightness of the star without needing to know any more information about it, such as its *actual* brightness, its distance or size.

Apparent brightness is a relative measure. The ancient Greeks allocated a magnitude measure of 1 to the brightest twenty stars in the night sky, calling those stars 'first magnitude stars'. Astronomers have since been a little more exact, and rated those twenty in order of apparent brightness, but roughly speaking, first magnitude stars are the brightest – stars like Sirius, Vega and Betelgeuse. They are easily visible with the naked eye, and can even generally be seen in cities and places where there are a lot of street lights and other sources of light pollution. Anything in the night sky brighter than those stars – like our Sun – gets a negative magnitude; anything dimmer – like all the other stars – gets a positive magnitude. The scale goes down, the brighter the object appears to be. The Sun has an apparent magnitude of −27, the full Moon is −12.74; Venus, meanwhile, is +4, and the dimmest object visible to the naked eye is around +6.5. Caroline's third comet had an apparent magnitude of +7 and so was just beyond the range of brightness visible without a telescope.

Caroline found her comet on 7 January and, because her brother was at home at the time, the discovery was announced by him on her behalf as soon as she told him. The number of people considered to be authorities in matters of science and astronomy in the late eighteenth century was small. Official announcements tended to be made to Sir Joseph Banks, president of the Royal Society, or Charles Blagden, its secretary. Nevil Maskelyne, the Astronomer Royal, was also often approached. However, very often, the Herschels would also tell their well-known amateur friends, such as Alexander Aubert, a friend with his own private observatory near Deptford, or Sir Henry Englefield, an aristocrat and recent author of a recent book on comets.

The title 'amateur astronomer' in the eighteenth and nineteenth centuries had different connotations than it does now. There were very few professional astronomers – there was the Astronomer Royal and professors of astronomy at Oxford and Cambridge (the only universities in England at the time) and, by 1790, at Glasgow and Edinburgh. In each instance, these men (they were always men) had assistants who would have been paid, and so technically they would have been professional as opposed to amateur. All other astronomy was done by amateurs: very rich individuals who had the resources and free time to build themselves private observatories and study whatever aspect of astronomy caught their imagination.

Even today, amateurs account for many discoveries in astronomy. In the eighteenth century, however, they accounted for almost all of them. 'Amateur', in the eighteenth century, meant unhindered by professional obligation, the freedom to pursue one's interests and integrity, since you had no need to satisfy an employer or patron with the 'right' results. The Herschels, although proud of their royal pensions, were keen to emphasise that these were without strings, so they might still claim the moral authority of an amateur. In terms of people to tell about a new discovery, the Herschels' amateur friends were as well qualified as the professionals to judge its validity. They only lacked an institutional means of passing that information on.

In the case of Caroline's third comet, William wrote first to the aristocratic amateur Harry Englefield, who immediately passed the information on to his friend, the comet hunter and editor of *Connaissance des Temps*, Pierre Méchain in Paris. Curiously, this comet was not announced in the *Philosophical Transactions of the Royal Society*. Instead, word was spread, always naming Caroline as its discoverer, through letters. The same people were informed, just by a different means.

This was the tail end of the 'Republic of Letters', an informal international network of intellectuals and institutions that existed in the seventeenth and eighteenth centuries. This network linked people across Europe with those in America. It was a way for ideas to travel, thoughts to be developed and published work to be passed on. These networks predated official journals. Indeed, to an extent journals developed out of these networks. They existed on paper, through letters, but they were also fostered through social interactions, membership of societies, attendance at literary and scientific salons, and visits within a grand tour. Gradually some of this work was formalised into journals and official society meetings, but there was still an important role to be played by correspondence and social gatherings, not least for allowing women to participate in science. The Herschels' home, with its newly installed iconic telescope, was an example of this network in action. Visitors would come to see the telescope, meet up with the Herschels and their intellectual neighbours and call on a few men and women of science in London along the way.

Scientific journals were still something of a novelty in the 1790s. While the *Philosophical Transactions of the Royal Society* had been around for over a century, and most other countries had some kind of equivalent, they did not have the capacity or interest to publish every single piece of work produced in every science. Even now, intellectual ideas do not develop simply through a series of published papers. Discussion and informal interaction with others in the field is always needed along the way. In the eighteenth century, this was even more the case, as academic publishing was new and what should or should not be published had not yet fully been resolved. In the 1790s, there was still only one major journal per country trying to cover ALL science – and anyway, it was still not entirely decided what constituted 'science'.

Science was still known as natural philosophy in the 1790s, and covered all manner of different interests and disciplines. There was huge variation in what constituted a scientific paper – what it should contain and how it should be written. Caroline's paper on her first comet and her brother's on her second were little more than transcriptions of their letters to Dr Blagden and Sir Joseph Banks respectively. Other papers in the same editions went into several pages, with considerable experimental detail, reference to other papers and conclusions. New comet discoveries, as with many other new finds, were not always announced, although who decided which to leave out – the discoverer/author or the journal's editor – is not always clear. Caroline's comets were always announced to *somebody*; letters were always sent. In this instance, William, and plausibly Caroline, seems to have felt it more important that the news was spread among fellow comet hunters – Englefield and Méchain – than to the Royal Society and its members.

In the case of Henry Englefield, this seems to have been the right decision. As soon as he received William's letter he acted immediately. Only after he had passed on Caroline's discovery to comet hunters in Paris did he stop to reply. 'Pray congratulate Miss Herschel from me,' he wrote, 'on her new career, which I hope she will follow and share the glory with you.' Word spread and soon the popular press across Europe was aware of this peculiar woman and her discovery of yet another comet.

The Herschels were living through an age of social change. It was the tail end of the Enlightenment, the age of satire, the age of wonder. A common theme of this period was a questioning of hierarchy and the social structures that had been inherited from generations before. The French Revolution across the Channel and the American Revolution further afield were just the beginning. In religion, these changes gave rise to Protestantism and other forms of religious dissent as some Christians attempted to take on greater responsibility in their religious lives. This took the form of new types of worship, emphasising a personal interpretation of the Bible over that promoted by the Pope and Church authorities. In science too, relationships with hierarchies were changing as experimentation and seeing for oneself was replacing the authority of the ancients.

In art and literature, satire was flourishing as cartoonists and authors held up to ridicule the social hierarchies as they then stood. Politicians, then as now, were an obvious and easy target for satire, as were many caricatured figures: the archetypal Englishman, John Bull; quack doctors and old maids. Besides these, however, were cartoons of contemporary, much talked about events. Some of these were political or military. Cartoons also portrayed publicly understood science ridiculing the pomposity of a certain type of intellectual or, more often than not, mocking the latest scientific theory by taking its conclusions to a ludicrous extreme.

Those areas of science that caught the satirists' attention were not necessarily the same as those that caught the attention of men and women like the Herschels, whose whole lives were immersed in the subject. It was often the curious moments, rather than the scientifically pivotal ones, that had somehow caught the public imagination. Four years earlier, Caroline had been the subject of fascination and gossip as the discoverer of the first 'lady's comet'. Now she had become established, not just among her fellow comet hunters but among the readers of newspapers and the buyers of prints, as a phenomenon in her own right. She was a lady comet hunter.

A month after she found her third comet, an artist called R. Haydeian produced a cartoon called 'The Lady Philosopher: smelling out the Comet'.[1] Not perhaps the most flattering depiction Caroline could have hoped for, but many intellectual women had fared a lot worse. The cartoon showed a woman at a telescope, scientific instruments strewn at her feet, with hands clasped, exclaiming, 'What a strong sulphurous scent proceeds from this meteor!'. Fart jokes, as my children will confirm, then as now, are always funny. Added to this, the fact that the artist has included a mix-up between comet and meteor suggests that either he did not know they were different, or just as likely, thought Caroline did not. Even though she had discovered a comet and he had not, the cartoon suggests that the artist may still have thought himself more knowledgeable on astronomy than a mere woman.[2]

Intellectual women, whose achievements were cerebral rather than decorative, were often the subject of derision and mockery. Caroline probably got off quite lightly, yet it is notable that no similar cartoon exists ridiculing her brother. A century earlier, Margaret Cavendish had tried to take part in discussions at the Royal Society and had her clothing mocked and was given the name 'Mad Madge'. Contemporaries of Caroline, meanwhile, who were openly interested in intellectual pursuits, such as members of the Blue Stocking Society, Hannah More, Frances Burney and Elizabeth Montagu, were often ridiculed for their unladylike interest in matters of the mind.

The Blue Stocking Society was set up in the 1750s to promote and indulge intellectual curiosity among women. For the women who took part, it was stimulating and empowering. It gave them an outlet in which to indulge their intellectual curiosity and to do so in a supportive environment. Not everyone, however, saw theirs as a just or admirable cause. By the end of the century, 'Bluestocking' had become a term of derision in many circles.

Outside of Britain, intellectual women who dared express too much curiosity or competency had to manage their public persona very carefully if they were to avoid ridicule. The life stories of women such as Émilie Du Châtelet in France, Maria Angela Ardinghelli in Italy and Maria Winkelmann in Germany all show the care women needed to put into balancing intellectual fulfilment with socially acceptable female roles. Some had class or a husband on their side to help shield them from ridicule, but those without had to try harder. In all cases, they needed to take care not to claim too much, lest their ideas be rejected out of hand. It was a very careful balance that women had to manage if they wanted to pursue their intellectual interests, receive credit for it and use it to help take their subject forward.

Like all these women, Caroline had some help along the way from sympathetic men, but so much was down to delicate social judgement on her part. We try to remember the women for their contributions to science, but their social astuteness and continual attention to detail (one slip could destroy them) also deserves some credit.

Given the contemporary mood, Caroline's depiction as a woman 'smelling' comets, and possibly mixing them up with meteors, seems positively affectionate. Elsewhere, the attention she garnered was generally kind and friendly. She was the discoverer of the lady's comet – several by now, actually. She was the dutiful assistant to her brother and modest and shy with those who met her. This final attribute was important in allowing her scientific contributions to be accepted and celebrated. She was no threat, since she was first and foremost ladylike in her modesty, shyness and good nature.

On meeting Caroline for the first time, Fanny Burney described the woman before her, 'She is very little, very gentle, very modest, and very ingenuous: and her manners are those of a Person unhackneyed and unawed by the World, yet desirous to meet, and to return its smiles.'[3] Mrs Papendiek – about whom Caroline was always very rude in private writing – wrote, 'Miss Caroline Herschel was by no means prepossessing but a most excellent, kind-hearted creature, and though not a young woman of brilliant talents, yet one of unremitting perseverance, and or natural cleverness.'[4] Both women seemed keen to play down any hint of active ambition, energy or talent in their descriptions of Caroline. Papendiek, in particular, seems almost insulting in her description of Caroline's lack of 'brilliant talents' in contrast to the gushing praise written elsewhere in her diaries of William's genius, but it may be they were doing her a favour. To have come across as too pushy as a lower-class, middle-aged and unmarried immigrant woman would have been disastrous. That she was able to appear to these women as almost invisible, gentle, modest and kind-hearted was just as important to her success and acceptance as having astronomers know it that was her eye that had spotted yet another comet in the night sky. While occasionally in her personal notes or family letters late in life, Caroline might let slip that a specific incident or person left her seething, she knew better than to let strangers or acquaintances see that side of her. Her success relied on her playing a part, and she kept dutifully to her script.

Just four months after discovering her third comet, Caroline again found herself with time on her hands as her brother and his new wife went on holiday. The happy couple were taking a tour of Yorkshire. Though they left little record of this trip, a standard eighteenth-century holiday in Yorkshire (people were just starting to take holidays – the middling classes anyway), followed certain patterns. They would very likely have admired the countryside, visited a seaside resort such as

Scarborough and taken a look at a rapidly industrialising town such as Leeds. While they were away, Caroline stayed in Slough. Her brother Alexander came to keep her company, busying himself with brass work and other mechanical work for the telescopes. This left Caroline with some time to herself and her little telescope on the roof.

William had tried to win her over to bigger telescopes. He had built her a new model after her third comet discovery, but Caroline was never entirely convinced. She liked her old, familiar little sweeper. She liked the independence it gave her. She could use her small telescope on her own, whenever she had a moment. William always liked to upgrade, but was also happy to call on Caroline or a workman whenever he needed an extra pair of hands, unaware or uninterested in whether or not they were busy doing something else. Caroline was not like that, she did not like to ask for help or feel that she could not manage on her own. She liked to be a help to others, but when it came to asking for help for herself she was a lot less comfortable. The big telescope her brother kindly made for her, following her run of successful comet discoveries, was always a little too big. She was a small woman – less than 5ft tall – the new telescope had a tube of 5ft. It was altogether too cumbersome for her, after the compact and easily manoeuvrable telescope she was used to. Her brother's gift was a kind present, but based very much on his view of what she should be doing, rather than on her own assessment of what she needed. She would use both, changing between the two depending on her mood and what she was trying to see, but she preferred her old 'small sweeper'.

Out on the roof, with her small sweeper on 17 April 1790, Caroline discovered her fourth comet. With William away, Caroline once again stepped up to the challenge and wrote personally to her fellow astronomers to make her announcement. Straightaway, the morning after her discovery, she wrote to Alexander Aubert. 'I am almost ashamed to write to you,' she began.[5] She had no need to be, however, as his reply emphatically stated. She also wrote to Nevil Maskelyne, telling them both that she would wait for their replies before spreading the news further.

While she wrote that she would wait, she then began to get anxious. Sir Joseph Banks was also a friend, but he was much grander than Maskelyne or Aubert and so Caroline was a little apprehensive in writing to him. Nevertheless, time was ticking and she was anxious to get news of her comet out, as well as assurance that it was her comet and had not been claimed by anyone else. 'I am very unwilling to trouble you with incompleat [*sic*] observations,' she began. However, she went on, it could be days before she got a reply from Aubert or Maskelyne, or her brother William and, in order not 'to be thought neglectful' and 'for the sake of astronomy',[6] she did not feel she could wait that long. Banks understood her concerns. He thanked her, assuring her that he would 'take care to make our astronomical Friends acquainted with the obligation they are under to your diligence', adding that he was 'always happy to hear from you but never more so than when you give me an opportunity of expressing my obligations to you for advancing the science you cultivate with so much success'.[7]

Two days later, a reply came from Maskelyne. Like Banks, he was encouraging and trusting of her abilities. Even before he had a chance to see the comet himself, he felt able to pass on her announcement to Pierre Méchain in Paris. She was, he wrote, 'my worthy sister in astronomy'.[8]

While the Herschels' astronomical friends and admirers had been intrigued by her first comet, impressed by her second and encouraging of her third, her fourth seems to have marked a shift in how she was viewed. She had become something quite unprecedented. She was now most definitely a comet hunter, and yet she was a woman, and not even one with the benefits of an aristocratic education. She was baffling – but in a good way. Nevil Maskelyne praised her 'meritorious attention to our science',[9] after her third comet. By her fourth, he and his colleagues almost felt compelled to treat her as a fellow astronomer. Caroline had quietly achieved something extraordinary.

In time, prizes from societies around the world would come to her, but for now, she had to make do with small, personal gestures. In July, Lalande wrote her a letter. His sister had asked him to name her new baby and to be the child's godfather. Lalande chose Caroline, so that, like her brother Isaac, the baby might be named after a hero of science. Caroline was quietly and reluctantly flattered. She was even moved to write, although she made a point of dismissing all his praise and kind words as exaggeration.

Despite her letters, especially the one to Sir Joseph Banks at the Royal Society, this fourth comet discovery was not announced in the *Philosophical Transactions of the Royal Society*. Her letter to Banks, unlike her earlier letter about a previous comet to the Society's secretary Dr Blagden, did not make it into the journal's pages. This comet, as with her third, would need to rely on the network of scientific and intellectual correspondence that spanned Europe and America. It was sufficient; soon everyone knew, although, by now, yet another comet discovery by this remarkable woman was hardly news.

In the meantime, the Herschels got on with their work. William and Mary came back from their travels, Alexander went back to Bath and Caroline and William returned to their old routines, with William at the telescope, and Caroline at her desk. By now, William had virtually stopped using the 40ft reflector and was back to his much less awkward large 20ft telescope. On 13 November, he spotted something very interesting that would need some thinking about. What he saw contradicted everything he had previously believed about the stars and how to better understand them.

Up until this, and later observations in November, William had been working on the assumption that the little blurry spots in the sky, the ones that looked too blurry to be identified indisputably as single stars, were in fact *groups* of stars. With bigger telescopes and greater magnification, he thought he could resolve the blurs into their constituent stars. They might be pairs of stars revolving around one another, or perhaps clusters of stars. They might equally be stars that were light years apart, which just happened to appear from Earth to be in roughly the same place. This was the rationale behind his building larger and larger telescopes, so that he could work out what they really were. His observation on 13 November, however, threw that theory.

The object William found on 13 November was one with true nebulosity. It had a bright star in the middle, but was then surrounded by hazy bright material. No amount of magnification was going to resolve the hazy material into anything, that much was clear. William would need to rethink his theory. He looked back over his observations. He had been categorising the nebulae he found into different groups, depending on their shape. He had 'planetary nebulae', which were perfectly round; large nebulae; small nebulae; rich clusters; and scattered clusters. His cataloguing system was not yet complete, but he was working on it. This example of 'true nebulosity' meant that he had to think again about what those categories might mean.

This seemingly small discovery which, let us not forget, William could only have made with Caroline's help, had big repercussions for the history of astronomy. William had already started to introduce new kinds of questions into his discipline. He had drawn the first ever map of our galaxy – the Milky Way – back in 1785, encouraging astronomers to consider the universe beyond our solar system. His cataloguing of double stars and star clusters had nudged astronomers towards pondering the distribution of stars in the sky. Stars had mostly just been seen as a backdrop to the more interesting goings on within our solar system. William's investigations were a first step in looking beyond, to looking more closely at the stars, not just where they were but *what* they were. The discovery of true nebulosity pushed that still further. It offered the beginnings of a line of thinking that would change how we saw the stars. No longer static, unchanging points of light, these curious distant objects were evolving.

7

FRIENDS AND FANS

C aroline did not make friends easily. Her family was very important to her, friends she seems almost to have classed as an
unnecessary luxury. A few people did manage to get to her,
though. Scattered through her life there were a small number of men
and women whom she came to consider friends. These were people
who were kind to her, who took some time to get to know her and
gradually gain her trust.

Her gregarious and socially comfortable brother was much more
outgoing. Visitors to the house always remarked on his intelligence
and cheerful manner which made them feel instantly at ease. In that
setting, Caroline could get away with being shy and retiring. When
he was away and visitors came anyway, she found it more troubling
but determined it her duty to entertain, and did the best she could.
William's easy manner meant he made friends easily. Caroline was
always in his shadow, she could benefit from the company he attracted,
but friendship took a little longer.

As a child, Caroline's days had been filled with schoolwork and an
overwhelming array of domestic tasks, while her brothers had been
busy learning the skills they needed to make a living as musicians.
No one in the household had had much time for friends. The boys,

however, had a professional reason for learning to behave in a way considered respectful and courteous but also friendly and entertaining. They needed to hone this manner if they were to get work as society musicians. Musical skill was only part of the selection process; performance and likeability were also important attributes for musicians hoping to be invited into homes and concert venues to play and teach. Caroline, at home surrounded only by family and neighbouring families, had much less need for such skills and far fewer opportunities to learn them. As an adult musician and then astronomer, William had made professional acquaintances and, over time, some of these had become friends. Caroline never really had that opportunity. There were her brother's friends, but no one she had sought out to become friends with herself. As her comet discovery tally grew, however, and with it her reputation within the scientific world, her relationships with people outside her family had a chance to develop, reluctant though she was.

Caroline grew up in a house full of brothers. Most girls in her neighbourhood, of her age and social class, were like her, expected to cook and clean and look after their families. Her opportunities for meeting and making female friendships were always going to be limited. That said, there were a few women with whom she made friends as a child and whom she remembered fondly in old age. These were the girls that had surprised her as a child, making time for her with no other motive than to be friendly. Naturally, they needed to be nearby and not take her too far away from her many domestic responsibilities.

When Caroline was about 16, she made friends with a young woman whose family lived in the same building. Every morning, Caroline and her new friend would get up at dawn to meet, chat and learn a few sewing skills from one another. Learning dressmaking allowed Caroline to frame this rather frivolous activity in a way that made it seem useful and less selfish than simply wanting to spend time with a girl her own age. They would meet at dawn and then at 7 a.m. would leave for their daily routine with their respective families. The young woman, Mademoiselle Karsten, was in fact dying. She was up early in the morning because she could not sleep and welcomed the company and distraction Caroline gave her. Caroline was her friend when she needed it most; she, in turn, offered Caroline friendship at a time when her life was in every other way about serving others. Their friendship lasted until Mademoiselle Karsten sadly died a year later.

A year or so after her friend died, Caroline found herself in the company of women once again. After some begging, she had persuaded her mother to let her attend classes to learn millinery. Her father had recently passed away, leaving her brother Jacob as head of the house. Their mother asked his permission for Caroline to attend the classes, and he gave it with the proviso that it was for making her own things only – she would not be learning a trade. With that agreed, her mother made arrangements, bargaining with the teacher to allow Caroline onto this rather prestigious course at a reduced rate. So it was that at 17 she found herself attending lessons alongside twenty-one elegant young ladies from genteel families. Caroline kept her head down, aware that she was there on reduced rates and not really like the other students. To her surprise, they took to her. Her teacher became a friend and tried to encourage her to stay on after she had mastered the basics. Even more surprising was the friendship she made with a young woman who would go on to become Madame Charlotte Beckedorff.

Charlotte remembered Caroline as a sweet, shy, smiley girl in her class. Thirty-five years later, they met again as adults, quite by chance, when the Herschels moved to Windsor, and they became firm friends. As Caroline wrote, looking back on the renewal of this friendship (or rather the start of it, since they had never really been friends as children, Caroline had been far too shy for that):

When I was introduced to her at the Queens Lodge [she] received me as an old acquaintance, though I could but just remember of having sometimes exchanged a nod & smile with a sweet little girl about 10 or 11 years old. But I was soon sensible of having found what hitherto I had looked for in vain – a sincere, and uninterested [disinterested] friend.[1]

By the time they met again in Windsor, Charlotte Beckedorff had become a lady-in-waiting to Queen Charlotte. While William's world of science was filled with men, the royal court had a vibrant community of women. Around Windsor, in circles that overlapped with the Herschels, were women such as Charlotte Papendiek, Fanny Burney and Charlotte Beckedorff. Caroline was never really comfortable in their presence. This was William's wife Mary's world more than Caroline's. Beckedorff was an exception because they shared a past, however slight. They at least came from the same place and could remember some of the same places and people. With the other women, Caroline simply had very little in common. They more or less dismissed her as the quiet, modest, less talented sister of the very interesting genius William Herschel. Since that was very much the image Caroline tried to project, she cannot have objected too much to such descriptions. However, there was a strong feeling of different worlds and different priorities. They considered her too quiet to be interesting. She, for the most part, found them irritatingly gossipy and vacuous. It did not have the ideal makings of friendship. That Charlotte Beckedorff made the effort to break that rather uncomfortable division was a kind gesture, and one Caroline very much appreciated.

Caroline had experienced similar problems with William's musical acquaintances in Bath. Some of the women who came to the house tried to be nice to her to ingratiate themselves with William or Alexander. There were rumours, for example, that Mrs Colebrook, a rich local widow, had designs on one of her brothers. This may perhaps have encouraged her to take an interest in Caroline and take it upon herself to help organise her cultural education tour of London back in 1776. Other women may not have had the same ulterior motive, but were nonetheless irritating to Caroline, rarely appearing to her as potential new friends. On a mother and daughter who would sometimes come to the house, for example, she wrote that they were:

… very civil and the latter [the daughter] came sometimes to see me; but being more annoyed than entertained by her visits I did not encourage them, for I thought her little better than an idiot. The same opinion I had of Mrs Bulman [William's housekeeper].[2]

Caroline was shy and always ready to make public claims to her lack of ability, intellect and talent, but in an odd way she was also rather confident of having those qualities. She might make a show of her amateur status, claiming to be nothing more than a 'puppy dog' or of little more use than 'a boy might be to his master in the first year of his apprenticeship', but she could be very unforgiving of those she thought were unintelligent.

Caroline made do with what she had. She learned to tolerate her brothers' wives and she even came to like Mary in time. She had William and Alexander, who needed her and felt a brotherly desire to protect her. More than anyone else, her brothers Alexander and Dietrich could probably be thought of as her closest confidants. William came gradually to have a similar role, although it was never quite the same. William was 12 years older than Caroline and had moved away when she was 7. Caroline barely knew him before she came to England, and afterwards she was always a little too dependent on him for home and work to ever completely consider their relationship equal. Nevertheless, they were close, closer than Caroline was to anyone outside her family.

Beyond this small group of siblings and in-laws, Caroline's circle was largely limited by her brother's gregariousness and willingness to introduce her to new people and maintain those relationships for her. Luckily, William was extremely outgoing, this trait allowing him to build up a network that kept him up to date with the latest news, spread word for them of his and Caroline's discoveries and allowed him and his correspondents to test out new ideas. For the much more reserved Caroline, her brother's sociability was undoubtedly an asset, but it was also difficult in its way. She was much slower to make friends, and perhaps would have chosen to mix with a very different set of people than her brother had it been up to her.

Nevertheless, she had her brother's friends and professional allies and they were very often kind and friendly towards her. This left Caroline in an odd position. They knew her through her brother, and were friendly to her, in part, for his sake. It was unclear to Caroline, with her natural reserve and lack of social experience, how much she should read into their gestures of kindness and encouragement. Jérôme de Lalande was always extremely encouraging in his conversation with her, but how much, she wondered, could that be put down to good manners? When Lalande named his niece after her, she reluctantly wrote to thank him, but at the same time was keen to emphasise that she did not take his praise literally. 'You, my dear Sir, certainly overrated them [her abilities],' she wrote firmly. If he was being kind, or worse, offering exaggerated flattery, then she would not allow herself to fall into the trap of appearing vain or gullible. This was not family she was talking to now, and she did not really know how to best present herself. She had been warned before about being 'her own trumpeter' and that advice remained at the forefront of her mind whenever kind words came her way. It was safer to appear overly modest and brush away compliments than come across as arrogant.

Writing back to Lalande on the subject of her namesake, she made an unusual reference to a mutual 'good friend', General Komarzewski. For Caroline, this was a very unusual turn of phrase. Very often in her writing she would speak of 'my brother's friend', or sometimes 'our astronomical friends', but it was extremely rare for her to write of someone in such affectionate terms as a 'good friend'.

Historical records give us very little about who General Komarzewski was. However, Caroline's comment alone suggests an uncharacteristically close bond. Jan Komarzewski was a Polish nobleman and military man. He had been in England since 1789 and apparently became good friends with the Herschels; while in England he had also begun to develop an interest in philosophy, astronomy and mineralogy. Although their correspondence after Komarzewski left England in 1793 is sparse, his short stay seems to have had a big impact on the Herschels and they stayed close friends. Komarzewski's burgeoning interest in their science must have helped – while in England he observed with some of their telescopes and even had a try at building his own and making his own speculum mirror alloy – so too must his sociability. Komarzewski seems to have mixed in very similar circles to the Herschels, both in England and after 1793 when he travelled in France.

As the Herschels became more established in Slough, and as William's scientific and aristocratic friends came increasingly to visit them and their iconic telescopes, it became easier for Caroline to immerse herself in that world. Early on, William had been on a rather formal footing with many of these people, corresponding by letter, offering and receiving scientific information, but not able to consider them friends. As William and Caroline's scientific reputations rose, however, that dynamic altered. They could consider themselves more as equals, and that change in status led William, and to an extent Caroline, to come to see many of these men of science as friends. Nevil Maskelyne and Jérôme de Lalande seemed often to make an extra effort to be kind and encouraging to Caroline, slowly becoming her good friends despite her natural unwillingness to let down her guard and open up to those outside her family. Komarzewski also clearly made an impression. Others were friendly, but not always considered so close.

The scientific world of Europe and America in the late eighteenth century was in a period of transition. On the one hand, there were the beginnings of structures that seem familiar to us today – journals, academic societies, the occasional academic post devoted to astronomy – on the other, there were still many traditions that lived on from earlier ages. There were still very few universities, let alone university positions. There was little in the way of industry, less still industrial research and development work. For the most part, prestigious science or natural philosophy remained the preserve of rich amateurs, and scientific activity carried out by the lower orders was viewed not as science but as work, labour or craft. Work in brewing or dyeing or cookery may have involved an extensive working knowledge of chemistry, but those doing it were workers and so it could not possibly be seen as proper science. Among the elites there remained a strong tradition of communication through correspondence. These were after all the literate classes, long before literacy was widespread. They no longer wrote in Latin, but they did correspond across geographical boundaries, often swapping between English, French, Italian and German as they did so. The scientifically inclined within these elites, and the clever few among the lower orders they allowed to join them, formed that international network known as the Republic of Letters.

While Caroline was never strictly part of this network (with William to speak on her behalf that would have appeared presumptuous on her part), she was still involved through her brother and through visitors. While he would write the letters, she would make a copy for his records. She would often have news that William passed on for her through these letters. Many replies would send messages to her (such as Lalande telling her about Madame Dupiery) or at least acknowledge her by sending their compliments. Like many scientific wives and daughters, she was involved in the correspondence network but at one step removed. When visitors came to the house she would get a chance to get to know them better or, just as likely, shy away, leaving the impression of the kind-hearted, smiley, modest sister.

The network changed all the time, but a snapshot of William's correspondence for the year 1790 gives a sense of its scope and how relationships were formed and developed. Among his most frequent correspondents were those fellow astronomers who lived reasonably close by. These were amateurs such as Henry Englefield, the comet expert; Francis Wollaston with his private observatory in Chislehurst; Alexander Aubert in Deptford and Hans Moritz Brühl, the German diplomat, living in England and in 1790 still in the process of building his observatory in Harefield. Unlike the Herschels, all these amateurs bought their telescopes from the famous London instrument makers of the time: Peter Dollond, Jesse Ramsden and John Bird. These men also featured in the international web of correspondence, as astronomers across Europe and America looked to London, the workshop of the world, for the best telescopes to furnish their new observatories.

Then there were the academics from across Europe looking to set up their own observatories. The 1790s seems to have been a period of emerging academic interest in astronomy. Up until then, observatories tended to belong to rich individuals, or to national institutions set up by a ruling monarch. The idea of a university observatory was only beginning to take shape. As it did so, the Herschels became an obvious point of call for those researching their options as they set about designing the state-of-the-art observatory for their given institution. Patrick Copland, professor of mathematics and natural philosophy at the University of Aberdeen, Johann Ludwig Herrenschneider, the recently appointed first professor of astronomy at the University of Strasbourg, and Giuseppe Piazzi, also recently appointed professor of astronomy at the University of Palermo, were all correspondents. All had made their cases to their respective universities that they would need to travel to visit observatories, meet astronomers and research their options. Piazzi was made professor of astronomy in 1787 and spent the subsequent two years travelling around Britain and France visiting observatories, astronomers and instrument makers. Herrenschneider, who was made professor in 1789, did much the same.

Other correspondents came from more well-established professional astronomical posts. While Piazzi and Herrenschneider had both recently become professors of astronomy (both were originally mathematicians), other posts had been around a little longer. Patrick Wilson, at the University of Glasgow, had been regius professor of astronomy since 1784 and the post had existed even longer. Patrick and William got on very well, and even Caroline found Patrick's sister reasonably tolerable when they had come to visit. As an academic from a Scottish university, Patrick turned out to be an extremely useful friend to William. Where those who had studied in England, and very often Cambridge, had been trained to be fiercely loyal to Newton and thus not learned very much French mathematics, the Scottish universities had no such prejudice. As a result, William would often turn to Patrick Wilson for help in understanding some of the work of his French colleagues, Lalande and Pierre-Simon de Laplace. Later, he would even look to his Scottish friend when organising the education of his son.

Astronomers from national observatories, those who job it was to carry out the laborious routine work of mapping the sky and producing very accurate astronomical tables for sailors, also formed part of this network of correspondence – and of William's network in 1790 in particular. There was Nevil Maskelyne, of course, at Greenwich, and Pierre Méchain in Paris. There was also Johann Elert Bode, in Berlin. While their paid work was to create and supervise navigational material for the military and merchants, they were also interested in the latest astronomical news and ideas and therefore acted as points of knowledge distribution within their respective countries. When Englefield wanted to pass on news of Caroline's comet discovery, he sent word to Méchain in Paris, knowing that it was a good way to pass on the information to all the major French comet hunters and mathematicians.

Closer to home, there were also several non-astronomers clustered around the Royal Society who were regular correspondents of the Herschels. Joseph Banks was someone William and Caroline would both turn to when they had astronomical news to share and, similarly, when Banks had news, William was often the Britain-based astronomer he turned to first. When an unknown astronomer had news to share, Banks would often ask William to check its validity before passing it on. Others around the Royal Society included Charles Blagden, the society's secretary who, like Banks, would get reports from the Herschels and others about new discoveries and ideas. Henry Cavendish, the extremely shy and socially awkward aristocratic chemist who worked in a similar area of chemistry to Joseph Priestley, James Watt and Antoine and Marie-Anne Lavoisier, was also part of the network. Like them, Cavendish was interested in the composition of different substances, including water, which he successfully identified as being made up of oxygen and hydrogen in 1783.

Another Royal Society friend of the Herschels was Tiberius Cavallo, an Italian physicist living in London. Like Cavendish, Cavallo was not an astronomer, but was interested in other aspects of natural philosophy which were popular at the time. While Cavendish studied the atomic nature of chemical reactions, Cavallo was investigating an equally popular scientific topic of the late eighteenth century: electricity and magnetism. William had dabbled in this area when he lived in Bath, mainly as an exercise in ingratiating himself with the members of his local literary and philosophical society. Now he was less involved, but the world of eighteenth-century elite science was small and the boundaries between different disciplines were hazy at best, and in many cases non-existent.

Many within the Herschels' correspondence network focused on one or other area of natural philosophy. William had astronomy, and his network was naturally rich in fellow astronomers. Banks, on the other hand, tended more towards botany; for Cavendish, it was chemistry; and Cavallo studied electricity and magnetism (which today we would categorise as physics). The Herschels' neighbour, Jean-André Deluc, was more of a geologist, although these categories mean more now than they did then. Geology and botany were often seen together as natural history, and all the different areas were generally thought of under the umbrella term 'natural philosophy'. While different individuals tended to focus their own research on a particular branch of natural philosophy, it was generally considered polite to have some broad understanding of the other branches. The Royal Society and its journal helped, allowing the different practitioners to get a sense of what others were working on; correspondence networks and travel helped too.

Caroline was a part of this network, just as much as William, but in a way that made her almost invisible. She could keep up with all the developments in different areas of natural philosophy by reading the *Philosophical Transactions*, but she could not join in discussion of them at the Royal Society. She could meet the various philosophers who came to their house, but she was much less able to correspond with them directly. William, as the man of the house and the man in charge of their scientific collaboration, was the one who convention and etiquette dictated should be the main correspondent. Caroline did, over time, correspond with a few of their mutual scientific friends, Lalande and Maskelyne in particular, but she was very cautious in doing so, and would only write after she had known them a long time and been heavily persuaded that it would be socially acceptable for her to do so.

Different women dealt with this dilemma in different ways. Some did not have a male relative or collaborator to speak for them and had to find other ways to participate in this network as independent women. Other women, certainly by the nineteenth century, developed their own networks of wives reinforcing male-dominated scientific networks and strengthening the same ties. Caroline was neither a supportive wife nor an entirely independent woman. When she did make friends, it was a big step, and she did not make friends lightly. The fact that she would list Madame Beckedorff, General Komarzewski, Jérôme de Lalande and Nevil Maskelyne among her friends speaks volumes of the depth of those relationships.

Elsewhere, she mentions old friends of William's as her own. These were scientific men who had been William's friends before he discovered Uranus: for example, Alexander Aubert and William Watson. Pierre Méchain might have written gushingly to William about Caroline's abilities and celebrity after she discovered a second comet and he had met her in Slough, but these were said at a distance. He did not attempt to approach her directly. He, like Francis Wollaston, who told William he put Caroline 'first as a sister astronomer',[3] admired her from afar. Theirs was perhaps the more typical scientific reaction to Caroline. While a small number made friends, most others simply looked on with bemused admiration. They were her fans, they told William how amazing she was and how proud he must be, but stopped short of approaching her themselves. She was an anomaly they did not quite know how to deal with; she was not yet an equal, nor a friend.

1791

8

RIOTS

Outside of the cosy surroundings of Observatory House, political passions were running high. Reverberations – fallout from the French Revolution that had begun two years earlier – were being felt throughout Europe. The Paris Commune was, for the time being, thriving and offering a world of possibility; an example of how a society could be run without a monarchy and with 'the people' in charge.

This was before the executions of priests, aristocrats and non-revolutionaries had begun, while the Commune was still in its peaceful stage, offering hope rather than terror. While their example was inspiring for some, it was worrying for others. The royal families of Europe were looking on nervously, as were many aristocrats and supporters of the status quo. This was an experiment that had great minds pondering on both sides, and then arguing loudly, angrily and with great passion.

In 1791 Thomas Paine published *Rights of Man*, a heartfelt, populist plea in support of the Revolution with advice on how to bring lessons from France across to Britain. Paine was a man of true revolutionary spirit. He had grown up in Norfolk, went to the grammar school then onto an apprenticeship as a ropemaker, producing rope for use in the shipping industry. He had worked for the Excise Office, dealing with taxes and imports. He had also been a school teacher. Then, in the early 1770s (at about the time Caroline was pondering where her life in Hanover might lead), Paine became involved in politics, petitioning Parliament for better pay and conditions for excise officers. In 1774, he was sacked and had to sell all his possessions to avoid debtor's prison; he also formally separated from his wife.

It was at that point that he was introduced to Benjamin Franklin through a friend. Franklin suggested he emigrate to America. And so, just as Caroline was emigrating to England and getting settled in her new home in Bath, learning to become a musician and helping her brother to take up astronomy, Thomas Paine was setting sail for America. With the help of Benjamin Franklin, Paine left England with the hopes of finding, or at least helping to create, a better, more equal and more enlightened society in the New World. Paine lived in America throughout their revolution (which lasted from roughly 1765 and 1783), writing pamphlets to inspire Americans to free themselves from British rule. His 1776 pamphlet *Common Sense*, in particular, set out to send home that message. *Common Sense* told its readers what Paine felt was wrong with the way America was currently being governed and how, with independence, they might do things differently. It was popular and widely read, to the extent that some commentators at the time claimed that without it the revolution would have been both aimless and unsuccessful.

By the 1790s, Paine had moved again, this time to Paris – from one revolutionary nexus to another. Once settled in France, Paine again began to write, voicing his support for the French Revolution and its aims. *Rights of Man*, which was written in France but for a British audience, was not only a celebration of the revolution, but an outright attack on the revolution's critics. In particular, it was directed at one popular and vocal critic, Edmund Burke.

Edmund Burke was a writer and politician. He was an Irish Catholic, one of the first to be allowed to study at Trinity University in Dublin after rules had been amended to allow non-Protestants to attend. Rules regarding university attendance were very complicated in eighteenth-century Britain, and Dublin at the time was still part of Britain. Universities were seen primarily as a training ground for future Church of England clergymen, lawyers and, to a certain extent, doctors, and until the late eighteenth century entrants had to be followers of the Church of England. Burke was an early beneficiary of a change to those rules. He was a Whig politician (the old left-wing party of British politics before Labour existed), who had supported many of the American revolutionaries' demands. He was not against the monarchy, but he had campaigned to restrict the king's power; he also felt America should be allowed to set its own taxes.

When it came to the American Revolution, Burke had been against absolute separation from Britain but he had suggested a set of resolutions that would have given the revolutionaries what they wanted in terms of self-rule and taxation, but still kept the colony British. In all situations, Burke was keen to find peaceful solutions above all else. He is sometimes credited with inventing early conservatism, in the sense that he did not like change. Where he saw problems, he would advocate minor changes, tweaks to the status quo, but he was firmly opposed to radical changes and revolutions were too violent and too unpredictable for him to ever feel comfortable with. When it came to the French Revolution, Burke had trouble offering support of any kind. The American Revolution had raised a number of issues with which Burke had some sympathy, and he had tried to solve these with compromise. The French Revolution he found more troubling. He did not agree with its aims. This revolution, he felt, was a step too far – or perhaps a step too close to home.

In 1790, Edmund Burke wrote a pamphlet on the French Revolution – a bestseller, no less – called *Reflections on the Revolution in France*. In it, he set out his response to the revolution across the Channel as it unfolded. At the heart of his criticism was his disgust at, as he saw it, the violence of the mob. As a rule, he was against all forms of unruly violence (war and armies were a separate issue), and for that reason alone, he felt he could not support the revolution in France. He also criticised the intellectual ideals of the revolution, suggesting they were not sufficiently grounded in any of kind of practical understanding of how to carry them out. Fundamentally, he saw no value in proclaiming that everyone had a right to food and medicine. Rights were useless without the mechanisms to put them into practice, and he did not have any faith in the revolutionaries' abilities to make those aims a reality. Abstract concepts such as liberty, fraternity and equality were too vague, they could easily be manipulated and used by the ruthless to obtain and abuse power. Practical solutions, on the other hand, were harder to dispute or misinterpret.

There was a lot of sound, rational argument in Burke's critique. At the same time, it came from a very cautious, conservative place that was at odds with how many were feeling at the time. He was all for gradual reform, not revolution, but that was inevitably partly because he was reasonably happy with the way the world was run. He saw little wrong with the monarchy, private property or the power of the Church. He acknowledged the need for minor changes, but nothing that would justify revolution. Less excusable was an underlying contempt for the revolutionaries and their supporters that came across in some of his criticism:

> Already there appears a poverty of conception, a coarseness and vulgarity in all the proceedings of the Assembly and of all their instructors. Their liberty is not liberal. Their science is presumptuous ignorance. Their humanity is savage and brutal.[1]

This was partly intellectual critique, but it also revealed a fear of and contempt for the common man and woman, with all their coarseness, vulgarity and savagery. The subtext to Burke's book, 'work the worker', was not lost on some of his more revolutionary readers.

A year later, Thomas Paine published his response, *Rights of Man*, in which he set out his arguments for why the French Revolution was a good thing, and how Britain could be made better and fairer. *Rights of Man* was first published in February 1791, then withdrawn (the publisher feared prosecution), then printed again with a new publisher in March. In it, Paine argued that the French Revolution was perfectly just because, in France, the rulers had become out of control. A government, he argued, should serve and protect its people, and when it stopped doing that it was perfectly reasonable for the people to get rid of them. Gentle tweaks of the kind advocated by Burke would not achieve that. Overthrowing a whole government and political class took a revolution.

For Britain, Paine recommended a few changes in light of the revolutionary spirit of the age. He was not suggesting, he assured readers, that the British government was anything like as out of hand as the former rulers of France. He proposed a national constitution for Britain, like that which had recently been drawn up in America. He advocated the abolition of aristocratic titles, subsidised education, lower taxes for the poor and higher taxes for the rich. While Burke garnered substantial support from the landed classes, Paine was enthusiastically read by Protestant Dissenters (those who had already rejected the authority of the established Church), skilled craftsmen and emerging industrialists. Paine's supporters were, by and large, people who felt their achievements had been earned rather than inherited. The battle lines were being drawn, just as in France: one class against another.

Among those Dissenters, skilled craftsmen and industrialists who found themselves agreeing with Paine were close friends and distant acquaintances of the Herschels. The Lunar Society in Birmingham was a particular hotbed of dissenting ideas and revolutionary causes. As a group, they started out very much as Herschel's Philosophical and Literary Society in Bath had begun. They were a group of like-minded neighbours who met once a month (when the Moon was full, hence the name), to discuss the latest ideas and experiments in science and philosophy. Among their best-known members were Matthew Boulton and James Watt – who together improved, manufactured and installed newly invented steam engines in factories and mills all over the country – and Erasmus Darwin, Charles Darwin's grandfather. In their meetings, they would discuss the latest experiments reported in the *Philosophical Transactions*, or talk about work of their own they had been carrying out. Outside their meetings they were even more productive, collaborating in experiments and inventing. Richard Lovell Edgeworth, a member up until around 1782, pioneered early experiments in child-led education; Joseph Priestley, who moved to Birmingham in 1780, discovered oxygen; James Watt invented his own type of steam engine. Boulton and Watt were early industrialists, as was fellow Lunar Society member, Josiah Wedgwood, who made pottery. These men were collectively at the forefront of great scientific, technological, commercial and, to an extent, social change in eighteenth-century Britain.

While as a group, what drew the members of the Lunar Society together was their shared passion for science and invention, but politics was also a major consideration for many. The group was never an official society. It never had a membership list or kept minutes of meetings, so establishing exactly who constituted a member and for what period is tricky. However, whether we consider them fully paid-up members, or simply friends and supporters of the society, many important players in the political and intellectual landscape of the time were connected to the Lunar Society. They included inventors and engineers, men of science, industrialists, doctors and political activists. William Herschel and his neighbour, geologist Jean-André Deluc, were both considered occasional members. So too was Benjamin Franklin, one of America's founding fathers, since he would join meetings when he was in Birmingham and collaborated with other members in experiments on electricity and sound.

They were an eclectic group: while many had family money, others did not. Their position broadly was that it was intellectual curiosity, business and a desire to use those things to make the world a better place that brought them together. Hereditary wealth might make life considerably easier, but it did not make anyone more fit to rule, or naturally better at science or business. They were not entirely free of the class- and status-based hang-ups of their age, but as much as possible they were happy to welcome anyone who had an interest and passion for learning into their circle. By and large, they were all men, although the women in their lives often played an important role, if more akin to Caroline's role in her brother's correspondence networks than as fully integrated members of the society themselves. The Lunar Society members, on the whole, were excited by the revolutions happening in France and America. In their world of science and business, they could see the world changing. It made sense that how countries were ruled should change too.

On 14 July 1791, on the two-year anniversary of the storming of the Bastille, supporters of the French Revolution held a celebratory dinner at a big hotel in Birmingham. The figurehead of this group was Joseph Priestley, part of the Lunar Society set and a dissenting minister with outspoken views. While his association with the Lunar Society was significant, it was probably his religious views that led him to become such a public and vocal supporter of the revolutionary cause. Up until around this time, those from dissenting religions had lived reasonably peacefully alongside members of the established Church in Birmingham. However, times were changing, and by the early 1790s, there had been some agitation among some of the more radical Dissenters (like Priestley) to have some of the laws restricting what Dissenters could do abolished.

Dissenters and Nonconformists were people outside of the established Church. They were neither Catholic nor Church of England but they were still Christian. While these groups grew dramatically in the nineteenth century, they were still a small – and to many a strange – minority in the late 1700s. In England, Nonconformists and Dissenters comprised groups such as the Methodists, Unitarians and Baptists – basically any kind of non-Anglican Protestant. Elsewhere in Europe, the distinction was between these various kinds of Protestant and the Catholic Church. These offshoots of Christianity emerged in the sixteenth, seventeenth and eighteenth centuries, and stood out from the rest for their rejection of any kind of central authority for their religion and interpretation of scripture. Reading, thinking for oneself, and questioning authority were all key values held by many practising Dissenters. Given their religious outlook, and their rejection of certain types of centralised authority, it made sense that support for the revolutions was higher in dissenting communities than elsewhere.

Priestley was a Unitarian minister, one of the first in England, and not only preached his and his church's views on religion and how to interpret the Bible, he wrote on it too. His rejection of centralised authority was not simply a private matter of personal belief. He was extremely outspoken on what he saw as the problems with other types of Christianity. His books, which carried titles like *A History of the Corruptions of Christianity* and *A History of Early Opinions Concerning Jesus Christ*, were never really calculated to appeal to the established Church or its followers. For Priestley, religious evangelism and political agitation were all part of the same thing. It is tempting even to say that Priestley sought out controversy.

Dissenters were not always as bold as Priestley in advertising their opinions or religious affiliations. They were still very much in the minority, they attracted suspicion from those who knew little about them, and in the 1790s there were still a number of old laws (and some not so old) restricting what Dissenters and Nonconformists were allowed to do. They could not hold public office, study at an English university or become civil servants. This meant that, in some cases, where they could, Dissenters kept quiet about their religion. Priestley was not one of those people. He spoke up about his religion. He was confident in his scientific claims and he campaigned to have laws that restricted Dissenters abolished. All of this made him a target, and when his name was linked to a meal which had been organised to openly celebrate the controversial revolution over in France, his detractors saw their chance.

There had, for a few days before the dinner, been the rumblings of discontent. Attempts had been made to scare the diners into cancelling, which they almost did; but in the end the dinner went ahead, although it finished early. Meanwhile, encouraged by some prominent figures in local government, an angry mob assembled ready to protest outside the venue. Dissenters and Nonconformists, attending their own churches and forming their own communities, were often seen as different to their neighbours. They were a curious and separate minority and many looked upon them with suspicion. That attitude was encouraged and played upon by some of the more unscrupulous members of local government. Finding the meal over and the diners gone, the angry mob moved on to Priestley's Old Meeting House (his church) and burned it to the ground. The protest had very quickly turned nasty. From there, the rioters turned to Priestley's home and those of other Dissenters and their supporters.

The Dissenters were mistrusted, and those who objected to their campaigns for equal treatment were quick to capitalise and turn it into something more angry and violent. When Priestley's home, church and friends were attacked, the authorities were very slow to react. They did not rush to calm the situation, put out fires or disperse the crowd. There were very few convictions following what became known as the Priestley Riots, and a lack of will to investigate. Further probing suggests that they were not just slow to react and condemn: many senior community figures were instrumental in facilitating and fuelling the riots. Fearing for his life and for his family, Priestley left Birmingham, never to return.

The Herschels, and indeed the rest of the country, looked on in horror. This peaceful celebration had ended in violence and no one, it seemed, was there to defend or protect those who spoke up in favour of a changing world. Priestley perhaps exaggerated his naivety when he wrote of his surprise:

> That a peaceable meeting for the purpose of rejoicing that twenty-six millions of our fellow creatures were rescued from despotism, and made as free and happy as we Britons are, could be misinterpreted as being offensive to a government, whose greatest boast is liberty, or to any who profess the Christian religion, which orders us to love our neighbours as ourselves.[2]

He was surely aware that the meal could have been interpreted in a variety of ways. However, he had no reason to expect quite such an angry and violent reaction, nor quite such a lacklustre response from the authorities and those supposedly there to keep him, his family and their fellow citizens safe. The riots signalled an end to the very vocal support for the French Revolution that Priestley had embodied among men of science. They would still discuss the issues among themselves, but after those rather alarming scenes in Birmingham, it took them a while to speak up again quite so loudly.

Even before the riots, not everyone within the Lunar Society or the Herschels' circle of friends had been as enthusiastic about the French Revolution as Priestley, nor so keen to show it. Even among the most dedicated members of the Lunar Society reactions varied. While Priestley and Wedgwood wrote excitedly of the great leaps forward it represented for freedom and liberty, others, like the engineer James Watt, were less impressed. Watt's objection was nothing to do with the ideas or philosophy behind the revolution, but rather the practicalities. The revolution had disrupted what had been an effortless flow of scientific information between the two countries. Now it was becoming increasingly difficult to get news of scientific work going on in France and this he found frustrating. Boulton, meanwhile, took the more pragmatic stance of purposefully not taking sides. He could see a strong business case for staying onside with the government, but at the same time he did not want to alienate any potential clients or collaborators.

The Herschels as a family were not very revolutionary in their political views, or at least saw no value and many potential pitfalls in expressing them openly. They seem to have reacted to the revolution in much the same way as Boulton and Watt. It was an inconvenience that slowed down correspondence with their French colleagues. It was also a political situation in which taking sides might potentially create problems for their livelihoods. These were not trivial matters for people like the Herschels, James Watt or Matthew Boulton. None of them had the security of family money to fall back on. Work failing had hugely damaging consequences for them all, and they could not afford to gamble in that way. The revolution was inspiring. It empowered people like them to take over the running of a country, and in doing so, potentially run it for the benefit of their class (or at least more so than the former aristocratic rulers). At the same time, change is always uncertain, and they were fine as they were, with no guarantees that life would be better with different rulers. They also could not afford to jeopardise what they had, particularly their relationships with people who held different political opinions to themselves.

There is also the very likely possibility that the Herschels and others like them did not see these great political changes and transfers of power from one group to another as anything to do with them. They did not run the country, nor did they have any ambition to do so. It was true that they were reliant on the current rulers for their income and status. The Herschels – and indeed their nephews, the Griesbach musicians – were employees of the king in the broadest sense. For William, this became less important after his marriage, since Mary Pitt had money and a position in local society, but it was nonetheless a consideration. There was also the fact that the king and queen had been good to them, giving them the money to give up music and devote themselves full time to astronomy, providing Caroline with her own income and funding the building of their large 40ft reflector. Their aristocratic visitors who came in a regular stream to see the 40ft telescope were, similarly, perfectly nice. They had no personal gripes with hereditary rulers or the aristocracy. To change them for people they did not know may not have seemed a cause worth fighting for.

At the same time, the Herschels were not unaware of or unsympathetic to the mood of the age. William had read Locke and Hume with enthusiasm, keenly absorbing the ideas they laid out regarding human potential and innate equality. He and Caroline were living proof of those theories about practice and training, and that no one is born with innate knowledge but rather has to put in the hours in order to learn. Within that world view, the idea of a class born to rule seemed ridiculous to many; much better to give power to those who had given the matter some thought. While any ruler might be expected to run their country for the benefit of all its citizens, the problem of having that role fulfilled only by those of a certain class, it was starting to be felt, meant they had little knowledge of or sympathy for the effects of their rule on those outside their class. Many felt a change was needed. The Herschels' views on philosophy and their personal experience of education certainly suggests they were sympathetic to the idea that equality and effort were more important than hereditary rule. England, however, already had a Parliament, the king had fewer powers than monarchs in other countries, and the revolution in France was the business of the French. To express support as a foreigner in England may have been felt to overcomplicate matters.

Those agitating for change were of a similar class to many within the Herschels' circle of friends. Many were supporters of the revolution in France and advocates of some kind of political shake-up at home, but the Herschels kept out of it. These debates were inextricably tied up with religion, and the Herschels kept out of that too. There were reformers like Priestley, whose support for the French Revolution went hand in hand with his campaigning for greater rights for Dissenters and Nonconformists. Others looked upon France, with the rise of atheism and the revolutionaries' attempts to separate Church from state, with suspicion. Religion, it was still felt by many, offered a moral compass. Without it, how could any state be kept in line, how could it be guaranteed to act with conscience and compassion?

As with politics, so too with religion, the Herschels kept quiet. It has been suggested by some historians that the Herschels were originally Jewish, although nothing conclusive has ever been proved. Their grandfather, Abraham, and father Isaac may have been Jewish (so suggested William's nineteenth-century biographer, Holden). By William and Caroline's generation, however, they were practising Protestants. Caroline was confirmed at a church some distance from her home and her only comments on this were about the inconvenience that the run-up to her confirmation caused her family. She missed out on seeing much of her brother William on his brief visit to Hanover from England and she also felt that she had neglected her domestic work since she had to walk all the way to church and back on a regular basis. All this, however, was thought worth it to have her confirmed.

Similarly, when the youngest Herschel, Dietrich, went to England with his brothers, their mother's primary concern was that they get him confirmed. When, after two years, they had failed to do this, she insisted he come home, regardless of how well he might have been doing as a musician in England. Beyond these instances, the Herschels spoke very little of religion. Probably they were Protestants (Dissenters), but of a type more common in Germany than England.

The Herschels rarely spoke about, or even gave any indication of their opinions on either religion or politics. Caroline was confirmed as a child, so they were Christian, but beyond that they offered few clues. Politically their silence was, if nothing else, pragmatic. William admired Joseph Priestley's science and was good friends with Boulton and Watt (he even testified as an expert witness for them in the 1790s). He visited their new factories admiringly on several occasions, but he never publicly endorsed or even mentioned their political opinions. Caroline was the same. While their friends might look around them and fight, the Herschels very resolutely directed their attention inward and upward.

While so much political change was happening all around them, the Herschels were careful not to express an opinion. They were careful to be anything but revolutionary in their political opinions. Scientifically, however, things were very different. The world was changing, and so was science. While others were rejecting long-held beliefs about who could and should rule, the Herschels were far more revolutionary in rejecting long-held beliefs about the universe. It was not enough just to look at the solar system as astronomers had done for centuries, considering the stars only as a static backdrop against which the planets appeared to move. Working together, systematically cataloguing and categorising the stars, the Herschels were now ready to reveal to the world a whole new understanding of the stars beyond our solar system.

9

ORDER IN THE SKIES

While their English friends and colleagues might have looked upon the revolutions in France and America with excitement, the Herschels had already lived through enough political upheaval and saw no thrill in it. For them, the thought of revolution offered little romance. William had spent time on the battlefield during the Seven Years War and had fled to England as a young man, risking the possibility of never seeing his family again. Caroline, meanwhile, had grown up in a town sometimes under occupation and often on the brink of war and invasion. Her father had been away at war for much of her childhood, coming home towards the end of his life, sick and severely weakened by the experience. For a time, she had lived in a house filled with occupying French soldiers.

Growing up within that war-torn environment, Caroline had learned to shut herself off from the world around her and focus on her work. She saw little to be gained from becoming involved in politics, or following too carefully the news of the dramatic events happening around the world. She listened out for news of her family, but beyond that she kept her focus deliberately narrow. Back in Hanover, she had thrown herself into her studies, domestic work and self-improvement. When she came to England she brought that same focus with her, using it to good effect to become first an excellent singer and performer, and then assistant and astronomer. The revolution in France was a problem for France, and unfortunate for French friends and colleagues. When she did think about the revolution it was with them in mind, their safety and the ease (or lack of) with which their scientific news could get through. Beyond that, she kept her mind on her work.

Caroline's lessons in astronomy had begun as an extension of her mathematics lessons not long after she first arrived in England. At first, her lessons had been designed very practically around the aim of teaching her the mathematics needed to keep the family's household accounts. They soon morphed into lessons more connected with William's new love of philosophy and astronomy than with the details of domestic expenditure. As time went on and Caroline's knowledge grew, these lessons began to take on a different feel again. They went from accounting to helping William with his understanding of his latest reading. By the time they had moved to Slough they had changed again, serving a new purpose for Caroline as she tried to better her understanding of what interested or puzzled her. The 'little lessons for Lina' in Bath had transformed into 'answers … to the inquiries I used to make when at breakfast'. No longer was William giving or imposing lessons on Lina; Caroline was now determining for herself what she was taught. She was taking charge, and the questions she now wanted answering were ones that would help her to become better at observing, and understanding William's current theories.

At first – back in Bath – Caroline's lessons had concentrated on the basics, 'A little geometry for Lina', 'A little algebra for Lina', and so on. Under her direction, those lessons had then moved on. She began to focus on algebraic trigonometry and logarithms. These were essential prerequisites, the steps she needed to learn before she could start to apply mathematics to her understanding of the stars. Before she could go any further, she needed to master the mathematical tools to describe the way in which the stars and their distances related to one another. She also needed to learn the rules for using her astronomical instruments, along with useful theorems like how to calculate 'the number of stars that have been seen in a sweep'. Once she became fairly secure in this mathematical basis for their work, William started to introduce new ideas. He began to explain and teach Caroline the ideas he was working through before he announced them to the world. Caroline was no longer just his student and assistant; she was now also his collaborator.

So, by the early 1790s William's lessons were now entitled 'The 8 classes of Nebulae' or 'The 6 classes of Double Star'. This was an entirely new area of astronomy. European astronomers, up to this point, had shown little interest in the sky beyond the solar system. When they had considered the 'fixed stars', their primary concern had been to plot them as a backdrop against which to describe the movements of the planets. Over the previous century, these fixed stars had gained a little more attention as comet hunting became more popular and observers needed a clearer description of what the different fixed stars looked like. However, their interest was still not really in the stars themselves, but rather the comet hunters needed a guide to stop them confusing nebula–like stars with comets.

Charles Messier had published the first catalogue of nebulae and star clusters for comet hunters in 1781 (the year William discovered Uranus). William and Caroline had then continued this data collection, although for different reasons, collecting many more nebulae, star clusters and double stars, and bringing the total up from Messier's eighty objects to around 2,000 by 1791. With all that raw data William, testing out his ideas on Caroline as he went, now began to try to categorise and understand these objects further. Just as an eighteenth-century natural historian would try to make sense of the natural world by collecting, cataloguing, naming and grouping his or her finds, so too the Herschels were trying to do the same with the stars. Within their broad categories of 'nebulae' and 'double star', William now subdivided his objects into classes. As he worked on this categorisation system, he talked it through with Caroline in the hope of better understanding it.

Gradually, through this process of collecting and studying the data, theorising, discussing and teaching, William began to develop a very different concept of the stars from anything that had gone before. By February 1791 he was finally ready to present these new ideas to the world. On 10 February 1791, William Herschel read his paper, 'On Nebulous Stars, properly so called', to the Royal Society of London.

Up until then, 'nebulosity' was just a term used to describe any blurred objects in the night sky that could not quite yet be resolved into stars. The term had been used for centuries as a catch-all term for anything unexplained. It comes from the Latin word for cloud, and was used in astronomy for anything that could not be unequivocally labelled as a single point source star. When William began looking at these sorts of objects, he had set out with the assumption that if only telescopes could be made with a little more magnifying power, those blurs could all be resolved into stars. He even stated as much in his catalogues and used the theory to justify the enormous expense of his 40ft reflector. After years of study, however, William had come to the conclusion that this was not the case. There *was* such a thing as true nebulosity after all, and his paper set out a challenge to his original assumption.

'Nebulae' was a term, he felt, that had been bandied about far too liberally. The aim of this paper was to make the term much more precise. He proposed to break up the blurred objects into distinct types. Like a natural philosopher, he wrote, categorising different animals, insects and plants, he would set about subdividing the sky. And just as they, 'arriving at the vegetable kingdom … can scarcely point out to us the precise boundary where the animal ceases and the plant begins', so too it was at first difficult for astronomers to distinguish between a blurred star and true nebulosity. Yet, by identifying all the stages between one extreme and the other, a boundary gradually becomes apparent. This was true for the natural philosopher, he asserted, and it was true for the astronomer.

In the rest of the paper, William then elaborated on his thesis. He gave various examples: the Milky Way appears nebulous, but actually it is just an area of the sky rich in stars; the Pleiades (sometimes called the Seven Sisters, in the constellation Taurus) appear nebulous, but with careful observation, even with the naked eye, this patch of sky can be clearly seen to be a cluster of stars, or star cluster. He then moved on to more ambiguous regions of the sky – an object he described as a 'planetary nebula' and another that was a 'round nebula'. These were nebulae in the truest sense, he argued. In the mid-1780s, he wrote, he began to notice a number of these true nebulae, objects that seemed often to contain a star or sun, but were also surrounded by luminous material. Slowly he began to ponder this luminous material and, step by step, draw some revolutionary conclusions.

There was, he felt increasingly certain, a connection between the star and the luminous material surrounding it. If that connection was to be supposed, then either it was a group of stars that could all be resolved with one incredibly bright one in the middle (far brighter than anything previously known), or it was a normal star surrounded by some kind of glowing fluid. He felt the second explanation was more plausible. He then went on to suggest that some nebulae might be this fluid on its own, and that the fluid was likely to be self-luminous since reflected light would never be bright enough to reach us from the distant stars. He then drew an extraordinary conclusion: 'If therefore, this matter is self-luminous, it seems more fit to produce a star by its condensation than to depend on the star for its existence.' Nebulae, he was suggesting, were the birthplace of stars.

To understand how revolutionary this suggestion was, it is worth taking a moment to look back on where astronomical thought was at the time. Only two centuries earlier, the Danish astronomer Tycho Brahe had shocked European astronomers (not the Chinese, they knew about these long before) with the discovery of a supernova. At the time, the fixed stars had been thought to be perfect and unchanging in accordance with the Christian understanding of the heavens. Brahe's supernova changed all that. A supernova is a point at the end of the life of a certain type of star. The star 'explodes': its middle falls in on itself and forms a very dense nucleus or core, while its outer shells expand outwards making the star appear suddenly very bright, the star then slowly dims over several weeks. Brahe's supernova transformed our understanding of fixed stars by showing that they were not so fixed, they could change. Now Herschel was suggesting something even stranger – stars could be born, they had a lifecycle.

It is difficult to measure the impact this one paper had on astronomy. The Herschels tended to be quite careful to play down their work, in order to keep the focus on the data and instrumentation. This rather wordy paper was peppered with strictly factual, observational information. His remark about the theoretical production of stars was mid-paragraph, mid-page towards the end of the paper. He ended with the hope that he 'had not launched into hypothetical reasoning', and reassured readers that he had provided all the necessary information for his observations to be remade by others. As in politics, so too in science, the Herschels were ever careful not to appear to be rocking the boat. He wanted the security of his claim to this theory in print, to prove that he had definitely come up with it first. At the same time, it was quite radical and could even be wrong, so perhaps better to tuck it away where only those as immersed in his particular, unusual area of astronomy might find it.

Looking at William's series of papers, it can sometimes feel like he was arguing with himself, positing his theory that all nebulae could be resolved into stars in one paper (his 1789 catalogue), then arguing against it two years later in this paper on nebulosity. The problem was that he was working on something that no one else was studying. He was trying to introduce the methods used in natural history – the idea of collecting many specimens and gaining an understanding of their 'rise, progress and decay' – into astronomy. Most other astronomers were more interested in calculating, in ever more detail, the exact positions and movements of celestial bodies. It is only when we start to appreciate the isolation of his new methods that the role Caroline Herschel played in her brother's work really becomes apparent. She was someone, possibly the only one, who was as immersed in this work as he was. He could talk to her, sound out ideas and hear her point of view.

For the historian, this kind of conversation is notoriously difficult to recover from historical record. Unless their conversation was conducted by letter, or they had some reason to write about it later, it tends to become lost forever, undocumented and ephemeral. For anyone who has ever been involved in trying to solve a problem of any kind, or even develop an academic idea or theory, however, this interaction is obviously essential. It is, after all, why academics have conferences and seminars and workshops. New work is very rarely developed in a vacuum. The process of discussion is important, and for the Herschels it was a central part of their relationship.

In writing about women in science (or indeed any of the other characters who, for reasons of class, race or geography are little discussed), we often tend to get bogged down in trying to extract work that was purely theirs from the record. We try to find something tangible that we can connect with their name so they can be returned to history. What we lose when we do that, however, are the ephemeral stories of process, unminuted discussion, teaching as a way of learning and companionship.

The Herschels spent the rest of the winter of 1791 observing and cataloguing. For a while, it looked as though Caroline's comet-hunting days might even be behind her. In the summer, as had become the family tradition, William and Mary went on holiday while Caroline had the house to herself. Professionally, William was growing in respect and dependence on his sister, but their correspondence during these holidays brought them back to a more traditional sibling relationship. As fellow astronomers, William would run through theories with Caroline. He would write about her in letters and journal articles in encouraging tones, announcing a discovery for her, for example, or assuring readers that he could confirm what she had seen. Caroline, meanwhile, would always write about how unimportant she was compared to her great and talented older brother and how desperate she was never to be an inconvenience to him. At the same time, she was always ready to help, and quick to involve him when she had something new to share with the world. Domestically, though, as their correspondence during William's travels suggests, their relationship stayed much the same as it always had.

The relationship that comes across in the letters is a far more typical sibling relationship than the one that comes through in their professional writings. William, twelve years Caroline's senior, would write with lots of news, assuming his little sister to be interested in his daily life. These stories would then be peppered with domestic requests:

> Be so good as to let Mrs Penny know that I want her to brew me the usual quantity of Ale as soon as possible, that it may be ready for drinking by the time I get to Slough.[1]

Occasionally, Mary Pitt would write in William's place to ask Caroline about preparing various pickles and such like to be ready on their return. Caroline would get on with these tasks, quite enjoying the authority it gave her among her brother's servants. At the same time, she did not seek out ways to be useful domestically while they were away as she had once; left to her own devices she would happily have spent all her time at her telescope.

Caroline, for the most part, seems to have been quite happy with this relationship: professionally supportive on the one hand, full of favours and requests to carry out useful domestic tasks on the other. It gave her a role, and a certain degree of power. In none of these exchanges was she herself expected to do the domestic work. Instead, she was being assigned the role of mistress of the house in lieu of Mary and, as such, given the power to instruct the various members of domestic staff the Herschels now had at their disposal since William's marriage. Although Caroline still had not quite come to terms with the changes to her family that William's marriage had brought, she was beginning, at least when her brother was away, to carve out her own role.

The uncomfortable domestic equilibrium that Caroline had been steadily maintaining since her brother's marriage could not last. While Mr and Mrs Herschel were away, Caroline had a clear and distinct role. She was the mistress in lieu of the house. On their return, she would expect to go back to her semi-solitary life, boarding above the study, sharing and yet not sharing a home with her brother and sister-in-law. It was comfortable enough – she had experienced worse – yet it was not an especially happy time for Caroline. There was uncertainty over how long it could comfortably last.

Before she had to worry too much about that, however, there came news that would transform their family's life dramatically, and in a way that both eased the tension and brought new-found joy and purpose to Caroline. William and Mary came back from their holiday with exciting news: Mary was pregnant.

The news was somewhat unexpected. William was, by this time, 53 years old, and Mary was 41 with a grown-up son from her previous marriage. While a new baby on the way was a cause for celebration, it was also dangerous. Around two in every 100 births ended with the mother dying, a figure that was higher in poorer households who could not afford medical aid, and that risk grew with age. It was by no means uncommon for women to have babies in their forties in the eighteenth century, but the risks both to the baby and the mother increased significantly. Émilie du Châtelet, the French mathematical philosopher, died in childbirth aged 42, as did Mary Wollstonecraft at 38, although it could strike much younger women, too. Princess Charlotte, for example, died in childbirth in the early nineteenth century, aged only 21. Therefore, while the Herschels were delighted, they were also apprehensive.

Nevertheless, Mary's pregnancy offered hope of a new beginning and a new family for the Herschels. The baby was due in March the following year and, all being well, it would bring the family together. Mary's ageing mother, Elizabeth Baldwin, lived nearby. Caroline – who had a good deal of experience looking after her younger siblings and her sister's children – was on site. Mary's son, Paul Adee, was also not so far away, living in London with Mary's brother and training as an apprentice chemist. Even Paul's old wet nurse was still local. After an eventful and disruptive few years as Mary and William's families came together in getting used to their very different ways of life, a new baby on the way offered hope of some peace and unity.

As Mary settled into her pregnancy, gradually stepping down a little in her array of duties as a wife and local landowner, William, and more particularly Caroline, went back to observing. While William cared for his pregnant wife and concentrated increasingly on developing his theoretical understanding and interpretation of all their raw data on nebulae, Caroline found herself with more time alone on her rooftop to observe.

On 15 of December 1791 Caroline discovered her fifth comet, in the constellation Lacerta (meaning 'lizard') while her brother was busy observing Saturn. Lacerta is a constellation invented by Polish astronomer Johanne Hevelius in 1687 to account for a small patch of sky surrounded on all sides by the ancient Greek constellations Andromeda, Cassiopeia, Cepheus, Cygnus and Pegasus in the northern hemisphere. Caroline told William immediately the moment she spotted the new comet and he looked at it for her through his 7ft reflector. A week later, he announced her discovery on her behalf in a cryptically titled paper, 'Miscellaneous Observations', which he read to the Royal Society on 22 December 1791.

While William rightly deserves credit for acknowledging his sister's work in print, in contrast to many of his contemporaries and their attitudes to their female collaborators, it is interesting to take a look at the paper and how he handled her discovery. The first sentence stated, 'My sister looked over the heavens, and discovered a pretty large, telescopic comet, in the breast of Lacerta.'[2] He did not mention her name there or anywhere else in the paper. Beyond this initial sentence, in fact, he did not mention her at all. Instead he followed this statement with an account of what he did next – he checked her observation by viewing the comet through his own telescope. He determined more accurately its position and rate of movement. He then observed it again with his 20ft telescope, in order to describe in more detail what the comet looked like. And that was it – the rest of the paper talked about observations of things other than Caroline's fifth comet.

Caroline, as ever, made no comment on her brother's handling of her latest comet discovery. Her first had been announced with great triumph. She had made the announcement herself as William had been away and, in the process, inadvertently made history as the first woman to be published in the *Philosophical Transactions of the Royal Society*. Compared to that, it is hard not to see William's casual dismissal of her latest discovery as something of a step down. The comet is not mentioned in the title of the paper; hers is just one of several interesting observations that William felt it timely to announce. She was not even named in the paper, except as William's sister which, given their level of fame by this time and the tight circle that was the fellowship of the Royal Society and readership of its journal, was not too ambiguous but still feels a little dismissive. Stoical as ever, Caroline made no comment on this, although compounded by her recent demotion from lady of the house following William's marriage, it must have left Caroline feeling a little lost. William had offered her hope when her life in Hanover had started to become unbearably insecure, and she never lost her sense of gratitude for his help at that moment. At the same time, it is hard to imagine there was not just a small part of her mind fuming over this, at best, lukewarm announcement of her latest work.

With the new baby on the way and a comet discovery just before Christmas, 1791 was certainly ending on a high for Caroline, and yet there was an edge starting to creep into her relationship with her older brother. With her steady stream of comet discoveries and increasing fame as a celebrated woman in astronomy, Caroline was very much on the rise. William was also making important strides forward in his theoretical work on nebulae, but the astronomical world was not quite ready for them and the reception of his papers had been, at best, muted. Caroline was no longer quite the doting, innocent, attentive student that she had once been. She was starting to find her own voice, to see the value in her own work and not just as a helper and sidekick to others. William, who had always led the way as chief musician, main instrument maker and project leader in their survey of the skies, was finding the transformation unexpected. He had already had to adjust a little, when he married a woman richer and more well established socially than himself. While Caroline represented no challenge to his standing scientifically, her emerging independence in that area was still unnerving. Change in the Herschel household was on the way.

Published Feb.ʸ.1,1785, by I.Sewell, Cornhill.

1. This engraving of William Herschel by J. Walker accompanied an interview with Herschel published not long after he discovered Uranus, as readers all over Europe were curious to learn about this new astronomical celebrity. The interview and portrait featured in *The European Magazine* of 1784; this is a reproduction of that image made the year after. (The Wellcome Library, London)

2. Antoine and Marie-Anne Lavoisier were among a number of scientific partnerships to choose to celebrate their collaboration in joint portraiture. This portrait (actually an engraving after the oil painting by Jacques-Louis David) from 1788 shows the chemist M. Lavoisier at work, writing his papers, surrounded by his scientific apparatus, while Mme Lavoisier leans in supportively. (Science & Society Picture Library)

3. This undated anonymous portrait of William Herschel's wife Mary Pitt is the only depiction we have of her. The portrait belongs to her descendants. (Herschel family archive)

4. This was the first Ordnance Survey map ever made of the Windsor–Slough area, in 1830. As well as showing clearly the distribution of properties and families living around the Herschels' family home, Observatory House, the map also shows the by then iconic landmark: their 40ft reflector telescope. (British Library historic map collection)

MASKELYNE.

London, Pub. as the Act directs May 1. 1815. by G. Jones

5. Nevil Maskelyne, the Astronomer Royal, became over time one of Caroline's closest friends and most enthusiastic supporters. This portrait shows Maskelyne at the top and a small, simplified sketch of the Royal Observatory at the bottom to give viewers a quick hint as to who he was. (The Wellcome Library, London)

6. Mme Nicole-Reine Lepaute was one of a number of female mathematicians and astronomers to work with Jérôme de Lalande over the course of his long career. Sadly very few portraits exist of these remarkable women, and for the most part they tend to have been made because the woman was aristocratic or had some other reason to be well known: a career in mathematics was rarely deemed enough.

Right: 7. This image of Caroline lovingly and patiently waiting on her brother, serving him a cup of tea as he concentrates on his telescope making, not even looking up to acknowledge her presence, was made long after the pair were dead. It was painted in 1896, by which time the image of exaggerated selflessness and passivity carefully created by Caroline had uncritically become a standard part of her story. (The Wellcome Library, London)

Above: 8. The Herschels' 40ft telescope, for a time the largest in the world, soon became an icon of British science. This image shows the telescope's set-up with its observing platform at one end of the tube and Caroline's hut at the other. The visitors walking round the edge give a sense of scale. (The Wellcome Library, London)

The Female Philosopher smelling out the Comet

Left: 9. 'The female philosopher smelling out the comet.' This cartoon ridiculing the female comet hunter shows just how much Caroline's story had sparked public imagination. This caricature dates from 1790, by which time Caroline had already discovered three comets. (Draper Hill Collection, Ohio State University, Billy Ireland Cartoon Library and Museum)

54   *Arcturus*

Aug.ᵗ 18, 1789

20ʰ 5′ Sid. Time.

    I suspect the object in the
figure to be a comet

21 30 I do not perceive any change
in its situation. but there is a very strong
Aurora borealis, and the weather hazy; so that
I can hardly see the object any longer.

22 ... Cloudy.

Aug.ᵗ 19, 1789.

The object I saw last night is fixed. It is
none of the Nebula of the Coniss. des temps.
therefore I suppose it to be one of my brother's
a great number have been discovered by him
in that neighbourhood. Cloudy

Oct.ʳ 15, 1789.

1ʰ 30′ Sid. time.
I saw the 5ᵗʰ Satellite, but forgot
to marke it.

10. A new nebula, August 1789. Although more of a fuss was made of Caroline's comet discoveries, then and now, she also discovered a number of new nebulae. This page from her notebook for 18 and 19 August 1789 shows her annotations, and even a small sketch to serve as a reminder of what she had observed. (Royal Astronomical Society Science Photo Library)

11. This portrait of Émilie du Châtelet by Maurice Quentin de la Tour shows the marquise at her desk, books open in front of her, a pair of compasses in her hand (to signify mathematics) and a slightly bored expression on her face. Unlike Caroline, du Châtelet had class on her side, and could afford to be slightly more outspoken and upfront about her abilities and ambition. Even so, in her published work she hid her interpretations and ideas within the standard female formats of translation and teaching aids.

12. Margaret Bryan was a school teacher who wrote books to help her and fellow teachers with their lessons. This portrait comes from the frontispiece of one of her books, *A Compendious System of Astronomy* (1797), and shows Margaret with her daughters, surrounded by scientific instruments. (Royal Astronomical Society Science Photo Library)

13. Like his father and aunt, John Herschel went on to have a long and successful career in science. He took a more conventional route, however. This portrait shows him as a student at Cambridge, where he studied mathematics. (The Wellcome Library, London)

Joseph Brown. sc.

Caroline Herschel.

ÆTAT 92.

14. Only three portraits of Caroline Herschel painted in her lifetime exist: one from the 1820s (after William had died and she had returned to Hanover) and another from when she was even older, showing her at a desk pointing to one of her comets on a diagram of the solar system. The last – this one – shows her aged 92, propped up in bed. (The Wellcome Library, London)

1792

10

BIRTHS AND DEATHS

John Frederick William Herschel was born on 7 March 1792 at the family home, Observatory House, in Slough.[1] He was baptised at Mary's church, the old church in Upton, and two godfathers were chosen for him, both old friends of William and Caroline: Sir William Watson and General Komarzewski.

Watson was an old friend from Bath. He had lived near to the Herschels and helped William to get started in astronomy. He had introduced him to the Bath Philosophical Society and various important people who would later help him in his career, including the Astronomer Royal Nevil Maskelyne. They had met General Komarzewski more recently. He was a Polish nobleman who had become a close friend to the Herschels during his time in England.

Caroline, of course, was present at the christening. There is no record of whether their brother Alexander came down from Bath for the occasion. On Mary's side of the family, it is not clear who was at the christening, although since most lived close by, most of them would probably have attended. None of Mary's friends, however, seem to have been chosen as godparents and there do not seem to have been many at the christening. On hearing of John's birth, Mary's grown-up son, Paul Adee, wrote to offer his congratulations. He was living away from home at the time in Birmingham as an apprentice chemist, apparently with family. Immediately he heard their announcement he wrote to send kind words to his new brother, his mother and his stepfather:

> Accept my most sincere congratulations at the happy conclusion of an event which has blessed you with a son & me with a Brother, the news of which has given great joy to all the family here & they join with me in wishing you all the happiness to see him grow up an honour to his father and mother.[2]

Friends, family and neighbours of Mary were also quickly informed of the news: Mary's mother, Elizabeth Baldwin, her 'Aunt Clark', and her brother, Thomas Baldwin. There were family friends such as Miss White, a well-known London hostess and friend of the royal household, who features several times in the Baldwin family correspondence.[3] Friendly neighbours – the Papendieks, the Linds, Delucs and so on – were all keen to congratulate the happy couple on the safe arrival of their healthy baby boy.

That spring, the house was filled with the excitement of this tiny new baby and with visitors after Mary's obligatory period of confinement. Women in the eighteenth century, as least those who could afford to, were generally expected to stay at home, resting, recuperating and recovering from the birth of their new baby in the first few weeks after labour. Some babies were sent out to wet nurses, local women who might breastfeed the child in lieu of their mother, but this does not seem to have been the case with John Herschel. By the 1790s the fashion was fading (though slowly), as medical experts began to advise against it, concerned with the spread of disease and whether or not breastfeeding might be a factor in it. Instead, it seems baby John stayed at home with his mother, father and Aunt Caroline, and through the exhaustion and anxiety of that shared care, gradually the tensions between them began to lessen. Caroline was besotted with her new nephew from the start, and was always happy and willing to lend a hand. Mary, aware that she would have work to return to, keeping on top of her family's various properties and investments, was delighted to have such a willing companion. Gradually, with baby John as their own shared project, the Herschel women began to tolerate and even like one another.

Outside the cosy cocoon of the Herschel home, the world was in political and military turmoil. After seven years of fighting across Europe over the boundaries of various empires in the Seven Years War, attentions had now turned to the threat of revolution and its possible spread beyond French borders. On 20 April, war was declared. This was the first of the Revolutionary Wars and was called the War of the First Coalition (1792–97). It was shortly followed by the War of the Second Coalition (1798–1802) and then by the Napoleonic Wars (1803–15). Today, it can seem as though there is always a war in the Middle East; back then, Europe pitched more of its battles on home soil and was, for several decades, the world's main battleground.

The first coalition against the rebellious French comprised several European monarchies – Austria, Prussia and the United Kingdom – all trying to bring down the new Republic of France. Things had begun with France declaring war on the monarchy of Austria (hoping that the people of Austria would rise up and join them). A few weeks later, Prussia had joined the fight on Austria's side. Britain, the Netherlands and Spain would all join the war the following year, but for now those countries just looked on with concern.

Back in Britain, a battle of a more intellectual variety was taking place. Following the spat between Burke and Paine over the appropriate British response to the French Revolution, novelist Mary Wollstonecraft had felt compelled to wade in. In 1790, she had written a pamphlet, *A Vindication of the Rights of Men*, attacking Burke's critique of the revolution and supporting Paine's position. Central to her argument was the idea that rights should come about because they made sense and were reasonable, not just out of tradition and habit. Two years later, however, a discussion within the French Assembly made her question her support for the revolution. Perhaps their aims and ideals did not chime as perfectly with hers as she had originally thought.

In 1791, Charles Maurice de Talleyrand-Périgord, an aristocrat, cleric and diplomat active within the republican government, presented his recommendations on a new system of universal education to the Assembly. He asserted that men and women should be educated differently. Rather than have a constitution that allowed equality between the sexes, he advocated teaching women 'not to aspire to advantages which the Constitution denies them'. Men, he argued, were well suited to public life and should be educated accordingly; women, conversely, were better placed in the home and their respective education should reflect that division.

The first to react to Talleyrand's proposed system of education was French playwright, feminist and political activist Olympe de Gouges, in her *Declaration of the Rights of Woman and the Female Citizen*. By 1792, Olympe de Gouges was fully immersed in the political debates of the day. She was a keen and early critic of slavery and, like Wollstonecraft, had originally been strongly in favour of the French Revolution. In 1791, she became involved in the Amis de la Verité (Society of the Friends of Truth), a political and intellectual organisation that aimed to make public intellectual debates about how the new republic should be run. Among their strongly held beliefs was that of equality between the sexes, although this was also one of their more controversial positions. Olympe de Gouges felt strongly that women could be equal to men given the right opportunities, and certainly they could, with the right education, be men's intellectual equals. This was her position and the position of the Society of the Friends of Truth. With these discussions from within the society fresh in her mind, Talleyrand's assertions about unequal education seemed like a betrayal of the revolutionary spirit she had once defended. It did not take long for Olympe de Gouges to formulate and publish her response.

Mary Wollstonecraft, over in England, responded in much the same way as Olympe de Gouges and her Friends of Truth had done in France. Just to make it absolutely clear, the book was directed at him. Wollstonecraft dedicated the whole volume to Talleyrand, with the remarks:

Having read with great pleasure a pamphlet which you have lately published, I dedicate this volume to you; to induce you to reconsider the subject, and maturely weigh what I have advanced respecting the rights of woman and national education.

As an indication of current thinking in the world in which Caroline was working, and making a public name for herself in science, it is worth taking a moment to look in some detail at Wollstonecraft's book. Although Caroline is not mentioned directly in the book (it is not overly weighed down with actual examples), it is plausible to suppose that she may have been one of the 'few exceptions' to whom Wollstonecraft referred when she wrote, 'That the civilised women of the present century, with a few exceptions, are only anxious to inspire love, when they ought to cherish a nobler ambition, and by their abilities and virtues exact respect'.[4] Women, she felt, should be less worried about being liked (or loved) and concern themselves more with trying to be good at things and demanding respect for those talents.

The book, she stated, was aimed at the middle class, 'because they appear to be in the most natural state', in contrast to the rich, 'the education of the rich tends to render them vain and helpless'.[5] The lower classes, she had not really considered. She continued with some advice that seemed to run contrary to the carefully crafted super-feminine self-presentation that Caroline had been steadily cultivating over the years:

I wish to persuade women to endeavour to acquire strength, both of mind and body, and to convince them that the soft phrases, susceptibility of heart, delicacy of sentiment, and refinement of taste, are almost synonymous with epithets of weakness.[6]

She went further:

Dismissing, then, those pretty feminine phrases, which the men condescendingly use to soften our slavish dependence, and despising that weak elegancy of mind, exquisite sensibility, and sweet docility of manners, supposed to be the sexual characteristics of the weaker vessel, I wish to shew that elegance is inferior to virtue.[7]

Wollstonecraft was homing in on language and self-presentation, suggesting that it was damaging to women and their ability to gain respect for their talents to talk of themselves and allow others to talk of them as delicate, fragile creatures. Caroline, in contrast, seems to have approached this problem in a completely different, less confrontational way. Like Wollstonecraft, Caroline was aware of the very different language used for women, but instead of insisting that women lose such language and adopt a way of speaking that was closer to that of men, she did something very different.

Instead of challenging traditional conventions about how to talk about women and how women should talk about themselves, Caroline made a point of using such language for her own gain. She was always very careful to convey her delicacy of sentiment and her sweet docility of manners, but had managed to do so to apparent good effect, using it to win allies and ease the reception of her work. That Wollstonecraft felt compelled to argue so strongly against such tendencies indicates just how prevalent it must have been. Caroline was an astronomer, she took no interest in politics, but she was aware of the social currency of language. As a singer, she had learned how to speak in social situations in a way that was appropriate but, without ideas like Wollstonecraft's at the time, she saw it simply as just the way of things. In fact, most people did. Wollstonecraft was advocating that women might change that. According to her, women did not have to continually disguise their ambition or downplay their role. She was not arguing against good manners, but simply that women did not have to, as Caroline and countless other had, present a self-image to the world that was so very modest and self-depreciating.

Caroline and Wollstonecraft had seen a problem in the way in which men's and women's language differed and tried to solve it in very different ways. On the subject of education, too, it is possible that they would have agreed on the problem but not the solution. In Mary Wollstonecraft's proposed educational system, she suggested boys and girls should be educated together in buildings with lots of outdoor space. Lessons should be short and full of activity, performance and conversation, and they should be broken up with time to play outdoors. All of which sounds very much like the education system we have today. However, while Wollstonecraft's proposed system seems very much designed to improve education for all and for girls in particular, it is debatable how much it would have helped children like Caroline. While the first part may have been an improvement on what Caroline experienced back in Hanover, Wollstonecraft then goes on to say that, from the age of 9, girls and boys 'intended for domestic employments, or mechanical trades, ought to be removed to other schools, and receive instruction in some measure appropriate to the destination of each individual', while 'the young people of superior abilities, or fortune, might now be taught, in another school'. Aged 9, Caroline was very much intended for domestic employment, or at least domestic labours. It is unlikely that anyone would have seen in her then the potential of what she would later become.

Wollstonecraft was not so very unusual in making such distinctions. The general assumption of the time was that while many individuals might aspire to leave the lower orders for the chance of a better life, maintaining a lower class was still a necessity for society. For all their talk of equality, most intellectuals still wanted someone else to carry out the domestic work and manual labour. They still wanted servants, although increasing numbers of the more liberal writers balked at actual slavery. While some writers were happy to make the distinction between those who had equality and those who carried out useful but low-status work along gendered lines, others found class, or that often intangible commodity 'ability', to be a more palatable division. Given the lack of sympathy for people of her background, it is possibly not surprising that Caroline took little interest in the political debates of her time. Nevertheless, as Wollstonecraft's views about female education and language began to make their way through society, a little of them may have reached Caroline's ears and given her pause to wonder and reflect.

Back in the Herschel household, plans were afoot for a grand trip – for the men of the house at least. Towards the end of May, when his tiny baby son was just 3 months old, William and the boy's godfather, General Komarzewski, set off for a grand tour of Britain, ending with an award ceremony in Scotland. William was to be given an honorary degree. He had never been to university; few had in the late eighteenth century and, for most, university was treated either as a male finishing school for the aristocracy or a vocational training ground for future lawyers, doctors and clerics. University was not a place for training men (or women) of science, or indeed any other academic discipline, although very slowly it was inching in that direction. In time, William would be awarded a number of honorary degrees and other awards and titles from institutions around the world. This award, from the University of Glasgow, was not his first honorary degree but he was keen, nonetheless, to use the opportunity to travel and meet a great many of the Scottish men of science whom he admired.

Herschel and Komarzewski set off from Slough on 29 May in the direction of Oxford. By the following day they had reach Warwick, where they stopped to visit William's old friend, Mr Greatheed. Bertie Greatheed was not a man of science: he was the son of an MP, an aristocrat, at least by marriage, and a dramatist. They were regular correspondents, and it was due to Greatheed's persuasion that William sat for one of his most famous portraits, by William Artaud in 1819.

From Warwick, they travelled to Birmingham where they met William's brother-in-law, Thomas Baldwin, and William's stepson, Paul Adee Pitt. William and Mary had been married for four years by this point, so William and Paul, and possibly William and Thomas, had very probably met before, though there is no record of those meetings. While in Birmingham, Herschel and Komarzewski also took the opportunity to visit the famous Soho works. This was Boulton and Watt's Manufactory, one of the first of its kind in the world and one of a handful of starting points for Britain's Industrial Revolution. At the time, the factory was powered by a waterwheel and produced various pieces of metalwork (buttons and buckles, for example). Metalwork of this kind would be a speciality of the Birmingham area until well into the twentieth century. A few years later, Boulton and Watt would replace their waterwheel with a steam engine, which revolutionised how industry could be powered, and where factories could be sited. William was fascinated by this and other factories he saw on his travels. He would make intricate drawings of the machinery and the mechanisms for transferring the power from the waterwheels to the factory floor.

From the industrial landscape of Birmingham, they travelled west to the rural countryside of Wales. Here, William found much that reminded him of his life back in Hanover. 'The inn,' he wrote in his travel journal, 'resembles in its situation those of the country about Hanover. They burn turf or peat, a farm yard with trees and cows in front and garden by the side or back.' He also found the markets similar:

> A great number of women had butter in baskets, others eggs, &c., in the manner of the German country villages. [However] the air of these women was ... totally different from that of the Germans; most of them are lean but of agreeable features and good transparent complexions, but rather pale and emaciated.

Sadly, he does not elaborate on how German women differed from this description. To add a scientific flavour to their tour of Wales the pair, accompanied by three guides, attempted to climb Snowdon with William's 7ft reflector telescope in tow. Unfortunately, cloud cover prevented them making any observations.

By 3 July they had reached Scotland. In Glasgow, they were met by the mayor and presented with the Freedom of the City. There was a grand dinner held at the university and William was presented with his honorary degree. He got to see his friend, Glasgow's professor of astronomy Patrick Wilson, who had helped him when he had on occasion struggled to understand the mathematics offered by his French colleagues. (It was very probably Wilson who was one of the main reasons why the university decided to award William this honour.)

And then it was time to move on. The following day, they moved further east and a couple of days later were in Edinburgh, where they were shown the castle, observatory and various telescopes. Edinburgh had also awarded William with an honorary degree, back in 1786. There he met some of the major figures who were busy shaping the Scottish Enlightenment: Joseph Black (chemist), John Playfair (mathematician) and James Hutton (geologist), among others. William and Komarzewski even dined with Black and Hutton before heading south on 8 July and gradually making their way home, this time down the east coast, arriving back in Slough on 19 July.

What were Caroline, Mary and baby John doing all this time? History, being what it is, offers little record of their activities while William was away. If they corresponded with anyone outside the family, those letters were not kept. Very likely they spent their time exchanging visits with local women – Mary's mother, Miss White, Mary's Aunt Clark – caring for the baby and managing household staff. Caroline would have continued her observing, catching up on her reading and writing up observations of papers. Mostly, however, they were probably engaged in the kinds of day-to-day domestic activity that fills copious amounts of time and yet leaves little trace.

While William travelled up and down the country, and Caroline and Mary stayed at home caring for a small baby and running their two houses, disturbing events were taking place back in their home town of Hanover about which, curiously, the Herschel siblings said very little.[8] On 23 June 1792, the papers reported that William and Caroline's older brother, Jacob, had been found murdered, strangled, in a field just outside town.

Jacob had been living in Hanover as a court musician for many years by 1792. He and William had originally escaped to England together back in the 1750s, when Hanover was at war and French troops occupied the town. While William had stayed and made a life for himself in England, Jacob soon returned home when an opening became available within the Hanoverian Court Orchestra. Sometimes he visited the England-based Herschels and his nephews, the Griesbachs who, thanks to him, were now musicians within the English court. Mostly, however, he had remained in Hanover, continuing to mix with the aristocrats, gentry and upper middle classes for whom he played, and getting himself into debt as he tried to keep up.

How and why Jacob was eventually murdered remains a mystery. His killer was never found and his case was never taken to court. Some historians have suggested that he found himself caught up in the wrong place at the wrong time, and his murder was in some way connected with the French occupation. However, Hanover was no longer occupied by the French in 1792 – it was not occupied by *anyone* in 1792. It was not even involved, as yet, in the European War of the First Coalition. It is not out of the question, however, that there may have been rogue soldiers or sympathisers about town, or that Jacob found himself involved in a political dispute that got out of hand. Equally plausible, however, if we consider all that Caroline has ever told us about her brother and his arrogance, profligacy and excessive spending, is that his debts eventually caught up with him.

Caroline never liked her older brother. His power over her life as a child and young woman was something she never quite forgot or forgave. Her view of him was always coloured by those early experiences, so perhaps the image she painted was exaggerated. From her accounts, Jacob's desire to live in the same state of luxury as the aristocrats he served was such that he would happily see his family starve and himself in debt rather than miss out on a party or look scruffy while socialising with his employers. Quite possibly it was this tendency, rather than the political climate of the time, that led Jacob to be in the wrong place at the wrong time.

William and Caroline never mentioned their brother's murder. Considering what a close-knit family they were in other respects – the way in which Caroline would drop everything to make each visiting brother feel comfortable – this omission seems extraordinary. It is possible that they did not find out straightaway. It is equally possible that the story did not reflect well on them as a family. While William and Caroline would willingly talk of dramatic events in their past as a means of demonstrating their grit and determination to succeed or their triumph in the face of adversity, this story would have served no such purpose. Caroline never liked her brother, so her omission is perhaps easier to understand than William's.

William and Jacob, in contrast, were at one time extremely close. After William first came to England and Jacob returned home, it was to each other that they kept up their most consistent and heartfelt correspondence. Perhaps any discussion of their murdered brother took place verbally, without a paper trail. It is likely they considered it no one's business outside their family, although presumably news of his murder must have reached them somehow. Perhaps those letters between Caroline, William, their surviving brothers, Alexander in Bath and Dietrich in Hanover, and their sister Sophia in Coppenbrügge have since been lost. It was not a story either sibling chose to retell in any later account of their lives, although by the time Caroline was writing her autobiographies she would almost certainly have known. Perhaps they did not know – or perhaps, when they did find out, William had another tragedy closer to home to contend with and felt this to be the lesser of the two.

In November 1792[9] Mary's grown-up 18-year-old son, Paul Adee, died of consumption (tuberculosis, or TB). He had been sick for a while, and had been gradually losing weight as the disease, as the name suggests, consumed him. William knew him only vaguely from the occasional meeting and odd letter. Caroline knew of him, but had not met her nephew. Mary alone in the house had any real memory of the son she had just lost. Her husband and sister-in-law might sympathise, but they could not fully share in her grief. As John grew, he was encouraged to keep his brother's memory alive although he had been only a few months old when he died. When, many years later, John's granddaughter was cataloguing the family papers, she found a picture of Paul Adee along with a note written by one of her uncles or aunts that this brother of John, although never known to him, was always present in his life as he grew up. John, the note declares, 'always knew his brother's worth'.[10]

Babies had a high mortality rate in the late eighteenth century. It was not uncommon for families to lose children up to the age of 5. Indeed, Mary had lost a son from her first marriage (whom she had named William) in his infancy, back in the yearly years of that marriage. William and Caroline had lost several siblings who had died as infants. Although devastating, families were in some ways prepared for a loss of that kind. To lose a child just as they were entering adulthood, however, was something different and unexpected. As Mary grieved, trying to keep alive the memory of her older son, Caroline did what she could to help care for Mary's new son, John Frederick William Herschel.

1793

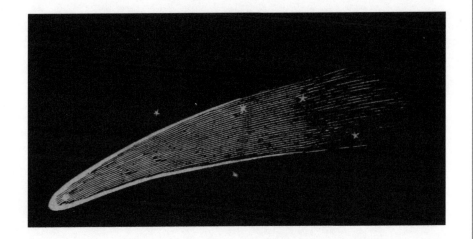

II

HOME LIFE

While William, Mary and Caroline were dealing, each in their own way, with the various births and deaths in their family, to some extent coming together as they cared for the new and grieved for the old, over in France the revolution had taken a turn for the worse. The guillotine was out and the royal family were on trial. After the execution of Louis XVI in January 1793 and Marie Antoinette in October, the atmosphere in France became increasingly fraught.

This was the Reign of Terror: a period when the rest of Europe was starting to fight back in defence of their own monarchies, and the new French republic responded by clamping down on any signs of insurrection within its own borders. The royals were two in a long list of enemies of the new state, guillotined for increasingly spurious reasons as the revolutionary republic began to fear for its own longevity. Besides the executions, which grew in number and frequency throughout the year, there were other changes too. The new rulers of the republic were banning numerous activities they considered threatening – all in the name of defending the cause.

Among the victims of the new regime was communication across borders: the passage of letters, journals and news in and out of the country ceased almost entirely. For the scientific community, this meant the Republic of Letters – the network that had kept information flowing so that practitioners could quickly learn of new developments and build on the work of others, regardless of location – was severely disrupted. French scientific men and women were, in effect, isolated from their colleagues across Europe. At the same time, they were also looked upon with suspicion by their own state and fellow countrymen for their supposed aristocratic sympathies.

Natural philosophy, very much like art, had for generations cultivated a close relationship with the rich and aristocratic across the world. It was an expensive hobby and could only be pursued by those who either had their own private wealth or could attract a rich or even royal patron. This connection with the old regime meant it was not always clear, in the battle between the new republic and the old aristocracies of Europe, which side the natural philosophers would be on.

For most, it was a pragmatic relationship: natural philosophers (and artists) sought out and befriended those with the money to fund their work. At the same time, their dependence on those with wealth meant they could not be seen to speak out against their patrons or the class that supported them. For the increasingly paranoid new French government, this silence made them potential enemies.

As the list of enemies of the state grew, it was uncertain whether the Herschels' scientific friends over in France would be safe. With no news getting through, the Herschels were naturally worried about them. Aware of their precarious political position, many of their friends had taken the precaution of changing their names: de la Lande became the less aristocratic sounding Lalande; de la Place similarly changed his name to Laplace, and so on.

In the end, not many men or women of science fell foul of the guillotine – the chemist Lavoisier was perhaps the most famous exception – but there were no guarantees at the time that this would be the case. The Herschels would not receive another letter from their friend Lalande until 1796. Occasional updates would reach them as friends managed to travel through France, reporting back any news they could garner of their French colleagues, but they were few and far between.

While all this was going on in France, the English aristocracy, including their own patron and many of the Herschels' friends and neighbours (large numbers of whom had connections to the royal court), were becoming increasingly uneasy. Numerous French aristocrats were making their way across the Channel to the safety of England, all with stories of their own innocence and the callous brutality of the new regime. The mood, at least within the aristocratic court circles the Herschels now found themselves in, was of righteous indignation. To show any sympathy to the revolutionary cause was increasingly to suggest support for violence and terrorism.

Beyond this small world of court society and intellectuals, the revolution was having a different kind of impact on people's thinking in a way that worried the British state. Reform societies were being set up across the country offering working men the opportunity to learn more about politics and their rights and to start to organise to defend them. After war broke out in 1793 such societies were banned in the name of national security. Just as in France, everyone was expected to show support for the state or be treated with suspicion and there was a sense that everyone should pick a side. Again, it was the men of science who were put under growing pressure to express open support of their own state over any claims of neutrality or support for the revolution. Given the fate of those French intellectuals who were seen to be allied to the old regime post-revolution, this was a difficult commitment to make.

In the Herschel home, meanwhile, everyone was for once getting along marvellously. Little John was growing up, learning to walk and talk and getting used to his unusual environment, and he did this all under the watchful eye of his doting Aunt Caroline. As one of John's obituary writers wrote many decades later, the household he found himself born into was one 'singularly calculated to nurture into greatness' a young mind such as his. He would go on to do great things, but for now he needed to concentrate on understanding his immediate environment and his aunt was always there and ready to help.

As Caroline occupied her daytime hours with cataloguing work, poring over Flamsteed's star catalogue and comparing his findings to her own and William's, John's nurse would often come and pay a visit with her young charge in tow. 'Aunty show me the whale!' she recalled him demanding when he came to visit.[1] An understandable favourite, this was the constellation Cetus, drawn in Flamsteed's catalogue as the most extraordinary looking sea creature. European astronomers at this time only had the very vaguest understanding of what an actual whale might look like.

On other days, John would play outside in the grounds of Observatory House with its several large telescopes, the busy work-shops all around, and very often workmen repairing, rebuilding or maintaining the various pieces of astronomical equipment on site. As he did so, Caroline was often to be found nearby, absentmindedly watching and listening. On one occasion Caroline described 'listening to his prattle', when 'my attention was drawn to his hammering'. When she went over to investigate further she found her young nephew destroying some of the newly erected building work. She hurriedly called over one of the workmen, 'a favourite carpenter'[2] called John Wiltshire, who was evidently very fond of John to sort it out. In the end, the damage was such that he had to bring over a bricklayer to undo what John had done. Then, as at other times, John Wiltshire was on hand and managed to rectify the problem.

John Wiltshire was one of the few workmen Caroline ever mentioned by name in any of her writing, but then he did make a special effort on behalf of her nephew. Not only was he readily on hand to amend without scolding the damage the young toddler did to work on the house, he also entertained him. Seeing John's interest in hammering, Wiltshire took it upon himself to find him some small tools of his own and teach him how to use them properly. As the only child in this busy working observatory household, John was very much a favourite, not just with his aunt but with many who worked in the strange home-turned-workshop in which he grew up.

In the summer, as had become tradition, William and Mary went on holiday. Caroline mentions in a letter some time later that they took John with them on these trips when he was between the ages of 6 and 9. This suggests that in the early years, when John was still a toddler, they left him behind with his nurse and Caroline for company. Everything about the way in which Caroline talked about her nephew, then and years later, suggests this arrangement suited her very well. She was never happier than when she had things to do and a sense of useful purpose. While her brother and sister-in-law were away – possibly in the countryside or perhaps at one of the newly emerging seaside tourist resorts; their records of these holidays were patchy – Caroline kept herself busy. She worked on her catalogues, read the latest scientific papers, copied out useful material and William's notes for him during the day. This she would intersperse with time spent with her nephew, watching him play and gently introducing him to her scientific world. Through Caroline, John became more familiar than the average toddler with the stars in the sky and the apparatus here on Earth that astronomers used to view them. At night, when it was clear, Caroline would go out on her own onto her roof and observe with her telescope. It is difficult to know when exactly she got any sleep, although she seems to have managed to fit in a few hours, perhaps at the end of a night's observing before she began her daytime activities.

On 7 October 1793, not long after William and Mary had arrived back from their summer travels, Caroline discovered another comet. Aware of the problems of priority claims, she wrote immediately to the Royal Society, despite having very little information to impart. Her letter to the society's secretary, Joseph Planta, was subsequently published as a paper in the 1794 edition of the *Philosophical Transactions of the Royal Society*, and must surely be among the shortest scientific papers in history. It simply read:

Sir,

Last night I discovered a comet near 1st (δ) Ophiuchi, but clouds covering the part of the heavens where it was, its place could not be obtained.

My brother has just now (7 o'clock) determined its situation, as follows.

The comet precedes the 1st (δ) Ophiuchi 6' 34' in time, and is 1° 25' more north than that star.

I remain, Sir, &c.

Car Herschel

Slough. Tuesday 8th October 1793[3]

All it said, in essence, was that Caroline had briefly spotted the comet near the fourth brightest star (delta, δ) in the constellation Ophiuchus, which is a constellation on the celestial equator, sometimes referred to as the thirteenth zodiac sign. She spotted the comet briefly, before clouds obscured her view. Her brother then confirmed the sighting, providing co-ordinates in terms of its distance from the fourth brightest star in Ophiuchus. Co-ordinates in the direction the Earth turns would have been given in time while co-ordinates in terms of how high a star is above the horizon would be given in angular height, or alternatively a star or comet could be described as being so many degrees away from another object in a given direction.

This was Caroline's sixth comet and she had announced it in Britain's most prestigious (and indeed, at the time, only) scientific journal. Yet this success was not to last. News was slow to leave France by this time, so there was some delay in finding out, but eventually it became apparent that Caroline had, in fact, been beaten to the discovery. Two weeks before she spotted this 6th magnitude comet in Ophiuchus, the famous French comet hunter, Charles Messier, had seen the same one, albeit when it was a slightly fainter 7th magnitude, on 24 September. Caroline was understandably disappointed. It had not been her best comet discovery, she had only caught a brief glimpse before the English weather got the better of her, but it was still one of her comet tally that she could no longer quite count as hers.

It is curious that Caroline chose to address this letter to Joseph Planta, who was simply one of the secretaries to the Royal Society, rather than the secretary in charge, Charles Blagden. Caroline had addressed other announcements to Blagden and, although not a close friend, he had been to the house and was reasonably well known to the Herschels. Blagden was, by this time, a key figure within the Royal Society. He is perhaps best known today as an organiser, a man who got things done and made connections, bringing important people together and helping them create their best work. Planta, on the other hand, was far more low-key. He was a librarian at the British Library, a post he had inherited from his father. He had been partly educated in Germany, and his sister, Margaret Planta, was a familiar face around Windsor as the English teacher to the royal princesses. Perhaps well aware that her comet discovery was not up to her usual standard, Caroline chose Planta as a less intimidating recipient for her announcement.

Despite confirming her discovery for her and offering detail on position, William did not make the comet announcement for his sister on this occasion. Instead, he left her to write her letter to Planta while he continued with work of his own. He was very interested in the planet Venus at the time, a planet closer to the Sun and therefore only visible in the early morning or evening (just before sunrise or after sunset). He wrote a paper in the summer summarising many years of sporadic observation, all made with the aim of better understanding the rotation, atmosphere and general appearance of the planet. William was branching out. He was starting to try and build his reputation in astronomy beyond his fixed stars specialism. With that on his mind, and the less than perfect conditions for Caroline's comet discovery, William was not as keen as on previous occasions to get involved. Caroline's announcement was short and to the point, but even before it turned out to have been found already by Messier, she knew this discovery was not her best.

For William, awards were now flowing in. Back in November 1781 he had won the Royal Society's prestigious Copley Medal for his discovery of Uranus. A month later, he had been made a fellow of the same society. In 1786 the University of Edinburgh gave him an honorary degree. In 1792, he was given an award by the French Académie des Sciences and an honorary degree from the University of Glasgow. In November 1793, he was contacted by Oberamtmann Schroeter of the Imperial Leopold Academy of Science with the offer of yet another award. The Imperial Leopold, otherwise known as the Leopoldina, was the learned society for the German states, and is roughly equivalent to Britain's Royal Society. As this point, Germany was not a country (this would not happen until 1871), but there was considerable communication and co-operation between various German-speaking states in the region we now know as Germany. The Leopoldina, named after Leopold I, Emperor of the Holy Roman Empire, slightly predates the Royal Society in its formation (it was formed in 1652 while the Royal Society was established in 1660) and remains a prestigious scientific society to this day. Schroeter was writing to offer William membership. By now, William was getting quite used to these kinds of grand gesture, although he was nonetheless flattered every time.

In the summer of 1793 discussions began about admitting William as a member of the Imperial Academy. These types of honour, along with awards and prizes, were one of the ways the international scientific community forged links across borders, showed solidarity and political neutrality and celebrated achievements in their discipline. Since William's discovery of Uranus, he had been a prime candidate for such honours. When Schroeter first wrote to William suggesting membership, William replied enthusiastically:

> In answer to the favour of your letter I can say that to be admitted as a member of the Imperial Academy of Sciences will be esteemed the highest honour that can be conferred on me, and I beg of you therefore to communicate these sentiments to the President of that Society.[4]

As with the honours list today, these were politically charged awards and diplomacy was needed in offering and accepting them. In contrast, when the French Academy of Sciences a few years later, during a brief truce in hostilities, tried to award foreign membership to several high-profile British men of science, they were under a certain amount of pressure from their fellow countrymen to refuse. Herschel, Nevil Maskelyne and Henry Cavendish, it should be noted, refused to bow to that pressure.

A few months after William had told Schroeter how flattered he had been to be offered membership, Schroeter wrote back with the results:

> The Imperial Leopold Academy of Science has entrusted to me the honourable task of conveying to you the enclosed Diploma with their best compliments, and I do this with the greatest pleasure and am ready to forward your acknowledgement.[5]

Grand gestures like this, for which she could show suitable deference and gratitude, were slightly thinner on the ground for Caroline. She could lay claim to the title of the first published female astronomer in Britain, the first paid female astronomer and nominee for the French Academy award in 1792 that was instead given to her brother. Awards and honorary memberships of societies would come her way in time, but the scientific establishment of her day needed longer to accept her as a woman scientist. Mostly, this recognition would come after her brother was dead and when her nephew was all grown up and a member of the scientific community himself.

She was awarded the Gold Medal and made an honorary member by the Royal Astronomical Society in the 1820s and 1830s respectively. This was a society her nephew helped to establish. She was given a Diploma of Membership by the Royal Irish Academy, by her nephew's friend the Astronomer Royal for Dublin, William Rowan Hamilton. Perhaps most impressive of all, she was awarded the Gold Medal for Science in 1846 by the King of Prussia, thanks to one of her nephew's heroes, Baron Alexander von Humboldt.

While whole committees, award-giving bodies and institutions took time to recognise Caroline's contributions, individuals were sometimes more forthcoming. Lalande and Maskelyne were always kind, friendly and encouraging towards Caroline, but they were not alone. Sometimes Caroline would receive and keep letters from supportive scientific colleagues who were virtual strangers. For example, Professor Karl Felix von Seyffer, a German astronomer at the University of Göttingen who had been in Britain briefly to carry out some measurements relating to the solar eclipse that took place in September 1793. During that visit, Caroline – his 'priestess of the new heavens' – and the Herschel home – his 'Temple of Urania, in Slough' – made quite an impression on the young professor:

> Permit me, most revered lady to bring to your remembrance a man who has held you in the highest esteem ever since he had the good fortune to enter the Temple of Urania, at Slough, and to pay his respects to its priestess. I still recall the happy hours passed in England in earlier days of sweet remembrance, and above all, those which I was privileged to spend near you in a society as genial as it was intellectual.
>
> Give me leave, noble and worthy priestess of the new heavens, to lay at your feet my small offerings on eclipses of the sun, and at the same time to express my gratitude and deepest reverence … How happy I should esteem myself if there were any service I could render you here, most admirable lady astronomer.[6]

Seyffer was a relatively new professor at this time, just 30 years old, and in awe of the veteran astronomers at Slough. Coming from a university environment, he would have had less experience of female colleagues than those who commissioned work from piecework computers, or the amateurs who frequented often female-run intellectual salons and soirées. Caroline was a surprise to him, and that made her understanding of his subject all the more impressive.

These were Caroline's rewards for her contributions to science. She was altering perceptions of who could be a competent astronomer,

one visitor at a time. More formal recognition of her work would
have to wait. As far as she let on, Caroline was not too bothered by
the disparity in formal recognition between her brother and herself,
at least within his lifetime. As she always told people, sometimes with
painfully exaggerated humility, she was only ever William's helper: 'I
am nothing, I have done nothing a well-trained puppy-dog would
have done as much: that is to say I did what he commanded me.'[7]
While her language seems to us today ridiculous in its self-depreciation, there is almost certainly a grain of truth in her statement
regarding how she saw her work. When she made an independent
discovery she was keen to ensure priority and clear her right to claim
credit, but these were minor occurrences that took place when she
had a moment free from her proper work. Her proper work was to
be a part of the team that produced William's catalogues, telescopes
and discoveries.

If Caroline's story and her way of telling it can teach us anything, it
would be that we should not be so quick to try to unravel the complex
weaving of social and professional connections that make our world.
At home with her family, or at work with her brother, she was part of
something that was collectively productive and important. She helped
to raise her nephew and was suitably proud of that achievement.
Similarly, she helped her brother create his surveys and catalogues and
analyse his data. Her brother received the majority of the praise for it,
because they lived in a time when all but a few people involved in any
enterprise were invisible. No one saw servants, workmen, labourers,
factory workers or family members when they looked at the products
of the working world. Caroline stood out in that world for finding
ways not to speak up directly, but to be visible and polite and have
others speak up for her.

Yet even Caroline had her limits. By 1793 she was exhausted. She
had discovered six comets, was struggling through an improving but
still imperfect relationship with her newly married brother and his
wife, and she was helping to looking after a toddler. It was a lot to take
on. That her brother was receiving international awards even as her

comet announcements became increasingly half-hearted shows how very different were the places that their similar paths could take them.

The year 1793 was a turbulent one in Europe. In Slough's own 'Temple of Urania', it was a time of settling down, reflection and taking stock for Caroline. In astronomical terms, it was not a very remarkable year for her. She had discovered one unsatisfactory comet and made note of it in her country's scientific journal. Her brother had received yet another award in recognition of their work, while she had received a rather uplifting, if less prestigious, note praising her abilities and importance to astronomical work. It was in her home life, however, that Caroline's fortunes had really begun to change. She had family; she was no longer just one of a pair (or occasionally a trio, when Alexander was around) of ageing siblings. Now there was a young child running around the house and grounds, brightening her days and giving her a renewed sense of domestic purpose. She was not just an astronomer, or her brother's indefatigable assistant – she was a devoted and loving aunt.

12

SOLAR ECLIPSE

Ordinarily, Caroline and William would have been asleep at 8.30 in the morning. The mornings were the part of the day they usually reserved for sleep as most nights would be spent observing, weather permitting. During the day, they tended to catch up on paperwork and reading as well as spending time with baby John. Early evenings were very often for visiting or entertaining visitors, of which this famous pair of astronomers and their home full of telescopes attracted a great number. This left them the mornings to get some sleep.

It was an unusual daily routine and not one that would have suited everyone, but it fit Caroline perfectly. Even before her life became filled with astronomy and scientific reasons for being awake at night, she preferred to stay up late than wake up early. When she first arrived in England and her brother had quickly piled on lessons and duties within hours of her settling in, her main complaint was not about the volume of work, but the early mornings. 'On the second morning,' she wrote, referring to the number of mornings she had so far spent in England:

... when meeting my Brother at breakfast, which was at 7 o'clock or before, (much too early for me, for I would rather remain up all night than be obliged to rise at so early an hour) he began immediately giving me a lesson in English, and arithmetic, and showing me the way of booking and keeping account of cash received and laid out.[1]

Although phrased as a statement about her introduction to many subjects, her complaint was not about her expected workload but about the earliness of the hour at which she was expected to start. She did not say a word about all William's other expectations regarding her readiness to learn all these different skills at once, and after so little time to get her bearings or recover from her exhausting journey from Hanover. That much she could take in her stride. She drew the line, however, at early mornings.

On 5 September 1793 Caroline had to make an exception for there were astronomical reasons beyond her control that demanded an early start. At 8.40 a.m., William, Caroline and a party of visiting aristocrats assembled in the grounds of Observatory House to view the predicted annular eclipse. This particular one was not of very much interest to most astronomers in the UK. The path of the eclipse (the line across the Earth along which it is possible to see totality) went (using modern-day country names and boundaries) from Iceland at sunrise, through mainland Europe, Poland and the Ukraine, ending at sunset in Afghanistan and finally Pakistan.

Even for a partial eclipse, no one would have recommended England as a good place to view it, yet William and Caroline persisted. Not only was England nowhere near the line of totality, but there was another reason the Herschels might have been unusual among UK astronomers for trying to see this eclipse. This was not the kind of eclipse that usually attracted attention. Annular eclipses are not the most spectacular, even when viewed in totality.

Solar eclipses come in two kinds: total and annular. In a total eclipse, the Sun and Moon are at such distances from the Earth that, amazingly, they appear from Earth to be exactly the same size. This means that when the Moon eclipses the Sun, it covers it exactly and all we see around the black disc of the Moon is the outer atmosphere of the

Sun, called its corona. In contrast, in an annular eclipse, the Earth is at a different place in its orbit around the Sun, and consequently at a different distance from the Sun. This time, the sizes do not appear to match up exactly. Instead, the Sun appears slightly bigger than the Moon. When the Moon eclipses the Sun in an annular eclipse, more of the Sun can be seen around the edge of the Moon. You do not get the same distinctive halo as in a total eclipse. You just see the Sun (too bright to look at directly, as usual) with the centre obscured by the Moon. The brightness of the part of the Sun that remains visible means the sky does not even go as dramatically and suddenly dark as it does during a total eclipse. Birds do not hurry back to their nests and wildlife does not go suddenly and eerily quiet.

Total eclipses have always attracted public attention. Often the attention was fearful, especially in more superstitious times, as their rarity and the sudden darkness they brought seem ominous and worrisome. In more recent times, total eclipses have drawn the interest of astronomers and then tourists. For astronomers in the nineteenth century, they proved to be useful as a way of viewing the Sun's corona, which would normally be very difficult to study. Because of the sudden darkness, total eclipses have also allowed astronomers to view the stars just behind the Sun, which would normally have been obscured by the Sun's brightness during the day. This was used in the twentieth century (I am not going to explain how) to test out Einstein's theory of relativity.

Annular eclipses, meanwhile, have been less obviously useful. While plausibly interesting in terms of helping us better appreciate the relative orbits of the Sun and the Moon, they do not offer the same broad opportunities to astronomers as a total eclipse allows. In the 1790s, however, eclipse study of any kind was in its infancy. They were clearly astronomical events, but how and why astronomers might want to view them had yet to be fully worked out. Total eclipses were more dramatic, but that did not mean pioneering astronomers like the Herschels could not find a way of using an annular eclipse in their astronomical research.

Not long after the eclipse, William wrote up his observations in a paper for the *Philosophical Transactions of the Royal Society*. The paper is a curious one, having no overall purpose exactly. It read more as an exploration of how astronomers might use annular eclipses in their research than a set of findings from the eclipse just viewed. The paper talked about seeing mountains on the Moon as it first began to pass across the surface of the Sun. It talked about the lunar atmosphere, stating that although he saw no evidence of the Moon having an atmosphere, this set of observations did not conclusively prove that one did not exist. He also wrote about viewing Venus during the eclipse. In short, the paper read as a series of interesting but ultimately unrelated observations. Some, such as his comments on the Moon's mountains, harked back to his much earlier astronomical interests, before Uranus and before he became known for his surveys of deep-sky objects. None, however, added up to any kind of coherent study. Instead, they came across very much as observations made to justify taking such an interest in this otherwise unremarkable astronomical event.

While William's paper tried to pass off his interest in the annular eclipse as a means of exploring how astronomers might use eclipses for their study, there was a more personal reason why the Herschels might have wanted to get up early to view this particular eclipse. For William and Caroline, this annular eclipse held a certain nostalgic attraction, especially seen, as this one was, far from the line of totality. Many years before, they had viewed an annular eclipse in similarly imperfect circumstances. It had been, for both of them, their first real introduction to observational astronomy and it was a memory that stayed with them both forever.

Nearly three decades earlier, back in April 1764, William and Caroline had stood, with their siblings and father in their backyard in Hanover. They all listened attentively as their father explained how and what they were viewing as they watched a partial annular eclipse reflected in a barrel of water. On that occasion they had not quite managed to be on the line of totality, and yet despite its lack of astronomical drama it was a moment that both siblings remembered for the rest of their lives. For the 14-year-old Caroline, it offered a brief respite from her many hours of cooking, cleaning and making clothes. It provided her with a break from her intensive preparation for her forthcoming confirmation. In contrast to all that isolating, continuous, laborious work, here was a chance for her to spend time with her family, not serving them, not studying, not improving herself or proving her commitment to God, but simply observing and marvelling at the world around them. It was a chance to see her father, not as the tired old man broken by war who worried and worked hard to prepare his children for their uncertain futures, but as a man sharing with her and her siblings his passion for knowledge and education even when it had no obvious utility. It was a chance to share this moment with her whole family, not just those she lived with, but also William on his one brief visit home after he had moved to England.

For William, the eclipse was a chance to spend time with his family, sharing what was then seen as a useless passion for knowledge and astronomy and the natural world. Most of his and his brothers' child-hood memories of their father were of him teaching them music, but here and there he could remember moments in which they were allowed a break from this vocational training. In those moments, Isaac would share with his children his interest in the latest philosophy or astronomy. He would encourage in them a passion for ideas and wonder. This was one of those moments. For William, the 1764 eclipse had an added poignancy, in that it was to be the last of those moments. Since he had moved to England, William had been able to travel to Hanover only very infrequently. Travel meant not working and he was not yet earning enough as a musician to be able to afford much time off. This visit would be the very last time he would see his father. Isaac died just a few years later, in March 1767. He would never know how successful his children would become. With the memory of that family gathering to watch an annular eclipse all those years ago, William and Caroline made what they could of the eclipse that would be just visible from Slough early on that September morning.

Eclipses, by the 1790s, were predictable, advertised and starting to be popularly viewed. Edmund Halley – second Astronomer Royal, friend of Newton and predictor of the return of the comet that bears his name – had used Newtonian theory back in the early 1700s and worked out how to determine exactly where and when a coming eclipse could be seen. He had then set about promoting this eclipse as a public astronomical spectacle, using maps to show where to stand for the best view. In May 1715, there would be a total eclipse visible from England, and to encourage people to go out and view this as an entirely harmless, predictable and exciting astronomical phenomenon, he had maps printed showing exactly where to go to view it. While eclipses had been predicted with less accuracy for centuries, this was the first time that people had been encouraged to see it as entertainment and an opportunity for scientific research. Previous generations had been more inclined to look upon them as bad omens.

Following Halley's enthusiasm, eclipses increasingly became a subject for scientific enquiry throughout the eighteenth century, although observers were not always entirely sure how to gain useful information from them. Later, with the invention of photography and spectrometry, and won over by the Herschels' arguments that our Sun and the stars were interesting to study, astronomers would use eclipses to study the composition of the Sun's corona and understand better the Sun's own make-up. In the eighteenth century, they were still finding their way in this, as in many aspects of astronomy, working out what to study, which questions to ask and how to go about them.

Since eclipses are about the Sun and the Moon, it made sense for astronomers to start there, to consider eclipses as a means of better understanding those bodies. Certainly, this was the approach William Herschel took. No one quite knew what the Sun, or indeed the Moon for that matter, was in the eighteenth century. William had for a long time considered both bodies to be inhabited, which made them particularly intriguing. However, he had been told off early in his career for writing with too much certainty about his theory that the Moon was inhabited. This was back in 1780, before he had discovered Uranus, and before he had been published in the Royal Society's journal. He had yet to learn the rules, such as they were, of what was and was not appropriate speculation for a scientific paper. Nevil Maskelyne advised him against claiming too much for his unproved theory about lunar inhabitants, and so William dutifully left it out. The idea still bothered him, though, and the eclipse gave him an opportunity to investigate further.

William thought it entirely likely that life could be found scattered throughout our solar system and, in this, he was not alone. James Ferguson, one of the authors William turned to in the 1770s to learn astronomy and whose book, in turn, he had passed on to Caroline, was a keen believer in life on other planets. The Herschels' friend Lalande, meanwhile, in his book *L'astronomie*, had described the Sun as potentially inhabitable, consisting as he thought, of mountains (sunspots to him were mountain peaks) and luminous oceans. Even Maskelyne did not rule it out. Maskelyne's objections had been about evidence, and how to back up claims; he was not dismissing William's theory about inhabitants on the Moon per se, only stating that in a scientific paper he needed to tone down his speculations and stick more strictly to the evidence.

In his paper about the annular eclipse, having learned from past mistakes, William was more cautious. He did not state outright in this that his interest in studying the Sun and the Moon was to find life upon them. Nevertheless, this was how he started his investigations, that others might follow in that direction. The eclipse had shown him that there may not be an atmosphere on the Moon, which would make life there unlikely, although he was reluctant to accept that as definite proof. As he said in his introduction, his paper on the eclipse was not about his results, but rather a guide to future researchers. He suggested:

The following particulars will at least serve to point out the way for similar observations to be made in other eclipses, where different circumstances may chance to afford an opportunity for gathering some addition to our knowledge, with regard to the nature and condition of the moon, or of the sun, and perhaps of both these heavenly bodies.[2]

Observing this eclipse had made William think not just about the possibility of life on the Sun or Moon, but also about how to safely study the Sun and what he might hope to find by doing so. This was a new departure for William. While he continued to survey the sky with Caroline's help, this new work on the Moon and Sun required less collaboration. He did not need to keep track of co-ordinates in quite the same way, and that made the need for an assistant less constant. This new interest in the Sun changed the way he worked further still, for the obvious reason that he would now need to spend less time observing at night, and more time observing and experimenting during the day. As a team, William and Caroline were starting to drift apart. This new work was taking William away from Caroline and that meant a loss for her, in the sense that he was taking with him some of her purposeful astronomical activity.

Oblivious to its possible repercussions for Caroline, William found his new interest in the Sun perfectly timed. He could spend more time working in the day, allowing him to keep more sociable hours, see more of his family and rest at night. He was well into his fifties by now and the cold nights especially were starting to get to him. He soon found that studying the Sun also offered a tricky technological problem to solve, which he found pleasing. It was well known that the Sun would damage the eyes if one looked straight at it. Their father had taught them that, insisting that they view the 1764 annular eclipse reflected in a barrel of water rather than looking at it directly. For telescopes, the problem was quite literally magnified.

Without a filter of any kind, a telescope trained on the Sun would take in its light and heat and focus it down to a concentrated point at the eyepiece, making it extremely dangerous to look at, and making the lens very likely to shatter. Coloured glass was generally used to filter out some of the Sun's light, reducing its strength in the eyepiece but this, William found, was still unsatisfactory and it was not unknown for eyepieces to shatter even using a filter. He also found that some filters worked better at reducing the light that got through, while others were better at absorbing the heat, but he could not see easily what the pattern was. Over the next few years William decided to systematically try to find the best filter to use and make it safer to observe the Sun, its sunspots, possible oceans and inhabitants.

William's daytime experiments on heat and the Sun, carried out, as far as his records show, alone and without Caroline's help, were eventually published in 1800. In these experiments, William used a prism to split sunlight into its rainbow of constituent colours. He then measured the temperature of each colour, placing thermometers beyond the spectrum too, as a control to measure the background temperature of the room. Measuring across the colours he found that the temperature increased from violet through to red, with red the hottest strip of colour. This part of the experiment was useful, but not entirely surprising. It gave him the results he needed to work out the best filters to use and introduced the possibility that the various colours might have other properties that differentiated them from one another. These observations were interesting, but no more than he expected to find. What was unexpected, however, was what he discovered when he looked at his control thermometer, the one placed beyond the spectrum to measure background heat. To his great surprise, he found that the control thermometer – measuring the space beyond red – was the hottest of all, hotter even than the red part of visible light. The other end, meanwhile, beyond violet, was cool, more in keeping with what he had been expecting.

Today we know that space beyond red as 'infrared' and that it is the first invisible part beyond light of the same spectrum as the visible light. We call this the 'electromagnetic spectrum' because of investigations and discoveries regarding the nature of light made by astronomers, philosophers and mathematicians who came long after the Herschels showed how light, electricity and magnetism are all related.

To William, this extension of the spectrum beyond red was a total surprise. He called the new, hot, invisible part of the spectrum 'radiant heat', considering it to be something *different* to light rather than a continuation of the same spectrum, as we understand it today. He was confident it came from the Sun, but decided to describe it as heat that radiated from the Sun, rather than giving it a name that would link directly to the visible light it came with. Language is very important in science, but it can also betray wrong turns. William was often overly cautious in his language, careful not to imply links where he did not see them. In these experiments, this led him to the term 'radiant heat'. We see it elsewhere in his coining of the term 'asteroid' in 1801 to distinguish newly discovered minor planets from his own real planet, Uranus.

By 1793 William and Caroline had worked together as an astronomical team for many years. He at the observing end of the telescope, she on the ground or in her small hut recording his measurements and adding her time readings. This arrangement worked very well for large-scale surveys of the sky, where quick and accurate recordings of position and time were essential. As their programme of work evolved, however, this working arrangement became less central to the enterprise. There was still collaborative work to do, but it was no longer all they did. After the 1793 eclipse, William's research interests began to drift. He began to take a greater interest in the Sun and, leading on from that, the brightness of other stars. He still observed at night, and had Caroline along to assist, but these observations were slightly different from before. There was also a greater daytime component to them, as he found himself having to look back over how historians in the past had thought about brightness and how he might do things differently.

Back in 1785, William had tried to use star brightness to map our galaxy, the Milky Way. At the time, it was commonly assumed that star brightness was the same as distance. All stars, it was supposed, were the same so if a star appeared brighter than another that must mean it was closer. William's Milky Way map, while fantastically inaccurate, was an important step in exploring this relationship and using it to better understand our place in the universe. The geocentric world view had long been discredited. The question was, if the Earth was not at the centre of the universe, then what was? Initially, the geocentric world view was replaced with a very similar-looking heliocentric universe. Instead of the Earth at the centre, we now had the Sun, surrounded by planets, surrounded by fixed stars. William's map was the first step in trying to get a better grasp of how those fixed stars were distributed and get a sense of how our star, the Sun, fit with all those that surrounded it.

William's time spent looking at the eclipse and studying the Sun and its brightness brought his attention back round to that earlier puzzle about stars and their brightness and distance. Coming back to the problem nearly a decade later, having spent a good deal of those ten years working with Caroline on the nature of and variation in the fixed stars, William was much less sure that the relationship between brightness and distance was as straightforward as he had previously thought. Current thinking at the time among other astronomers on the subject of star brightness, he felt, was also unsatisfactory. By the mid-1790s he began to consider the problem systematically, in the only way he knew how. He started a new set of catalogues, this time listing – and each time remeasuring – the brightness of stars in an attempt to bring more rigour and uniformity to the systems used by previous astronomers. Magnitude measurements were all very well, but that system dated from ancient times and there was a lack of consistency in how stars were ranked.

This change of programme, although reasonably subtle, was enough to push William and Caroline's working relationship off-kilter. Their working dynamic of over a decade had changed. It was less obvious to Caroline how she was contributing, especially with William's time away from the telescope measuring temperatures and theorising about magnitudes. She still had a role when her brother was at his telescope, and she was dutiful and conscientious about carrying it out. The rest of the time, however, she was starting to feel at something of a loose end. First Mary had come along, leaving Caroline to lose and then rebuild a role within the family, then their professional astronomical partnership had begun to fall apart.

When William and Mary married, Caroline had found herself without her old role of woman of the house, and so she had thrown herself into her work. Now, as her working arrangements were becoming less certain, she gave more of herself to her family, poring over every small achievement her baby nephew made. While she cherished her role as devoted aunt, always happy to help out, she did not shrink back into domesticity and leave her astronomical work entirely. She had, by now, a professional reputation to uphold, one she was proud of and keen to maintain. As her brother's work changed, she looked around to see how hers might change too. Their working relationship might not be quite as intertwined as it once was, but she could still contribute and create work that would make the whole Herschel enterprise better.

1794

13

ORIGINALITY BY STEALTH

In 1794 Caroline began to look around for a new project to occupy her time, especially her daytime hours. Her spare nights were still given over to her small telescope on the roof and her hunt for new comets and nebulae. So far, she had fourteen new nebulae and six comets to her name.[1] More were to come. She had her work with her brother, helping him with measuring and recording as he observed with one of his large telescopes. Her royal pension gave her a sense of independence, as did her growing reputation in scientific circles thanks to her discoveries and the support she had been given by her brother. The praise heaped upon her by influential astronomers such as Nevil Maskelyne and Jérôme Lalande also helped. Her home life within the family was improving as she began to feel a little more secure now that she was able to contribute in a way that felt necessary, providing some much-needed assistance in the daily care of her young nephew. But none of this was quite enough for Caroline. As her brother began to drift away from their surveying project, branching out to look at the Sun and experiment in daylight hours, she began to feel she needed more. She was always on the lookout, as she wrote in her autobiography, for 'work with which I could proceed without troubling him [William] with questions'. In 1794, she found just the project, one that would keep her busy for quite some time.

This was a turbulent year for the Herschels' friends over in France. Charles Messier, their friend and fellow searcher of nebulae and comets, lost a dear friend and collaborator when the lawyer, mathematician, natural philosopher and patron of the sciences Jean-Baptiste-Gaspard Bochart de Saron was guillotined on 20 April. A few weeks later, on 8 May, chemist Antoine-Laurent de Lavoisier was also led to the gallows. Messier himself was spared, although he lost all his money, his publications were delayed and at one point found himself so poor he had to borrow oil from Lalande for his lamp or work in darkness. The astronomer at the Paris Observatory, Dominique Cassini, survived too, although the observatory was raided and he was imprisoned in February 1794.

Other friends did what they could to keep themselves safe. Laplace, who had always tried to keep out of politics, left Paris. Lalande protected himself by becoming an outspoken atheist, very much aligning himself with the politics of the new regime. While there was considerable overlap between the work of the Herschels and that of many of their peers across the Channel, for very understandable reasons their colleagues were, for the time being, preoccupied with other things. At the same time, little correspondence was getting in or out of France, so any work they were able to carry out stayed, at least for now, in France.

Caroline would, in time, lose priority on one of her comets once correspondence channels opened up again with the French. As it turned out her sixth comet, discovered in October 1793, had been spotted a month earlier by Messier. That loss of priority was of course small price to pay, she concluded, for finally knowing that her friends had survived. Nonetheless, it was nice to have a project less dependent on timing and communication. For her new project the international correspondence network of philosophers, astronomers and mathematicians was less crucial; she was mostly working with very old data, and so the breakdown in communication was less of a problem. For this new project, Caroline needed only time, patience, old data, a sense of purpose and a meticulous dedication to detail.

William and Caroline's big surveys of the sky, their catalogues of nebulae, star clusters, double stars and, more recently, the brightness of stars, were important and time-consuming observational projects. Each star needed to be seen and described by them before it could enter their catalogues. Measurements had to be taken and recorded and calculations made on the observations to turn that raw data into useful information. At the same time, the catalogues were also building on work that had gone before. Charles Messier had previously produced a catalogue of nebulae and star clusters. Earlier still, but yet to be superseded, John Flamsteed's catalogue of northern hemisphere stars visible from the telescopes at Greenwich remained the standard reference for star positions in the northern sky. For the Herschel catalogues to be useful to astronomers, they needed to contain their observations but also to relate those observations back in some way to the findings within the older catalogues. If they could easily compare catalogues, astronomers – the Herschels included – would be able to see if and how stars had changed over time, which, if any, had disappeared and which were entirely new discoveries.

The problem was, the old catalogues were set out very differently to the way in which the Herschels observed. Messier was their contemporary and inspiration. Eight years older than William, but an astronomer from the start, Charles Messier had produced his first catalogue in 1771, just before Caroline came to England and the Herschels had started building their own telescopes. When William discovered Uranus, Messier was already so well established that he was one of the French astronomers Nevil Maskelyne approached to ask that he and his colleagues study and calculate the orbit of this new object. Messier had passed on details to his friend, Bochart de Saron, who was one of the first to calculate Uranus's orbit and to establish it as a planet rather than a comet.

Messier's catalogue was an important impetus to the Herschels' decision to study and catalogue the nebulae, double stars and star clusters in the night sky. Although William had been sweeping the sky before that, section by section, it was not until 1782, after he had discovered Uranus, that his friend William Watson gave him a copy of Messier's catalogue and the Herschels decided to make one of their own. Theirs was an extension of Messier's catalogue and, to some extent, superseded it. Certainly Messier was aware of how much more their catalogue contained than his. Trying to explain the continued relevance of his own work in a much later publication, he wrote:

> After me, the celebrated Herschel published a catalogue of 2,000 [nebulae etc.] which he had observed. This unveiling of the Heavens, made with instruments of great aperture, does not help in the perusal of the sky for faint comets. Thus my object is different from his, and I need only nebulae visible in a telescope of two feet. Since the publication of my catalogue, I have observed still others: I will publish them in the future in the order of right ascension for the purpose of making them more easy to recognise and for those searching for comets to have less uncertainty.[2]

The relationship between the two projects meant that their catalogues were reasonably similar and comparable. Flamsteed's catalogue, *Atlas Coelestis*, was a different publication entirely, however. His catalogue was completely different in aim, content and size.

John Flamsteed, Astronomer Royal at the Royal Observatory in Greenwich from its foundation in 1674 to his death in 1719, was employed by the king to produce a detailed and accurate map of the night sky using a telescope stationed on the Greenwich meridian. The aim of this map, and an accompanying table of lunar positions, was to give navigators at sea the raw data needed to calculate their longitude. The purpose was not to further knowledge of astronomy, but rather to protect lives and valuable cargo. Without these maps, countless ships were being lost at sea, as navigators thought they were further from land and rocks than they were. Others were lost believing themselves closer to land and the end of their journeys than they were and running out of food and drink. The royal patronage of science in this instance was more political and financial than intellectual.

Flamsteed's task was to list the position of every visible star or star-like object in the northern hemisphere. His primary concerns were with position and completeness, not to differentiate between stars and star-like objects. It was the position that was important, not what the object was. His purpose was to serve navigators and his aim was to list all the 'stars' that he could see with his telescope, rather than pick out particular objects as Messier and the Herschels would do later.

Although the royal imperative to create a new observatory and employ a full-time astronomer just to produce a map for navigators at sea was new, the idea of star maps to aid navigation (and astrology) was very old indeed. In producing this catalogue and plotting every star to help sailors find their way at night, Flamsteed was joining a centuries-old tradition. Hipparchus and Ptolemy had listed them for the Greeks and Al Sufi and Ulugh Beg had continued the tradition in the Islamic world. Flamsteed had updated those same maps again, in the same tradition, which meant listing all the stars he could see, in order of constellation. For each constellation, Flamsteed listed each star from the brightest to the dimmest, giving their position and magnitude (or brightness).

The Herschels' survey was something of a departure from this old tradition of star maps. They were not in the least bit interested in the concerns of navigators. They, like Messier, were instead trying to help astronomers. The Herschels did not think so much in terms of constellation, as in terms of strips of the sky, or zones, each of which they systematically scanned or swept for interesting objects. Back in 1781, William tried to explain this process and its benefits, claiming that this method of systematic sweeping made his discovery of the planet Uranus not accidental but inevitable. It was not luck that enabled him to spot his planet, it was not 'a lucky accident that brought this star to my view', rather 'it was that night its turn to be discovered'.[3] When he moved on to surveying and cataloguing the sky for particular objects, he continued to do so in the same manner, sweeping section by section, zone by zone.

The Herschels needed to check the observations they made (by location first, and constellation second) against Flamsteed's lists to see if any stars had moved or changed in brightness since Flamsteed had made his observations nearly a century earlier. They needed, they soon discovered, to check in case Flamsteed had made a mistake or an omission that they could then correct. Unfortunately, the way the Herschels had their telescopes set up and their method of observation were not the same as the way in which Flamsteed had worked. For them to fully get to grips with Flamsteed's catalogue, they needed to see not only the catalogue itself but Flamsteed's original observations and have a quick way of checking the various numbers against one another.

Back in June 1787, while her annoying brother Jacob was staying, Caroline had begun to rectify the problem of cross-referencing their observations with other catalogues in her 'Temporary Index'. Now, in 1794, she began to take that work further, producing a more focused and thorough 'Index to Mr Flamsteed's Observations of the Fixed Stars'. In this index Caroline went through Flamsteed's work, systematically comparing his observations and conclusions to his *Atlas Coelestis* and accompanying catalogue.

The resulting index very simply listed the star, the number of times Flamsteed observed it and how those observations differed from one another. Her results from this exercise were revealing and extremely useful. Some stars were found to be duplicates, having been on the edge of a constellation and mistakenly catalogued once as belong to one constellation and again as belonging to its neighbour. Other stars were found to be other things – for example, Flamsteed had unwittingly observed Uranus several times, but thought it to be a star rather than a planet. Other stars were found to be listed in the catalogue but never actually observed by Flamsteed or any of his staff. Still more were found in Flamsteed's observations but not in the catalogue. These missing stars, numbering several hundred, Caroline collected and catalogued separately.

None of this is to say that Flamsteed was a bad astronomer. He was, in fact, a very good and conscientious astronomer. He observed night after night for over thirty years as Astronomer Royal. He trained up a series of assistants to help him, including his wife, Margaret, who was responsible for finishing and publishing his catalogue after he died. He worked with an instrument maker to design much of the observatory's apparatus and even paid for some of it out of his own pocket. His attention to accuracy was such that when Edmund Halley and Isaac Newton became impatient and stole his results, publishing them without his permission, he sought out every copy of their edition he could find and had them burned. Yet, despite all of this, he made some mistakes.

Flamsteed's catalogue was new in many important respects at the time. It was the first comprehensive survey of the night sky to be made with a telescope. Catalogues had been produced before, but they were all based on naked-eye observations. His was the first to use observations from a telescope. It was the first to be produced at Greenwich, which would go on to produce data like this year after year for nearly 300 years. It was the first to be government-funded and made for the specific purpose of improving navigation for the nation. Despite its errors, it was still the most accurate and comprehensive celestial map of the northern hemisphere for nearly a century. For most purposes, it was entirely adequate. It was made to help seafarers find their way by the stars and in that it mostly served its purpose. However, the Herschels, with their interest in the stars for their own sake rather than as landmarks to aid navigation, brought with them a need for a different level of accuracy.

Caroline's work studying this catalogue – work that many historians now consider to be her greatest contribution to her subject – shows what real scientific work is all about. While we tend to hear only of the great breakthroughs, the big discoveries and the amazing new theories, most scientific work is quite different. It is about being able to hold on to the bigger picture in order to be able to devote untold hours to detailed, repetitive, laborious and often boring work. Caroline's real skill, her gift to astronomy, was being able to see the importance of what she was doing, even as she meticulously sifted through observation after observation searching out the occasional error, omission or duplication. It was a job that not even William could bring himself to do. It took a very specific set of very much undervalued skills.

Caroline had spent her whole life being extremely busy at the behest of others, although over the years her life had morphed beyond all recognition. In some ways, Caroline's childhood and early adulthood spent labouring away at 'low prestige tasks',[4] household chores that were always needing to be done again and were invisible until they were not done, prepared her perfectly for this work. Unlike her brother, she had no expectation of applause or recognition for her work, only a well-rehearsed need to be busy and useful. Meticulously working her way through Flamsteed's catalogue and identifying individual stars that were not recorded quite right helped her brother. It allowed him to see which catalogue entries he could trust, which genuinely represented where stars were and their past brightness, and which were less reliable. It was the kind of work that suited Caroline's lifetime of training. She liked to be busy and useful, and she was happy to hide behind the work of others – in this case, her brother and Flamsteed, who was providing the raw material – in order to appear suitably modest and undemanding.

The index that Caroline began work on in 1794 was relating Flamsteed's catalogue references to his original observations. This was a necessary, if time-consuming and laborious, step to discovering which observations to trust and which to question. If there was inconsistency in his observations, for example, errors would be much more likely to creep into the catalogue. If the observations were fairly uniform, then the catalogue entry was probably right. That was Caroline's initial aim – she wanted to make it easier for herself and her brother to look up what they had seen in the sky and check it against what Flamsteed said he had seen around a century earlier. What she found was even more significant. In the process of drawing up the index, she was able to identify errors. She found omissions, where the star was catalogued (presumably just copied from earlier naked-eye catalogues) but not observed. She found duplications too, where – because this was the first time a catalogue had been made with such magnification – dimmer stars on the edge of one constellation were inadvertently observed and then catalogued twice, in that constellation *and* its neighbour. She also found in her cross-references that some stars were assigned different levels of brightness on different observations. This inconsistency had bled through into Flamsteed's catalogue as another source of error.

It was about this time, as Caroline pored over Flamsteed's catalogue and her young nephew John was entering his 'terrible twos', that John's nurse must have started bringing John in to visit his aunt as she worked. As she systematically ploughed through Flamsteed's atlas, John got to see the elaborate illustrations representing each of the constellations. This was also when he developed his affection for the 'whale', or Cetus, and learned to be familiar with the idea of constellations and with the pictures and names of this strange menagerie of characters. Not only was Caroline helping astronomers to make new use of this old catalogue and aid her brother in his work, she was also beginning the process of teaching a new generation. As she pored over her catalogue, indulgently explaining to her young nephew about the pretty pictures her books contained, she was surreptitiously planting ideas and teaching the language and imagery of science that he would carry through into adulthood.

Buried within her essentially administrative task, Caroline made discoveries and was able to present them in a feminine way. She was not challenging Flamsteed's authority or expertise by showing his mistakes, she was merely annotating his work to make it more useful to her brother and other future astronomers. She was simply performing the long-held female role of note keeper and copyist and, in doing so, was following – possibly unwittingly – a long history of covert female writing.

While few women in the eighteenth century presented themselves as practitioners of science, and certainly even fewer were allowed to attend meetings, hold professional titles or publish, one area of science was notable for the visibility of the fairer sex. A significant number of scientific translations were carried out by women. Within science, as elsewhere in eighteenth-century life, there were specific roles that were deemed appropriate for women to perform. In science, these roles included assistant, copyist and proofreader, or hostess of informal scientific gatherings such as a salon or a soirée. In published work too, although it was seen as a principally male domain (one only has to look at the trouble certain contemporary female novelists had), there were certain areas that were considered acceptable for women.

Translations of scientific work were one such area: these were projects that would allow the work of one male philosopher to be read by another, via the linguistic skills of a woman translator. Translation of scientific texts has rarely, if ever, been a straightforward process. The meaning has to be fully understood in order for it to be explained in another language and this often meant that translators needed a deep understanding of the subject, and sometimes also needed to repeat experiments or observations to ensure their translation was accurate. Yet translation has often been dismissed as a simple paper exercise that those on the periphery, not real philosophers or men of science, might be able to carry out. For a long time, European historians dismissed nearly a millennium of scientific work in the Islamic world as just translation (from Greek to Arabic). The work of many eighteenth-century European women has, until recently, been dismissed in a similar manner.

Another form of scientific writing that was available to women was that related to teaching. Provided their work was presented as teaching material, to teach sons or even daughters about the latest scientific or mathematical works, then women could write as they pleased and find acceptance and publishers. Again, this allowed women to use their scientific knowledge and introduce their own ideas without immodestly demanding recognition within elite scientific circles. Instead, these educational books allowed women to write scientifically while still adopting the acceptable feminine role of teacher to the next generation.

Within these restrictions, many women in the eighteenth century turned out to be extremely enterprising. The French philosopher and mathematician Émilie du Châtelet⁵ produced both a translation of Newton's *Principia* and a textbook dedicated to the education of her son. In both cases, she managed to weave in considerable new material, based on her own experiments and theorising, through careful wording and, in the case of her translation, copious footnotes. Similarly, Marie-Anne Lavoisier, well known for her work assisting her chemist husband yet never mentioned in his publications, found a way to express her views and interpretations on her science through translation. In England, Margaret Bryan,[6] who knew Nevil Maskelyne and kept a girls' school near the Royal Observatory, found ways of having her ideas on a range of scientific subjects published by writing textbooks to be used at her school and further afield.

Caroline's index and subsequent catalogue of missing stars was a development of this trend. She was writing it, so she always insistently maintained, because it would help her brother in his work. In that sense, her index was very similar to the translations of earlier women. Like them, she was translating Flamsteed's work into a form that would be useful to her brother. The only difference being that there was no language barrier to hide behind. She could not present this as Flamsteed's work made newly accessible by a change in language. She had to admit that she was changing and improving on his work to make it more useful to the astronomers of her day. Plausibly, she could have argued that she was translating a work designed for navigators into a form that would be useful to astronomers, but to do so would have been a gamble and would have involved admitting to her understanding of the technical language of both – not a very feminine claim. Luckily, she had her brother on hand to argue on her behalf for the importance of her work, and she had several years of developing relationships and a reputation, through which astronomers had got to know and trust her and her work. She had, by this time, supporters and allies – her brother, Maskelyne, Lalande – but it was still a bold move for an unmarried, non-aristocratic, middle-aged woman to claim to be improving the work of a venerated male astronomer from the past. Even the aristocratic Émilie Du Châtelet had claimed only to be changing the language when she rewrote Newton's *Principia* for a French-speaking audience.

It was an extremely fine line that Caroline had to walk. On the one hand, she needed to keep busy and produce something worthwhile that would improve her discipline. On the other, she could not overstep her mark and claim, as a woman, to be showing the boys how it was done. Under the circumstances, it is not entirely surprising that she should be so anxious to present herself in meek and modest terms.

1795

14

THE INDEFATIGABLE
ASSISTANT

Away in France, as the Reign of Terror subsided and the spate of public executions and draconian lawmaking began finally to subside, the Herschels' old friend Jérôme Lalande decided to lighten the mood with some writing – it was time for a new edition of his earlier book, *Astronomie des Dames*. Jérôme Lalande had first published his celebration and encouragement of women in astronomy in 1785. In 1795, he decided it was time for an updated second edition. Lalande's book was essentially an introduction to astronomy, and a very popular one at that. Its claim to be for women followed a tradition established a little over a century earlier by one of Émilie du Châtelet's tutors, Bernard le Bovier de Fontenelle. To suggest that a book was for women was to widen its readership considerably. It meant its readers might include women certainly, but also it reassured the less well-educated gentleman or less academically confident man that it would not contain anything too challenging.

Fontenelle's *Conversations on the Plurality of Worlds* started a genre. His was a book designed to allay readers' fears that a science book might be too complicated for them by presenting it as a book for women. The book set out to introduce new readers to all manner of mainly astronomical ideas – from the heliocentric model of the universe to whether life might exist on other worlds – through a series of conversations. The conversations were in French (rather than Latin) and they were between a philosopher and a marquise. They took place over a series of nights in her garden.

Back in 1686, books on astronomy were mainly confined to books of tables, atlases, and philosophical and mathematical treatises. For many centuries, the number of people who could read was extremely limited, so this lack of range was not a huge problem. In the 1600s, literacy rates began to increase and, just as important, science, philosophy and astronomy began to move beyond the confines of the monasteries and universities and became topics of broader interest. Fontenelle was part of this world of broader interest. In France, salons, which were often run by women, were formed offering like-minded people of the right class an opportunity to meet and discuss the latest discoveries and experiments. When he arrived in Paris as a young man, Fontenelle attended many fashionable salons, including those held by women such as Madame de la Mésangère, the Duchesse du Maine and Madame Tencin. Drawing on those experiences and conversations, he set about writing his introduction to astronomy, presenting it as a conversation between the well-educated, well-informed philosopher and the intelligent and interested marquise.

Fontenelle's image of the man of science, as portrayed in his book, revolutionised the subject. Not only was it a topic suitable for the intelligent woman, but the man of science himself was also transformed. No longer was he a reclusive pedant, celibate, cloistered and living a secluded life in a monastery or university. Instead, Fontenelle's philosopher was a charming wit, seducing women with his knowledge and insight. Both sexes were flattered and sales and imitations soon followed.

Fontenelle's book was translated into many languages, spreading his ideas and the book's novel format throughout Europe. In England, Aphra Behn produced a translation in 1688, helping to secure her title as the first woman in Britain to earn a living as an author (she also wrote plays, poems and fiction). Following this spate of translations came imitations throughout Europe. Authors capitalised on this new genre as a way of selling books to an eager but uninformed public. In England, for example, John Harris – a clergyman who wrote books and delivered lectures in coffeehouses – published *Astronomical Dialogues Between a Gentleman and a Lady* (1719). Meanwhile, Benjamin Martin – an instrument maker and travelling lecturer – produced *The Young Gentleman and Lady's Philosophy* (1759), in part, like Harris, to help build his audience. In Italy, Francesco Algarotti wrote *Newtonianism for Ladies* (1737), while in France, continuing this same trend, Lalande wrote his *Astronomie des Dames*.

In his preface, Lalande acknowledged his debt to Fontenelle. Fontenelle's book, he said, served as a model, showing that it was perfectly possible to write about complex ideas in a comprehensible way. The book that followed covered various areas of astronomy from the movement of the Sun, to comets, to the possibility of life elsewhere in the universe. Before he moved on to that, however, Lalande deviated a little from the standard formula of earlier books by taking the opportunity to lavish praise on an extensive roll call of women philosophers and astronomers through the ages. This was astronomy for women, but it was also a celebration of women in astronomy.

In each edition, the list got longer. His second edition, in 1795, began with a message addressed directly to his student and protégée, Madame du Piery (who also featured in his list). There then followed a long poem and preface. In his 1795 edition, the women in science picked out for special mention were:

Hypatia (the ancient Greek philosopher)
Maria Cunitz
Marie-Claire Eimart Muller
Jeanne Dumée
Hevelius's wife (this is how he describes her, not by name but by association)
Manfredi's sisters (as above)
Kirch's three sisters and his wife, née Winkelmann

La Marquise de Châtelet

Madame Lepaute

Mrs Edwards (from the *Nautical Almanac* in England)

Madame du Piery

His niece, Lefrançois de Lalande

Miss Caroline Herschel

Caroline Herschel was new to this edition. He introduced her for her *'travaille avec [son] frère; elle a déjà découvert cinq Comètes'* ('work with her brother; she has already discovered five comets'). By 1795 the total was technically six, but communication between the two countries was such that Lalande may not have known, or not have heard in time for publication. Tucked away within a book that followed the old convention of regarding women as uneducated, but willing and appreciative audiences to the erudite man, Lalande had managed to smuggle in a more controversial message. In his roll call, he was quietly drawing attention to the fact that women could participate in astronomy, and to such a degree that their names and contributions would be celebrated for centuries to come.

Caroline was now a woman of science on the world stage. When lists were made of women in astronomy – and many have been since Lalande's – she was up there alongside Hypatia and Émilie du Châtelet. Back home, she was also finding her status improved, with her usefulness around the house now more than ever fully exploited and appreciated. Gradually she was finding that she could be of some real use in helping her brother and his wife raise their son. He had a nurse, and the family had several other servants to keep everyone fed and clean, and several of the workmen, such as John Wiltshire, took an interest where they could, but it was Caroline, possibly even more than John's own parents, who helped to introduce this young infant to the unusual world of science and enquiry that surrounded him at Observatory House.

Caroline's help with John and the steady continuation of domestic life at Observatory House became especially important in early 1795 when, after a long illness, Mary's aunt, Miss Clark, died, leaving Mary money and property. Mary's account book from this period shows just how much property she owned by this time, inherited presumably from both her first husband and her Aunt Clark. They present a rather different side to Mary from the loving wife and concerned mother offered elsewhere. In these accounts, a rather more ruthless, business-minded woman surfaces. Mary appears to have owned considerable land within the Slough and Upton area, and to have been entirely unsentimental in wringing every last penny from that investment. Rents were collected from: Mr Jones, Mr Boscowen, Mr Hevens, John Piearce Mr Brown, Mr Gilbert, Mr Moore, James Walden, Mr Pye and Mr Lovegrove. Also listed among Mary's accounts were references to rents paid for board by both Caroline Herschel and Mary's own mother, Elizabeth Baldwin. Curiously, while other rental properties were listed as belonging to Mary, the Crown Inn in Slough was listed as having been rented out by William to Mary's brother, Thomas Baldwin.

Mary seems to have lent money too, although not as a matter of course, and to have expected interest back on the loans. She lists interest on money lent to her brother, Thomas Baldwin, by her son, Paul Adee, and also on a loan to a Miss Hernon. Scattered among these listings was the occasional reference to money brought in by William, although in comparison to hers it seems very little. Over the period 1795 to 1822 he sold a total of fifteen telescopes; he also charged a fee for coming out to clients to clean and polish the speculum mirrors when that needed doing.

The family's main income, however, was from property and Mary, in her guise as a local landowner, was extremely thorough in her running of that business. When her Aunt Clark died, increasing her portfolio of properties, Mary understandably had less time to devote to running her own home and looking after her young son. Caroline, however, was happy to step in and be on hand wherever she was needed and, as the former lady of the house with many years of experience helping to raise her siblings and on occasion her sister's children, she was the obvious choice.

Caroline's position was starting to feel nicely secure. In her quiet, self-depreciating way, she could maintain the calm, continuous, smooth running of the Herschel home and observatory as the lives of her brother and sister-in-law changed around her. William had his astronomy, and increasingly his experiments on the Sun and heat. Mary had her many properties to attend to and the legal, financial and administrative burdens that accompanied them. Caroline, meanwhile, had her index, but she had designed it specifically to fit round her other work. She was their anchor, to provide help at the telescope, in the home or at the workbench whenever needed and so quietly, almost invisibly, she allowed her family to achieve so much more than they ever could have without her.

In June of that same year, William read a new paper to the Royal Society on an old subject. This was his official announcement of the value and importance of his great 40ft reflector telescope. 'The uncommon size of my forty-feet reflector,' William began, 'will render a description of it not unacceptable to lovers of astronomy.' He then proceeded over the next sixty-two pages to describe his journey into instrument making, how he had learned and showing the various designs he had experimented with along the way. When he came to discuss the construction of the 40ft itself, he carefully thanked the generosity and wisdom of the president of the Royal Society and the king before making it absolutely clear that, although he did not make every part, he designed and oversaw it all:

> In the whole of the apparatus none but common workmen were employed, for I made drawings of every part of it, by which it was easy to execute the work, as I constantly inspected and directed every person's labour; though sometimes there were not less than 40 different workmen employed at the same time.[1]

He used 'common workmen', he said, thus implying that their contribution was purely physical and they had added no expertise or specialist help, but were instead guided by his drawings and overseen by his inspection and direction. Throughout his description, he emphasised his part in the process, mentioning others sometimes to explain mistakes (one mirror failed because of 'mismanagement of the person who cast it'), but just as often simply to acknowledge that he had help. This was by no means a universal style of scientific writing, often the contributions of others would simply be implied or glossed over entirely, but that was not William's style. This was a large-scale project, only made possible by the contribution of many bodies, and William wanted them acknowledged. Since it was often women whose roles were glossed over – the wives, mothers, sisters and daughters who assisted, especially in science carried out in the home – William's style of scientific writing was of particular significance to Caroline's career.

William's introduction to his paper ended with his first discovery with the 40ft reflector telescope – the sixth moon of Saturn, Mimas, on 28 August 1789. There followed a very detailed description of the telescope's design, with diagrams that went on for the best part of forty-five pages. Towards the end of this description, William offered an account of how he and Caroline went about using this very large, cumbersome piece of astronomical apparatus. The observer (William) and assistant (Caroline), he wrote, were linked by a 'speaking pipe'. The assistant sat at a table with various apparatus before her; 'on the signal of the observer' she then read off the required information to plot the star. She would then guide him:

> By a catalogue in zones the assistant may guide the observer, who is
> with his back to the objects he views and who ought to have notice
> given him of such stars as have their places well settled, in order to
> deduce from their appearance the situations of other objects that
> may occur in the course of a sweep.[2]

Back in 1783, he observed, when they had begun this programme of sweeping the sky, no such catalogue in zones existed. Thanks, however, to his 'indefatigable assistant Carolina Herschel', a working copy had now been completed and another was very much in progress. He went on to note that the 'evident use of such a catalogue must undoubtedly soon have been perceived by every person who was acquainted with the method I used for sweeping the heavens'.[3] Halfway through a paper promoting and proving the worth of his very expensive giant telescope, William took the opportunity not only to praise his sister, but to write of the importance of her up-and-coming new work.

Curiously, while unnamed workmen were acknowledged at the beginning and Caroline was named as William's 'indefatigable assistant' halfway through, no mention was given to their brother, Alexander. He had worked with William and Caroline from the start on their telescope building. He had a keen eye for detail and liked to work with his lathe, producing precision parts and clockwork mechanisms. When William had an idea, he would often turn to his brother to work out how to make that idea become reality. The zone clock is a case in point. As William described in his paper, the zone clock was designed to tell the workman moving the telescope when one zone was complete and signal that he needed to change direction:

> It strikes a bell when he is no longer to turn one way; that is, when the telescope has come to one of its limits of the zone, which if it be after going down, is called the bottom bell; and it strikes another bell when he has made the same number of turns in a contrary direction.[4]

Letters between the brothers suggest quite strongly that while William may have had the idea for the clock, it was Alexander's design that brought it into being. Unlike the rest of the paper, William made no claim to have designed or built the clock; instead, he carefully removed himself or anyone else from his description of the zone clock's design. He described it, but gave no indication of where the design came from.

Despite her careful, well-chosen words – not wanting to claim too much, or to bother astronomers unnecessarily – it was clear by 1795 that Caroline wanted recognition for her contribution to her brother's work. William's nod to his 'indefatigable assistant', diligently praising her current cataloguing project for its usefulness, both to himself and others, was his way of providing that recognition. Alexander, in contrast, seems to have been much happier staying in the shadows. He had chosen not to move to Slough with them, and when he visited liked to stay among friends and close family. He was not a public figure and it would seem that William was just as happy to accommodate that desire for privacy as he was Caroline's yearning for credit.

William read his paper to the Royal Society in June. In the summer he and Mary, possibly accompanied by John and perhaps even John's cousin Sophia Baldwin (certainly she used to join them on later holidays), went away. Caroline stayed home to look after the house and was probably joined by their brother, Alexander. The nights were short so little observing could be done, but the siblings both had daytime activities to keep themselves occupied. The pair also had a comfortable enough relationship that they could happily go their own way for hours at a time. Caroline buried herself in catalogues and worked long hours on her tables. Alexander, meanwhile, would have shut himself off with his lathe and other tools and worked away on various mechanisms and small parts.

As the nights drew in and Alexander went home to be replaced by William and his family, Caroline could return to her telescope on the roof. Still snatching hours between assisting her brother, dealing with guests and helping around the house, she nevertheless managed a significant amount of observing. We can never know for sure how much time she spent on her own sweeps, as she did not always record sweeps that found nothing. As she explained in her observing journal:

> Sweeping for comets has not been neglected at every opportunity which did offer itself. But as I always do sweep according to the precept my brother has given me, and as I often am in want of time, I think it is very immaterial if the places where I have seen nothing are noted down.[5]

On 7 November, in the course of her regular sweeps for comets, Caroline found something she considered worthy of noting down.

Wasting no time, she quickly wrote to Sir Joseph Banks, who read her letter – as if it were a full scientific paper – to the Royal Society on the 12th of that month. With each new comet announcement, Caroline had changed her approach, subtly trying new ways to get her voice heard and her observations taken seriously. 'Last night,' she wrote on 8 November, 'in sweeping over a part of the heavens with my 5-feet reflector, I met with a telescopic comet. To point out its situation I transcribe my Brother's observations upon it from his journal.'[6]

The paper that followed was mostly her brother's observations of her comet. She ended these with a brief note of her own: 'As the appearance of one of these objects is almost becoming a novelty, I flatter myself that this intelligence will not be uninteresting to astronomers.'[7] That part was signed 'Carolina Herschel', and was followed by two more pages of 'Additional observations on the comet' by William Herschel.

Although the paper and the discovery were Caroline's work, much more space was given to William's observations. By this time, Caroline had understood how to get her voice heard. She had her name on the paper, her name linked to the discovery, but she had also found a way to address the concerns of many within the scientific community that a woman's word on its own was not enough. Using her brother's authority, she had given her assertions weight. With his observations of her comet, astronomers could see that what she claimed was credible, there really was a comet observable through a telescope in that part of the sky over the course of those few nights.

Unfortunately, on this occasion Caroline turned out not to have been the first astronomer to have discovered this comet, although it would take several decades to find that out. Caroline's seventh comet was one with a very short period. Comets are balls of ice and rock that loop around the Sun in a big elongated ellipse which takes them right to the edges of our solar system and back again. The period of the comet is how long it takes to cover that loop, how long it takes from when we see it near the Sun to its next pass near the Sun. Halley's comet, for example, is considered a short-period comet because it has a period of seventy-five years, that is, it returns roughly every seventy-five years. For others, it can be centuries before we see them again.

Before Halley, comets were assumed to be one-off events, and in even earlier times as portents of doom. Halley theorised that they made a loop around the Sun and out to the edges of the solar system, and to prove it he predicted the return of the comet that now bears his name. As he predicted, his comet returned in 1758 and then again in 1835, 1910, 1986 and will return again in 2061. After that, it became a standard problem for all new comet discoveries to try to calculate their orbit and period. This was not always easy, since it depended on taking very accurate observations over a long enough period of time to be able to essentially join the dots and mark out the loop. In the case of Caroline's seventh comet, for example, it would take nearly twenty-five years to obtain the information and calculating ability to work out its period.

Caroline's seventh comet, like Halley's, turned out to be a short-period comet, and once that was established it was found that it had been spotted before. Any comet with a period of less than about 200 years is regarded as a short-period comet. Caroline's comet turned out to have one of the shortest periods of any comet ever discovered, certainly any bright comet. It was eventually discovered that it has a period of just 3.3 years. It was a German astronomer, Johann Franz Encke, who finally calculated its period in 1819, tracing the comet back through various sightings, including Caroline's, to find that it was in fact the Herschels' friend Pierre Méchain who first saw it back in 1786.

Caroline was, by this time, 45 years old. She had been an astronomer for just over a decade and was starting to make a solid name for herself, thanks in large part to the support she had from the men around her. Lalande had listed her among his female pioneers of astronomy, following many years of supportive correspondence and promoting her name within his own scientific circles. Her brother had also spoken up, naming her his indefatigable assistant and promoting her work in his paper. He had offered his support to her comet discovery announcements, turning her polite observation of a new comet that might interest astronomers into a weightier declaration of discovery.

Caroline had achieved a considerable amount on her own – from her comet and nebulae discoveries to her continuing work organising and correcting Flamsteed's catalogue.

For these contributions and those of helping her brother achieve his scientific ambitions to be considered the work of a proper astronomer, she needed the help of a well-established male patron. Cleverly, Caroline had managed to cultivate three strong and vocal supporters of her work. Fighting her corner she now had her brother to speak up for her, along with her good friends Jérôme Lalande over in France and Nevil Maskelyne, Astronomer Royal and producer of the *Nautical Almanac* in Greenwich. With their help, she could quietly, politely and modestly break down walls and revolutionise contemporary perceptions of a woman's place in science.

15

NEVIL MASKELYNE

N evil Maskelyne was an important figure and an important friend to have in the world of eighteenth-century British astronomy. He was the Astronomer Royal, and had been since he had taken over from Nathaniel Bliss in 1765. That made him the fifth astronomer to hold the title, and with each new incarnation the observatory had grown in size and responsibility, if not yet in personnel. He was director of the *Nautical Almanac*, the yearly publication of tables for sailors that would ensure the Greenwich meridian was eventually chosen as the point of zero degrees longitude for Britain, and ultimately the world. He was also an influential voice at the Royal Society and an authoritative correspondent with natural philosophers all over Europe. William had found his advice invaluable when trying to get his early papers read to the Royal Society and had soon found him to be a supportive ally, fellow astronomer and friend. Caroline, although less naturally disposed to making friends outside her family, was gradually finding Maskelyne to be equally encouraging and supportive of her. By 1795 she might even have started to think of him as a friend of her own.

Unlike the Herschels, Maskelyne (who was just one year older than William) was born English and wealthy. Nevil's father had been a civil servant and when he died in 1744 (when Nevil was 12) he had been working for the Duke of Westminster. The duke seemed to take it upon himself to help out the Maskelyne family left behind by his death and obtained a post for Nevil's brother Edmund in the East India Company. Such posts were very prestigious; they offered guaranteed work and were available only to those with a close connection to an existing East India Company member who could recommend them. For the duke to offer Edmund a post was a considerable gift. Edmund in turn found Nevil's sister Margaret a suitable potential husband out in India, Robert Clive (Clive of India), whom she dutifully married. The oldest brother, William, meanwhile inherited a sizable estate from an uncle on their mother's side. He was sent to university to learn the requisite mathematics and social graces (and make the right connections) needed for running such an enterprise. That just left Nevil without property, position or spouse.

Following the educational path already trodden by his older brother, William, Nevil attended the University of Cambridge, beginning his studies the year his mother died. He went as a 'sizar', meaning that his fees were reduced in exchange for working within his college, but later managed to get a scholarship. When it came to exams – at this time Cambridge offered one route to graduation: the Mathematical Tripos – he came seventh in his year. This gave him the option to become a fellow, which he did, and then to take holy orders so as to become a clergyman.

So far, Nevil had followed a fairly standard, if academically impressive, path as the second son in a landowning family. While older brothers inherited the land, the younger boys tended to become clergymen, lawyers or doctors, these being the three professions for which a university education equipped its students. As a clergyman and fellow of Trinity College Cambridge, Nevil Maskelyne had a secure income. At this point, he began to deviate from the standard path of a boy of his upbringing, using his security to pursue his scientific interests with some enthusiasm. He had already dabbled in astronomy, showing an early interest in scientific instruments and being very taken with the chance to observe a solar eclipse with a camera lucida back in 1748. With his financial situation stable, he now began to work in more depth in both mathematics and astronomy, making friends with several mathematics professors and a number of astronomers, including those with their own private observatories. By 1758 he had made friends in sufficiently high circles that he could be nominated as fellow of the Royal Society by, among others, two mathematics professors and the Astronomer Royal James Bradley.

In 1761 an astronomical opportunity presented itself which would allow Nevil to make his name as a dedicated and serious astronomer. Roughly twice every century the planet Venus is visible passing across the face of the Sun. This is called the 'transit of Venus' and for eighteenth-century astronomers it appeared to hold the key to calculating very accurately the size of the solar system. This was an important question for astronomers at the time, who saw their main aim as being to model the solar system as accurately as possible and use that model to make predictions. For them, astronomy was all about getting to know the solar system, testing out Newton's laws (still new science in the 1700s) and understanding in detail precisely how the bodies within it moved.

To use the transit of Venus to measure the size of the solar system, astronomers needed observations to be taken of exactly when Venus appeared to start crossing the Sun's surface and exactly when it left the Sun's surface. And they needed to do this from two points on the Earth's surface, as far away from one another as possible, yet still close enough to have their daytimes coincide for the duration of the transit. They did this to measure 'solar parallax'. To imagine how this works, you need to look at something far away with one eye, and then look at the same thing with the other eye. The object will appear to shift slightly. From this shift, you can calculate using triangles the distance that object is from you. This is parallax. Much the same happens, only scaled up, if you look at Venus crossing the Sun from two points on Earth that are very far away from one another. From that shift, measured properly, you should be able to apply some complicated mathematics and use it to work out the distances between the Sun, Venus and the Earth.

In 1761 the Royal Society was very keen to measure solar parallax using the transit of Venus and funded two expeditions for that purpose – one to the island of St Helena and the other to Bencoolen in Sumatra. Nevil Maskelyne was appointed as one of the astronomers on the St Helena expedition and they set sail with many scientific instruments and a team of astronomers aboard. In the event, the expedition was not a complete success. Cloud cover prevented observations being taken of the transit so plans were made to observe the other transit in that century's pair, eight years later in 1769. Maskelyne, however, made sure the trip was not a complete waste. While he could not find the size of the solar system, he could test out a new navigation technique for finding longitude at sea and did so on his way there and back.

Longitude is your position around the globe, east to west and west to east, and can be found by measuring the time in your location, and comparing that with the time at some arbitrary baseline point, a point of longitude zero. The longitude problem in those days was how to carry the time with you before suitably accurate clocks, unaffected by the movement of a ship at sea, had been invented. Clocks at the time were all pendulum clocks, no use at all on a rocking ship in the middle of the ocean. The Board of Longitude had been set up in 1714 to judge a competition, thrown open to anyone and everyone, to find a solution to the longitude problem. The prize money was substantial, but the problem was extremely difficult and had still not been resolved conclusively by the mid-1700s.

The technique of finding longitude at sea that Maskelyne set out to test on this voyage was called the 'lunar distance method' and he found it to be an extremely good method in principle, although he felt it needed some work. He liked particularly that it required only a single robust piece of navigational apparatus (a sextant) and a set of astronomical tables. This made it a financially accessible method for most ships. His continued support for the lunar distance method throughout his life would make him a controversial figure in some later histories.[1]

In time, a rival method for finding longitude at sea would be put forward by John Harrison. Harrison's method was very simple. He could take a clock onboard, set to Greenwich time. As a clockmaker, Harrison felt he could design the kind of clock that could keep time even on board a moving ship in the middle of the ocean. The problem with Harrison's clocks was their expense. For Maskelyne, the cheap lunar distance method was more practical than expecting every ship to carry an extremely expensive clock on board such as that designed by John Harrison. In time, Harrison would be seen as the victim, but it is worth noting that sailors as late as the 1950s were still being taught how to use a sextant and find longitude by this method. While clocks like Harrison's eventually made their way onto ships, it paid to have a less technological back-up in case anything should go wrong with their more sophisticated onboard navigational equipment.

After his return from St Helena, Maskelyne continued to work for the Board of Longitude, testing out other methods of finding longitude at sea on other voyages. John Harrison's clocks had, by this time, impressed the commissioners of the board enough for him to be awarded some money to develop his idea. By 1763 he had perfected his design and it was this clock, H4, that Maskelyne was sent to test. His verdict was mixed. It was a good method, but he was not convinced it was a device that could be manufactured cheaply enough to be of practical use aboard most ships.

All this work on astronomy and navigation made Maskelyne the ideal candidate for a government post such as, for example, Astronomer Royal. When the fourth Astronomer Royal died suddenly (having only been in the post a few months), Maskelyne was the obvious choice. He was appointed in 1765 and moved, as the job required, into the observatory where he would work for the next forty-six years.

As Astronomer Royal, one of the first things Maskelyne did was to set up the *Nautical Almanac* to turn the regular observations taken at the Royal Observatory into data that sailors could use to find their position at sea, including the information needed to make use of the lunar distance method. When Maskelyne had tested the method back in 1761, he had found the main problem was the need for more accurate data about the positions of stars and the Moon. This was, in large part, why Maskelyne set up the *Nautical Almanac*. It was a way of publishing the observations made at the observatory in such a way as to be useful to navigators trying to calculate time at Greenwich while they were at sea. In time, the almanac would become so successful and so widely used that sailors from all over the world came to use Greenwich as their baseline longitude zero.

While the production of the *Nautical Almanac*, with its one clear aim, might sound relatively straightforward, it was not simple – to turn the observatory's raw data into useable tables required several hours of complicated calculation. To do so single-handed would have taken more than a lifetime, by which time the tables would have been horribly out of date and utterly useless. So, Maskelyne set up a workforce of piecework human computers to whom he would send books and mathematical tables, raw data and a set of instructions. They would send back tables that he could use in his nautical almanacs. Two computers were given the same month to compute and a third 'comparer' was then sent their work to check for inconsistencies and weed out errors. At any one time, Maskelyne might have to keep track of around ten home workers, all contributing to the same volume of the almanac. In all, thirty-five people were employed by Maskelyne as computers; some stayed for a few months, others for several decades.

Maskelyne kept a close eye on his computers. He did not employ just anyone. He wanted serious, conscientious workers with some mathematical ability and a keen eye for detail. Beyond that, he did not discriminate. While the observatory itself would not employ women until the late nineteenth century, and even then only as an experiment, Maskelyne had two female computers working at the almanac. He had several schoolteachers too, a couple of assistants from the observatory, several clergymen, surveyors, booksellers and also some instrument makers.

Given Maskelyne's encouraging support of Caroline, it is worth considering for a moment how the two female computers found themselves working with him. Mary and Eliza Edwards were the wife and daughter of John Edwards, a clergyman and instrument maker who had also been a computer for Maskelyne up until his death in 1784. Maskelyne knew the whole family and was friendly enough with them to have probably known, even before John died, that Mary (who was almost exactly the same age as Caroline Herschel) had been the one doing most of the calculations. After John died, Mary continued as she always had on the calculations, only now she was able to take over his place officially. In his record books and accounts, Maskelyne simply replaced the name 'John Edwards' with 'Mary Edwards', and carried on as before. He made no fuss about it, nor seems in any way to have felt that the change needed explaining or drawing attention to. In the end, Mary became one of Maskelyne's longest-serving computers, working for him for forty years.

Eliza Edwards had been just 5 years old when her father died and her mother took over as computer. As she grew up, she began to help her mother with the computations, taking over fully when her mother officially stopped at the age of 60. Eliza continued as a computer herself for the *Nautical Almanac* until 1832. In that time, her dedication to her work was such that she never married, never had children, nor did she extend her role and take on teaching, writing or instrument making as many of her male colleagues had done. Instead, she led a quiet life, and when she died in 1846, left her house to her servant, and presumably by now close friend, Selina Jones.[2]

At around the same time that Mary was taking over from her late husband, another woman was allowed to join the Royal Observatory. In 1784, after nearly twenty years living as a bachelor within the living quarters of the observatory, Maskelyne married Sophia Pate Rose. Sophia was one of two illegitimate daughters of John Pate Rose, owner of an estate in Northamptonshire and another in Jamaica. The Jamaican estate was probably the source of his wealth, it produced rum and sugar thanks to the labours of his many slaves, but it had been sold sometime after his death and before Sophia and Maskelyne met.[3] Although illegitimate, Sophia's father had left her and her sister money and paid for an expensive education. Nevertheless, their status meant that finding husbands was much harder for them than many of their peers. Sophia's sister did not marry until she was 33, just after their mother died, and then she married a widower, Reverend Sir George Booth, very much her senior. George Booth was Nevil's cousin. A month after their wedding (at which both Nevil and Sophia were witnesses), Sophia, then aged 32, married the 52-year-old Nevil Maskelyne. A year later, Sophia gave birth to a baby girl whom they named Margaret after Nevil's sister.

Like William, Nevil married relatively late in life, in the 1780s, and had just one child. Both John Herschel and Margaret Maskelyne[4] grew up in curious circumstances, surrounded by large telescopes and few other children, with a steady flow of scientific and aristocratic visitors to their respective homes. While Margaret had no Aunt Caroline to encourage her to take an interest in the work she was doing, she did have her father, and nearby there was the influential schoolteacher and writer Margaret Bryan and her daughters. Margaret Maskelyne was said to have been very interested in astronomy, helping her father at the observatory as she grew up. As an adult, she plausibly dabbled in the sciences too, certainly her son went on to have a career in science as a professor of mineralogy at Oxford.

The Maskelyne's neighbour, Margaret Bryan, ran a small girls' school in Blackheath (just across the park from the observatory), where among other things she taught the girls science and astronomy. Her lessons were so popular that by 1796 she had been persuaded to put some of the lessons together and publish them in a book she would call *Compendious System of Astronomy, in a Course of Familial Lectures*. The book, as was common practice at the time, was published by subscription and contained a list of all the subscribers whose contributions made publication possible. Among those listed was the Reverend Nevil Maskelyne, although he was not the one Bryan chose to publicly endorse the publication at the beginning of the book. That honour went to Maskelyne's friend and occasional computer at the *Nautical Almanac*, Charles Hutton, professor of mathematics at the Royal Military Academy, Woolwich.

In his professional, domestic and geographical position, Maskelyne had more involvement with educated, intelligent and able women than perhaps was the case for many of his scientific peers. He had come to know the Herschels in 1780, when William was introduced to him in writing by their mutual friend William Watson. After William discovered Uranus and he and Caroline moved to Slough, they found their paths crossed more frequently, and gradually William and Maskelyne became friends, although Caroline came round a little more slowly. Soon after, Maskelyne met his future wife, Sophia, when his cousin married her sister. Although the records are sketchy for Sophia, she is known to have had an expensive, if not necessarily good, education. She was sent away to boarding school and appears to have been able to read and write and, if nothing else, be sufficiently mathematically competent to keep track of her own accounts.

Sophia and Nevil Maskelyne married in 1784 and, a year later, their daughter Margaret was born. At the same time (also in 1784), John Edwards died suddenly from inhaling arsenic as part of an instrument-making process involving mirrors, and Maskelyne found himself employing a woman for the first time at the *Nautical Almanac*. Nearby, Mary Bryan set up her school and perhaps even came over to the observatory now and then to top up her astronomical knowledge in order to teach astronomy to her young ladies.

All these women appeared in Maskelyne's life over a very short period of time. Nevertheless, Maskelyne seems to have taken it all in his stride. With clever women in his life and a daughter to think about raising and educating, Maskelyne seems to have been perfectly primed to receive news of Caroline's first comet, back in 1786.

By 1796, Nevil and Caroline were good friends and Caroline had become quite used to receiving praise and encouragement for her work from Maskelyne. A few years later, in 1799, she would even break the habit of a lifetime, leave the cosy security of her family circle and go to stay with the Maskelynes for a few days. She went on 19 August 1799 and stayed until the 30th, ostensibly so that she could copy 'the memorandums from my brother's second volume of Flamsteed's Observations into Dr Maskelyne's volume'. In the event, the trip turned into far more of a holiday than a professional visit, with all sorts of interesting 'amusements' put on for her. She was quite swept away by the attention and wrote affectionately after her return, not only of Dr Maskelyne but of Sophia and their teenage daughter, Margaret, too.

Her short visit with the Maskelynes was a big moment in her life and her consideration of it afterwards accidentally revealed her fears and insecurities, often kept hidden behind a wall of false modesty and exaggerated humility. After her stay with the Maskelynes, presumably following some conversation they had had in that time, Maskelyne sent her some binoculars and a 'night-glass'. Her response to the gift is heartbreaking, revealing feelings that both explained her reticence to mix too much beyond her family circle and the closeness she must have felt to the Maskelynes to let those feelings show. The gift she had just received, she wrote:

> Makes me hope that during the time I had the honour of being in the company of such esteemed friends, I have suffered no loss in their former good opinion of me, which was a circumstance I often feared might have happened; for I have too little knowledge of the rules of society to trust much to my acquitting myself so as to give hope of having made any favourable impressions.[5]

In fact, Caroline had long ago made a favourable impression on Nevil Maskelyne and it would take more than a few slips in etiquette to shake the high regard in which he held her.

Despite her worst fears, she also tended to make a very good impression on women – at least those who had any dealings with the Royal Society and men of science. She was their proof that women could be the intellectual equals of men, and also be polite and modest with it. Even the more gossipy women around the court, whom she tended to despise, thought her sweet. Her fears of how she might come across, which prevented her making more of the society on her doorstep, were entirely unfounded.

In the decade and a half Caroline and Nevil Maskelyne had known one another, each had helped the other see the world a little differently. Maskelyne piled praise and encouragement on Caroline. When responding to the discovery of her second comet, he offered the rather odd, but kindly meant plea that for the 'benefit of terrestrial astronomy' she should not think of flying away with her comet. More concretely, he also spoke up for her comet and offered additional observations of his own, thereby giving it more weight when her announcement was passed on to Sir Joseph Banks. When she wrote with news of another comet in April 1790, he encouraged her even when weather had prevented him from confirming the observation, telling her that her second letter 'gives me fresh spirits as to the certainty of it being a comet'. In the same letter, he told her he had already 'sent intelligence of your discovery to M. Méchain in Paris', despite having not yet seen it himself. At a time when her papers were almost always accompanied by additional words from her brother or another male astronomer just to have them taken seriously, Maskelyne's confidence in her meant a lot.

Caroline, meanwhile, gave Maskelyne more proof that women could work well in science. Just as he was getting to know her and her work, he was also taking the bold step of officially employing his first lady computer, Mary Edwards. He was encouraging his neighbour Margaret Bryan too, subscribing to her book and helping her to get closer to publication. He was encouraging these women to make their way in a male-dominated field; they were helping him, in turn, by being extremely good at what they did and leaving as little scope for criticism as was humanly possible. And, of all these women, Caroline was taking the biggest, boldest steps into that world, yet with all the timidity and poise expected of her sex and station in life.

It is a testament to Maskelyne and his family's kind nature and generosity that they became the family friends with whom Caroline felt most comfortable so that she was even happy to visit. Their back-grounds could not have been more different. Maskelyne came from money, received an expensive education, sailed the world and was adept at making important friends and connections. Caroline, in complete contrast, grew up in poverty expecting to spend her whole life serving her family and rarely left home. Her education was practical, limited only to what would make her useful to others. Her sights were set low and she shunned society, only socialising when it was imposed upon her. And yet they became good friends, and helpful to each other, encouraging and inspiring one another in such a way as to make science, and scientific life, just that little bit better, more complete and more equal for everyone.

1796

16

THE OTHER BROTHER

As the years went by, Caroline was becoming more comfortable with the scientific circles in which her brother moved. For roughly the last fifteen years, the Herschel home had played host to a steady stream of important visitors. Touring aristocrats, men of science, diplomats and friends of the court and their scientific acquaintances all stopped at Observatory House. Although almost always described by those visitors as meek, quiet and shy, Caroline nonetheless made an effort to be present. Increasingly, after all, those visitors had come to see her – the lady astronomer and discoverer of comets – every bit as much as they had come to see William and the telescopes.

Scientific high society was being gradually won over by Caroline, and she, in turn, was slowly finding herself more comfortable with them, although they still could not compare with time spent with her family. The passing visitors were always polite and admiring of her. Those who had by this time become family friends made even more of an effort to put her at ease. Maskelyne was always kind to her, Lalande never less than effusive – when his letters got through, which by 1796 was finally becoming possible again – but nevertheless she was never completely relaxed in their company. She needed her family.

As a child Caroline, with her busy schedule and hours spent on the care and maintenance of her home and family, had rarely had time to make friends. Her world was her family and anything beyond them was an indulgence, entertained only in so far as it made her more useful to her family. The friendships she did manage to foster – the girl with whose family hers shared a house, the other girls in her millinery class – tended to be short-lived. The situation had not been much better in Bath. There her time had been filled with domestic duties once again, and music lessons. She had had to learn a new language, new customs, new cooking. Friends had been a luxury, a diversion from her work, and there had never seemed a good time to learn how to make them or maintain those relationships. Her siblings were her friends. They were always around and had always needed her. For none of her siblings was this truer than for her closest brother, Alexander.

Caroline and Alexander were the middle children. While Dietrich was the baby and Sophia, Jacob and William were all grown up and had moved away, Caroline and Alexander grew up together, sharing a childhood. Together they comforted their mother when their older brothers left under cover of darkness for England. They went to school together. They would have had dance classes together, had their mother been able to find the money at the time. When Caroline came to England it had been largely because Alexander had missed her and worried about having left her alone in Hanover with only their mother and Jacob. He had been her buffer against their worst excesses and without him there, Alexander had worried about his little sister and her future. It was Alexander who suggested to William that she be brought over to live with them, and when she arrived it was Alexander who was the one to follow her to market and keep her safe.

Johann Alexander Herschel was born 13 November 1745; he was five years older than Caroline and seven years younger than William. Like William, he went to school (the same as Caroline) during the day, and before and after took lessons or practised music as taught him by his father. As a child, he showed talent at music but, as Caroline noted, by the age of 11 'he had such an aversion to practising, looking into a book or improving himself in writing' that his parents did not quite know what to do with him. When he was 12 he was sent away to live with their older sister, Sophia, in the nearby town of Coppenbrügge to become an apprentice to her husband, a musician called Johann Heinrich Griesbach. This may have been to help out Sophia and her husband more than for Alexander's benefit, since Griesbach's job as town musician required him to have an apprentice and Sophia had just become a mother for the first time. It may also have been to keep Alexander away from the military band that had employed his father and two brothers and placed them in danger on the battlefield.

Alexander's apprenticeship meant he could continue his training as a musician, and he could also help out his sister with her growing family which, judging by the fond reminiscences of his nephews and niece, he seems to have done kindly and affectionately. He arrived shortly after Sophia's first son, George, was born and remained with the family for six years, in which time Sophia had two more boys (in all, she would have five boys and a girl). Griesbach was, by all accounts, not a kind man, sometimes even violent, and Alexander had a fairly miserable time under him, but he saw out his apprenticeship, only returning to Hanover when it was done.

Alexander arrived back in Hanover just in time for William's visit and the family viewing of the 1764 eclipse in a tub of water in the courtyard of their house. On his return, Alexander found work as a musician, first in a royal regimental band, then at court, although on half salary, since he had to share a single post with another musician.

When their father died in 1767, Alexander supplemented his income by taking on many of his father's old pupils, and when Jacob went to England, Alexander extended his role at court, taking over his brother's position while he was away. His family worried about him being led astray while Jacob was away, as he could sometimes be easily led, but he does not seem to have been as bad as Jacob. Quite the opposite: he spent many evenings quietly at home with his family.

On his free evenings, Alexander would stay at home with his mother and sister and little brother, Dietrich, building things by the fire as the women got on with their various jobs. At this stage he was just dabbling, keeping his mind and his hands busy, but even then, he showed aptitude for mechanical work. He tried his hand at pasteboard tubes, such as you would make a telescope from, and some clockwork. At one point, Caroline remembered him tinkering away trying to make a cuckoo clock that might keep time for a week. At other times, he drew, and he may have made globes like his brother, William, all the time chatting amiably with Caroline, telling her stories about the high society he played for and mixed with – a world she, as yet, knew very little about.

Once Alexander moved to Bath and began finding work as a musician there alongside William, he discovered quickly that his dabbling might be put to good use helping his brother along with a pet project. Soon that interest in mechanical tinkering became more focused and directed towards telescope building, as William went about learning what he would need to build telescopes and turn them on the night sky. As Caroline bemoaned, the house was soon given over to lathes, metallurgy and manure-made mirror moulds. Each sibling gradually fell into their own particular role and specialism within the family team. It soon became apparent that Alexander's talents and interest lay squarely in mechanics and clockwork. Without expecting or wanting any credit for his contribution – he seems to have actively shunned any kind of attention – Alexander worked away, designing and making fine metalwork for William's telescopes. He started as William began to make telescopes and carried out much the same role for the next fifty years.

When William and Caroline moved to Slough in 1782, Alexander was invited to go with them, but chose to stay in Bath. His impending marriage may have had something to do with it (he was married – unhappily, according to Caroline – in 1783). His musical work in Bath may also have been a contributing factor since by this time he had made friends and a home in Bath and had regular work in various venues. He was settled and not looking for a change. He could have gone with William and Caroline, but he chose not to. He could have joined his brothers Jacob and Dietrich in Hanover: they had asked him and tried to arrange work for him. He chose not to go there either. Instead, he stayed in Bath although he always made a point of visiting Slough every year when the Bath season was over, to keep Caroline company while William, Mary and later John went away over the summer. Years later, John would comment on these visits to his brother-in-law in an attempt to explain the character of this odd uncle:

> He never moved away from his own home, except to pay a yearly visit to his brother's [William's] family and then invariably came accompanied by his turning lathe and other implements, and getting himself & them established the moment of his arrival, in the workshop (now H's observatory) scarcely left that apartment during the whole period of his stay … He used to go away after his stated week of visitation had expired having scarcely seen his friends all the time, but declaring himself quite delighted with their society.[1]

More than any other, John's anecdote seemed to sum up Alexander's character. Like Caroline, he was not interested in mixing in society. Instead, he was at his happiest at home with family and, more importantly, with his work. While letters between the siblings suggest that William was heavily dependent on his brother's skills to make his telescope dreams a reality, Alexander, unlike Caroline, did not seek credit for this work. Instead, he seems to have just wanted to be left alone, to be helpful and busy. Perhaps this was why he and Caroline got along so well, their shared desire (and understanding of that desire) to be quietly useful and busy.

Although trained differently and with very different expectations placed upon them, Alexander and Caroline were in many ways very similar. They wished quietly to be useful, felt most comfortable among their families and never asked too much of others. The fuss made by both William and Caroline in Slough and Jacob and Dietrich in Hanover over where Alexander should live after William and Caroline left Bath shows that the family concern went two ways. He felt most comfortable with them, and they, in turn, banded together to try to protect him and keep him safe.

They all worried about leaving Alexander to his own devices in Bath. Similar concern seems to have been expressed when Jacob went over to work for a while with William in England. In both cases, Alexander seems to have managed. He found a wife (after several broken engagements) and seems to have become a notable feature in the Bath music scene. He had a number of regular pupils and played for the theatre and other venues about town. Every summer, when the Bath season ended, he would visit his siblings in Slough and work on their telescopes and other scientific accessories.

Caroline seems to have understood him better than William, both psychologically and linguistically. Although William often made requests relating to astronomy and the tools he thought Alexander could make for him, he did not always understand Alexander's replies. The task of translating Alexander's designs into a language William could understand fell to Caroline. Yet another in a long list of seemingly invisible yet essential jobs she did within the family's scientific enterprise to help them work efficiently and well. 'I do not wunder [*sic*] at your not being able to make anything of it,' Alexander wrote, referring to his very technical description in a previous letter, 'I think if you was [*sic*] to get Carolina to read it over and see what she can do for she is perhaps better acquainted with my roundabout way of describing things'.[2] And Caroline would rise to that challenge and explain to William the meaning contained within the letter from her other brother.

Every summer Alexander would go to stay in Slough; sometimes staying for a few days, sometimes weeks, sometimes longer. William's wife, Mary, may well have found these visits a little difficult, at least to begin with. The Herschels were not a typical family, and Mary was used to her friends and relations in Slough and at court. When William and Mary had been planning to get married, Mary's main sticking point had been the question of where they lived, how they divided their time and where William's family – namely Caroline – fit into the picture. That every summer her home was invaded by yet more of William's strange family, with their limited sociability and obsessive interest in scientific tools and apparatus, must have taken some adjustment. By the 1790s, however, this pattern had become routine. John grew up knowing no different – the summers were when his 'eccentric' Uncle Alexander came to stay and that was that.

Alexander eventually grew too old to continue working as a musician. Staying in Bath, without any family and no work seemed too odd, even for him. So he returned to Hanover, to live with the one Herschel sibling who had remained there his whole life. Dietrich, the youngest, was also a musician. Where the others were interested in mechanics and astronomy, however, he seems to have favoured natural history and moth collecting in particular. Dietrich married his landlord's daughter and remained in his home town raising their son and three daughters. It was to their family home that first Alexander and then Caroline retired in old age. Again, Caroline was wonderfully rude about her sister-in-law, as she had been of Alexander's wife, 'Mrs Smith', and William's wife, Mary Pitt. Describing Dietrich's wife, she wrote that she was 'a short corpulent woman upwards of 60, dressed like a girl of 20 without cap, her brown hair mixed with gray plaited and the temples covered in huge artificial curls I almost shuddered back from her embrace'.[3] One wonders what she could have written about William's wife in those ten years of journal entries that deserved destroying, when so many of her other comments on the other wives were left untouched. Sadly, Alexander would die in Hanover before Caroline arrived.

While, for Alexander, 1796 was just another year, another season playing concerts and giving lessons and another summer spent quietly with his siblings, tinkering away at his lathe, for the rest of the family time was moving forward. John was, if not yet growing up, then certainly coming closer to an age of presentability. In January, just coming up to his fourth birthday, he was taken to meet the queen. Although they lived near the palace, had lots of friends at court, nephews in the queen's band and William and Caroline were technically employees of the royal couple, this was nonetheless a momentous occasion.

On 9 January 1796 John was taken with his mother by Miss Margaret Planta to meet the queen and the princesses. Planta was the princesses' English tutor and companion, she was also the sister of Joseph Planta, librarian at the British Library, fellow of the Royal Society and a friend of the Herschels. At this meeting, much to his mother's delight, Princess Elizabeth presented John with a china cup and saucer. Mary put this away in a safe place as a keepsake to have when he was much older. A few months later, in April, he was taken again and given a small box to 'keep sugar plums in'. This again was put safely away for later, stored with the cup and saucer and a note, where it appears to have remained until John's daughter, or possibly even granddaughter, catalogued it.

The close proximity of the visits to one another suggests that perhaps more visits followed, now that he was old enough to behave appropriately when the occasion required it. Back in Slough, he could run around among the telescopes, watched over by Caroline, his nurse and the workmen, but alongside this playful scientific education John was also being introduced to a new and different way to behave within a higher social class and cultural world.

For William and Caroline, 1796 also marked an important step forward in the establishment of their new observing project. In February, they announced to the world their first catalogue dealing with star brightness, or magnitude. The same month William read his paper, 'On the method of observing the changes that happen to the fixed stars', to the Royal Society to accompany the catalogue. This, he set out, was their new interest; they were studying the brightness of stars in order to spot and study how those stars might have changed over time. He was presenting his catalogue and Caroline had her index, also a contribution to this same project.

Once again, the Herschels were tackling a problem in astronomy that no one had really considered before. So, to begin, William had to explain why it was important, interesting and worth doing. His paper began, 'The earliest observers of the stars have taken notice of their different degrees of brilliancy, and, by way of expressing their ideas to others, have classed them into magnitudes.'

So far so good – early astronomers noticed that stars varied in their brightness and came up with a system of 'magnitudes' to label these from brightest to dimmest. However, he went on to explain, having looked over other catalogues and compared them to the sky, he could find no standard (therefore concluding that it must be an 'imaginary standard') against which the magnitudes were assigned. In other words, no one seemed to agree on which magnitude to assign to which stars. Either that, or a huge number of stars had changed in magnitude. For example, eleven stars in the constellation of Leo alone, he wrote, seemed to have changed magnitude since Flamsteed wrote his cata-logue less than a century before. Since this was unlikely, the conclusion must be that the system of assigning magnitude measurements to stars had, until this point, been at best approximate.

As his paper's title would suggest, William's aim in cataloguing the stars by their brightness had a very distinct purpose: he wanted to be able to trace actual change in brightness in the fixed stars. Caroline's indexing would help him to do this, allowing him to see which of Flamsteed's magnitude measurements to trust, and which to treat with greater caution. She also found new stars which Flamsteed had missed entirely. A second catalogue would follow in June, and another two after that in the following years, suggesting that this was very much at the centre of the Herschels' research at the time. While they would eventually return to cataloguing nebulae and star clusters (their next catalogue on that subject was published in 1802), for now the bright-ness of stars alongside studies of the Sun were their main focus.

Over in France, 1796 offered the hope of change and new starts, too. After a long period of broken communication, some news from France was starting to get through. In April, after a gap of nearly three years, the Herschels received their first letter from their friend Jérôme Lalande. It was a short note, all in French, commiserating the lack of news he had had about William and '*votre aimable Caroline*'. He declared that the 'troubles' in France had not dampened his spirit nor changed his views on his work. But then he, unlike many of his fellow scientific countrymen, had sailed through the revolution relatively unscathed. In 1795, he had even received a promotion, becoming director of the Paris Observatory. In his note to the Herschels, having asked after them both, Lalande introduced the chapter he was sending him, from his book *L'histoire de l'astronomie*, telling them he planned to enrich it by adding news of the Herschels' work.

Lalande produced several works under the title *L'histoire de l'astronomie*. He produced annual accounts of astronomical work for the years 1801 to 1806. In his 1801 volume he mentioned both William's planet discovery and his telescopes several times, although never in very much detail. He also published a bibliography of astronomy with a history of the discipline from 1781 to 1802, which was later used by his student to write a more detailed account of the history of astronomy. The start date for this bibliography, 1781, was in its way a subtle reference to the Herschels and their importance, since that was the year William discovered Uranus. Which chapter of which book he sent in that first letter since the start of the revolution is unclear, but Lalande certainly kept his word, including mention of the Herschels in several of his later works.

For a while it had seemed that although astronomers respected the Herschels, few were quite sure they understood or could see the point of their work. As William and Caroline, helped by the instrument-making skills of Alexander, had toiled away cataloguing and analysing and theorising about the fixed stars, other astronomers continued to concentrate on the solar system. The Herschels were seen as an anomaly, doing their own thing on the periphery while well-established astronomers studied the planets and particularly the way in which they moved. Gradually, though, by the mid-1790s this seemed to be starting to change. Certainly, their work was seen as important enough to feature in another French publication, and not one by such a close family friend as Lalande. In his 1796 book, *Exposition du système du monde*, Laplace wrote admiringly of the importance of the Herschels' nebulae:

Herschel, while observing the nebulae by means of his powerful telescopes, has followed the progress of their condensation, not in a single instance, as such changes would not be sensible to us till after the lapse of centuries, but among the whole collection, as in a vast forest one could follow the development of a tree from the condition of the several individuals found there.

These words from such a well-respected international figure were a significant endorsement of William's work. Not only was he agreeing with William that nebulae were well worth studying, he was also echoing his natural history approach to the subject. Comparing the study of stars within the sky with the study of trees within a forest was exactly right. William was borrowing from natural history and applying that same way of thinking, naming, cataloguing, organising and drawing conclusions to astronomy.

Step by step, friend by friend, book by book, William and Caroline were gradually making themselves and their work known to a larger audience. They had started out as oddball Hanoverian musicians turned self-taught instrument makers and astronomers. By the mid-1790s they were slowly becoming recognised as contributing something important and new to European astronomy. Their names were becoming well known, thanks in large part to the praise they were getting from their growing army of important friends and supporters.

While William and Caroline actively courted this attention, albeit in very different ways, Alexander continued through all of this to work and live in much the same way as he always had. Every summer he would come to Slough, armed with his lathe and other instrument-making tools. He would set himself up in the workshop and quietly tinker away, making detailed brass-work components and clockwork mechanisms for the telescopes and timepieces. The varying astronomical projects his siblings were involved in, as they shifted focus from labelling stars as nebulae, star clusters and double stars to cataloguing their brightness, mostly passed him by. They were, after all, still looking at the stars, and for that they needed essentially the same apparatus.

As for all the attention, he seems happy to have left them to it, hiding away in his workshop and quietly sloping off back to Bath at the end of each summer to teach and play music.

1797

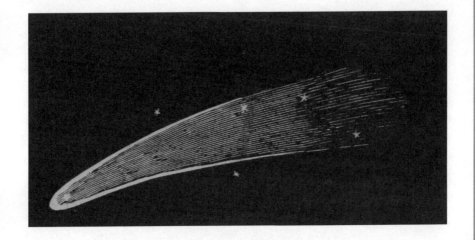

17

NEW BEGINNINGS

William, Alexander and Caroline would always be very close. They shared an upbringing and history as immigrant musicians making their way in Bath society; their shared love of astronomy and instrument making also helped unite them, bringing them closer still. At the same time, in certain ways as they aged they were growing apart. Variations in their personalities and desires were starting to show through.

The differences between Alexander and Caroline were never more starkly apparent than in the year 1797. While Alexander continued to be quiet, busy and useful, Caroline was slowly blossoming into a quite ambitious and persistent lady of science.

William's report of his 40ft reflector a couple of years earlier had carefully praised Caroline's contribution and hidden Alexander from view (although acknowledging that someone had designed and made those components and implying strongly that this person had not been William). Alexander seems to have actively shunned public attention when it came to his instrument-making contributions. He refused to move to Slough, hiding away in the workshops when he came to visit, and seemed not to have wanted credit in print. Caroline, meanwhile, was the exact opposite.

Caroline's brother was not the only one speaking out for her in print. There were now a number of scientific friends she could rely on for support, including important and influential figures such as Lalande, now director of the Paris Observatory, and Maskelyne, the Astronomer Royal. She could also expect encouragement from their lower-key scientific friends, such as the amateur astronomer Alexander Aubert and William Watson, their old friend from Bath. As her list of achievements grew she began to become bolder. With her contributions to William's telescope observing programme and her rising total of comet discoveries all acknowledged, Caroline was starting to expect a little more in terms of recognition from her scientific contemporaries. She was still careful not to overtly demand such attention, but every now and then that facade would slip and she would become more forthright in her language.

In March 1797 Caroline's little nephew John turned 5 which, in the Herschel household, meant he was old enough to be sent away to school. The first school he attended (he went to several) was a local institution run by a Mr Atkins. According to Caroline, he would stay there all week but would be brought home on Sundays to receive extra tuition from private tutors in 'writing, arithmetic, geography &c'. This comment has left several biographers pondering what he might have been studying all week at Mr Akins school if all those subjects were missing. William was, by all accounts, a very academically ambitious father, so it may be that those subjects were covered but John was perhaps not making sufficiently fast progress to satisfy his father.

What little documentation survives from John's school days suggests his progress was fairly impressive, at least by today's standards, but that does not mean it met with William's approval. In the Herschel family archive there remains a short, formal, very neatly written letter home from this school by the 5-year-old John. It reads, 'Dear Mama, I hope you have had a great deal of pleasure in London. We took a walk.' The handwriting is beautiful, the spelling perfect and phrasing surprisingly sophisticated for a 5-year-old. Yet William still seems to have wanted to add to this with private tutoring at home.

In the end, John only stayed with Mr Atkins a year – perhaps because his progress was too slow for William's liking – before moving on to a different school, one run by Mr Bull in Newbury. After a few years there, he went to Eton very briefly and then Dr Gretton's school.

The first move to Mr Atkins, however, was for Caroline the biggest. This was the beginning of the end. John was now gone, he may have come back for holidays and the occasional weekend, but he was no longer a permanent, full-time resident at Observatory House. Without her young nephew scurrying about, the Herschel home felt emptier to Caroline. For most of the week they were now back almost to the way they had been before John was born. They had had time to get to know each other better, and Caroline and William's work had moved on, but still it felt like there was less keeping her at Observatory House than once there had been.

In May, William delivered another paper to the Royal Society. It was his third catalogue of the comparative brightness of stars and it was accompanied by:

An introductory account of an index to Mr Flamsteed's Observations of the fixed stars contained in the second volume of the Historia Coelestis. To which are added, several useful results derived from that index.

The paper began by suggesting that William had originally assumed Flamsteed's catalogue (or, as he called it, 'the British catalogue') to be 'faultless'. He had assumed any stars missing were new additions to the night sky, and similarly, any difference in magnitude between that stated in the catalogue and that which he observed, was down to a change in the star itself. Gradually, however, he notes that he started to doubt his original assumption. Having doubted, he now 'wished it were possible to find some method that might serve to direct us from the stars in the British catalogue, to the original observations which have served as a foundation to it'.

This was, of course, the project Caroline had taken upon herself to carry out and had been working on for the past few years. While Caroline had described it as something she had adopted because she could see its utility and wanted to keep busy, William described it in this paper as his idea assigned to her. It would be a time-consuming and laborious task, he wrote, and he could not see himself ever having the time to carry it out and so 'I recommended it to my sister to undertake the arduous task'. Reassuringly for readers, he then claimed absolute control of the project and the way in which it was carried out: 'At my request, and according to a plan which I laid out, she began the work about 20 months ago, and has lately finished it.' Towards the end of his introductory notes, William explained how, in the course of putting together the index, a number of stars (about 500–600) had been found, observed by Flamsteed but omitted from the catalogue. 'These additional stars,' he went on, 'will make a considerable catalogue, which is already drawn up and nearly finished by Miss Herschel, who is in hopes that it may prove a valuable acquisition to astronomer.'

Caroline was on a roll. Her brother had openly and forcefully promoted her work in his paper. He had even protected it from easy dismissal by including a significant role for himself within the project. That her work came out of his and was endorsed by him gave it considerably more weight than it would have had she claimed to have come up with the project alone. Ten years of getting Caroline's work noticed had taught them that much.

Her year of great moments, however, did not stop there. While her routine of filling the time and keeping busy with work was bearing fruit, her occasional observing was offering its own rewards. That summer, with William, Mary and John away on their annual holiday and Alexander staying for his yearly visit, Caroline got to spend some time on her roof again, observing and seeking out comets. On 14 August she found one. This was her first comet discovery in over a year and a half, and the last had been a rather unsatisfactory find (having, it turned out, been spotted a decade earlier by Méchain). This new comet was to be her eighth discovery. It would also be her last.

At 9.30 on the evening of Monday 14 August 1797, Caroline decided it was dark enough (the nights had started to draw in slightly by mid-August) to get out on the roof and start observing. It did not take her long to spot her comet – according to her journal, she saw it almost 'immediately'. Experience had taught her what she needed to do next. She went to get her brother, Alexander, to ask him to help her with the clock so they might get some detailed figures about its location and movement to pass on to other astronomers. On her way, however, she was held up by visitors, an occupational hazard of living at Observatory House. These gentlemen – Lord Storker and a friend – had come to visit William and his telescopes. They obviously did not know much about him, nor had they made any attempt to make an appointment. If they had, they would have known that William was away, as he was every summer, on his family holiday. Caroline explained to them about William being away and tried to get across the urgency of her own situation. She had found a comet and needed to pinpoint its exact location and announce it as quickly as possible. They seemed slowly to get the message. In the end, she showed them the comet and that seemed to satisfy their astronomical curiosity enough for them to leave.

With the visitors out of the way, Caroline and Alexander got to work quickly, studying and recording the position and movement of the new comet. Then came the problem of making her announcement. Caroline had lost out on priority claims for a couple of her previous comets. There were now more and more comet hunters as it was becoming a popular hobby among the growing leisured classes. This made the urgency of the situation ever more pressing. She needed her announcement to reach the Astronomer Royal and the Royal Society – someone with the authority to accept such an announcement – before anyone else. The post, although more reliable than today, could sometimes take a couple of days. Under the circumstances, she could not risk her announcement being delayed that long, especially if after that time the weather turned, which it frequently did in England, and the Astronomer Royal had to delay confirmation of her discovery until the skies cleared.

Having thought through her options, Caroline decided there was only one thing for it. She would have to saddle a horse and ride the nearly 30-mile journey from Slough to Greenwich to deliver the news herself. In preparation she took a quick nap and then, an hour later, set off. To get some sense of what a significant step this was for her, and what a driven woman she had become, it is worth noting that Caroline did not like to leave home. In the past five years, as she later told Sir Joseph Banks, she had only ever made short 2-mile journeys at a time. She had never ridden this many miles in one go, not even in daylight. This journey was going to take her through London in the very middle of the night.

Caroline's original plan had been to stop in town and deliver a letter about her comet to Sir Joseph Banks on her way through to Greenwich. However, once on her way, she could not bear the thought of adding even a short detour to her already extremely long journey. She knew the Maskelynes would look after her once she reached Greenwich, but she did not know Banks quite so well and did not feel she could impose herself on him in quite the same way. So, instead she rode on to Greenwich to announce her comet.

Maskelyne was very accommodating, as she had known he would be, and encouraged her to rest and worry about sending word to Banks when she was ready and not before. When she was fully rested, possibly a little bit sooner, given her fears about overstaying her welcome, Caroline got back on her horse and rode home again. Three days later, she wrote to Banks with an announcement, or rather:

> Not a letter from an astronomer to the President of the Royal Society announcing a comet, but only a few lines from Caroline Herschel to a friend of her brother's, by way of apology for not sending intelligence of that kind immediately where they are due.[1]

She may have been steadily growing braver, but she knew better than to be too bold in her claims to such a figure as the president of the Royal Society. Nevertheless, Caroline's haste had been well founded. She arrived at Greenwich on the morning of Tuesday 15 August. That evening, Maskelyne received a letter from Stephen Lee announcing the same comet, which he had first seen, like Caroline, on the 14th. Caroline was still at Greenwich when the letter arrived, noting in her observing book, 'I had the pleasure to find that my observations agreed perfectly with Mr Lee's'.[2] Although it was galling that someone else had spotted the comet at the same time as her, it was comforting that, between them, she and Alexander had correctly gauged the information they had recorded of her observations. That her data agreed perfectly with Lee's made it all the more difficult to dismiss, even without William's added observations to support hers.

The comet was also seen in Paris by astronomer and fellow comet hunter, Alexis Bouvard. In the end, it was he and Caroline who shared priority for the comet (Lee was evidently a little too late), and it became known as C/1797 P1 Bouvard-Herschel. Perhaps because of this confused battle for priority, there was no announcement of this comet in the *Philosophical Transactions of the Royal Society*, despite Caroline's very polite letter to the society's president. Not all her comets were announced there, although most were. Perhaps there was too much ambiguity over priority for a quick publication this time, or perhaps Banks had taken Caroline at her word and believed quite genuinely that she was not announcing a comet, but only sharing news with a friend of her brother.

That was Caroline's last comet discovery. She had done everything right. She had found her comet – almost the moment she went out that night to observe – she had got her brother to help her observe, measure and record the details of its position. She had proceeded quite as she was supposed to – she knew this because she had looked at Lee's letter and seen that his information was exactly the same. She had then raced across the London with almost no sleep to ensure she was the first to tell the key figures and to announce its existence. Yet, none of it was enough. The comet was not even announced officially at the Royal Society. Although, of course, a great achievement in itself, it was a little dispiriting to have her comet treated with so little excitement or applause.

Back home, she was feeling less appreciated than in previous years, too. John had gone off to school, leaving her very little to do domestically. Mary now ran the house with a team of servants to help her. It was very difficult for Caroline to find a role within that set-up, now that there was no child to raise, to occupy her time and make her feel useful. Even her independent cataloguing/indexing project was coming to an end. William still needed her as his astronomical assistant for some of his projects, although not all of them any more. All his work on the Sun and 'radiant heat' (or, as we know it, infrared) did not seem to require her help. She was starting to feel as though she might need a change. Independence, in some form or another, was calling.

Despite her repeated claim to all who would listen that she was happy only to serve and be useful to her brother and family, Caroline had for most of her adult life felt a small, mostly abstract, hankering for some form of independence. Family needed always to be nearby, but she did not like to feel she was a burden, or worse, that her position was precarious and could be lost at any minute. She did not strive for independence as any form of defiant ambition – it was more practical than that: she wanted security, and that meant not having her lifestyle and livelihood dependent on the whims of others. She had worried about this when she was 22 years old and had seen her siblings all leave home, her parents age and her father die. She had felt it too when she was 38 years old and William had got married and she had not known where she might fit into his new domestic set-up. All the changes that were happening at home and in her working life made her start to crave that security (as she imagined it) of independence once again. She was now 47 years old.

Independence was attractive. She had toyed with that idea of being financially independent and self-sufficient back in her singing days when she had been offered a job to sing in Birmingham without her brother and had seriously thought about taking it. She had dipped her toes in those waters when, after that, William had helped her set up her own (short-lived) millinery business in Bath whose folding had prevented her joining William on the night he discovered the planet

Uranus. Now, with her pension from the queen, she already had some financial independence. She had the means, and with little to keep her at Observatory House, she now had the will to make that leap again. In October 1797, Caroline left Observatory House to move into her own lodgings nearby, as a boarder in the home of one of her brother's workmen.

Over time Caroline found independent living could be just as precarious as depending on her family to look after her. In one of the places she boarded, her landlord went bankrupt and bailiffs came to take possession of the house and all its contents. Other places she found to be simply too far away from Observatory House to be workable, given her commitment to helping William observe. Eventually she moved to some rooms in Mary's former house in Upton and that seemed to suit her. The house was just a short half-mile walk across fields from Observatory House. In daylight, she would happily make the trip alone and at night there was a local boy she could call upon to accompany her with a lantern across the fields to her brother's home. She stayed in that house for seven years.

No sooner was Caroline settled in her new home (at this point it was still the rooms in the house of one of the workmen) than she received some very exciting news. After much deliberation, the Royal Society's secretary, Joseph Planta, told Caroline and her brother that the society had decided to print Caroline's index as an appendix to Flamsteed's *Atlas Coelestis*. This was huge news. This was her publication, entirely independent of her brother's work. It was a vindication of her years of hard work and dedication to a task that, to many, would have seemed too time-consuming and laborious to even contemplate. She was delighted. She was, in fact, so pleased with herself that she appears almost embarrassed by her reaction, although by now she was old enough and secure enough to put that down to society's expectations rather than any personal flaw.

Caroline was aware that this was a great moment, but she also knew it had only been made possible by the friendships she had cultivated and supporters she had gained over the years. She was grateful to her brother for his words of encouragement and assertions of the work's importance in his last paper. She was also aware that Maskelyne must have had a hand in making this quiet, secret aspiration a reality. 'I have for a long while past felt a desire of expressing my thanks to you,' she wrote to him, on hearing the news that her work would soon be published. She wanted to thank him, she went on, for his interest in 'the little production of my industry' and, more directly, she wished to thank him for 'being the promoter of the printing of the Index to Flamsteed's Observations'. She then very carefully distanced herself from too much gloating by claiming she would have been quite satisfied that her time had been well spent if the work had only been of use to her brother. However:

> Your having thought it worthy of the press has flattered my vanity not a little. You see, Sir, I do own myself to be vain because I would not wish to be singular, and was there ever a woman without vanity? Or a man either? Only with this difference, that among gentleman the commodity is generally stilled ambition.[3]

Fighting talk! The level of trust Caroline must have had in Maskelyne at this point, to have revealed so much about herself and her thoughts on social convention is breathtaking. Caroline had come a long way in the past ten years. She was no longer hiding behind polite protestations of disinterest, at least not to those she had come to truly trust. Instead, she was boldly standing up, declaring her feelings not just about herself and her work, but about all those years of judgement and of hiding from judgement as a woman in a man's world.

Early on in her musical career Caroline had been told off by a well-meaning lady for being her own trumpeter. Her comeback at the time had been to claim she had to be because no one else was going to do it for her, but she had been cautious ever since. She had been very careful never to speak too boldly about her own work, announcing each new discovery instead with a timid desire that another astronomer might take it under their protection, or that news of it might be of interest to other astronomers, or that she wanted only to pass on information for the 'sake of astronomy'. And yet, finally, after several years of praise from others, she allowed herself a little pride, a little vanity of her own. More than that, she allowed herself a little anger that men were allowed that emotion all the time and were even congratulated for it, only terming it 'ambition' instead.

Following her brother's marriage, Caroline destroyed nearly a decade's worth of journal entries. That decade, as we have seen, was the most astronomically productive ten years of her life. In that lost decade of achievement in which Caroline made discoveries and produced work that drew praise from astronomers across Europe, perhaps her diaries were not just filled with bitterness and anger at her brother's marriage. Perhaps, instead, they were filled with vanity and ambition. We will never know for certain, because she destroyed them, perhaps in some way to preserve an image of herself with which she felt happier. But maybe she did not just write bitterly about her sister-in-law in those active and astronomically productive years. Perhaps she wrote of her pride in her work, pride that as a woman she was expected not to express for fear of being labelled vain. Maybe that is why, ten years later, she was happy to start writing again. Secure in the recognition that now she was a celebrated woman of science and she need not worry about those petty double standards any more.

EPILOGUE

aroline Herschel never lived with her brother William and his
family at Observatory House again. She discovered no more
comets. Her active research and publishing life came to its
natural end, although she did carry out one more significant piece of
independent work in the 1820s, after William died.

In 1828, Caroline was awarded the Gold Medal of the Royal
Astronomical Society for her work 'reducing' (a mathematical term
for taking raw data and making it useful) and publishing William's last
nebulae observations. Beyond that, her publishing days were mostly
behind her. Following the pattern of many researchers, before and since,
she moved in her later years from the ground-breaking research of her
youth to a more mature role of mentor, inspiring and encouraging future
generations. For the next twenty-five years she lived in various lodgings
in and around Slough. Never too far from Observatory House, and
always within walking distance so she could continue to assist her brother
as she had before. After William died in 1822, she moved to Hanover.
Alexander had retired there a few years earlier and their younger brother
Dietrich had been there the whole time with his wife and children.
Dietrich was her only remaining sibling (Alexander died in 1821), and
Caroline decided to move to Hanover to be with him after William died.

Despite the distance, Caroline stayed close to her nephew John. They corresponded regularly. She offered advice and encouragement and he kept her updated with his research (continuing the work of William and Caroline) and, in time, with his growing family. Towards the end of her life, John took his eldest son, William, over to visit her.

Thanks to Caroline's help and advice, John could continue his father's work long after William died. He could also bring something new to it. Thanks to his close relationship with his aunt, he learned to see the value not only in the collection of observations but in the organisation of that work, the long, laborious, detailed organisation of that data into a form that would be useful to others. That, as much as her assistance of William, her comets and her index to Flamsteed's catalogue, might be seen as her legacy.

Caroline's influence can be seen elsewhere, both in her family and the role of women in science beyond. John grew up to have an unusually wide circle of scientific female friends. Mary Somerville found in him a sympathetic ear and a helpful editor to her work. Maria Edgeworth was often turned to in John's family as a source of wisdom, whose arguments on science, child-rearing and education were always respected and admired. Had any letters survived (they do not seem to have done), Ada Lovelace, who worked with John's best friend, Charles Babbage, would quite possibly also have seen John as a supportive ally.

John, the 'incurable castle builder', as Babbage called him, was forever falling in love and getting engaged. When John finally married at the age of 37, he chose a wife more impressed by his aunt than himself. Margaret Brodie Herschel cited Caroline Herschel, not John or William, as her scientific hero, and for years after tried hard to cultivate a friendship with her and learn everything that she could from her. Delighted to have married into such an illustrious family, Margaret turned to Caroline throughout her life for advice on how to raise her daughters to follow in her footsteps.

Those daughters, in turn, grew up with access to an education far superior to Caroline's. They learned from an early age to participate in science (one even studied at Cambridge once it began to let women in) just as their great aunt once had; they also learned to revere and celebrate the achievements of their Great-Aunt Caroline.

Beyond her own family, Caroline was celebrated in her own lifetime and for generations to come. In Hanover, visitors came, just as they had to Observatory House, but now they came unambiguously for her – not William, nor the telescopes, but to see Caroline. Alexander von Humboldt visited in 1837, George Biddell Airy (the then Astronomer Royal) visited in 1846. Various royals visited too, as did dignitaries, philosophers, astronomers and mathematicians. So frequent were these visits that Caroline was moved to complain to her nephew that 'two or three evenings in each week are spoilt with company',[1] shortly after arriving in Hanover.

She was given awards from scientific institutions across the world. The Royal Astronomical Society made her and Mary Somerville 'honorary' fellows (so as to get around the problem of electing women as actual fellows). She was made a member of the Royal Irish Academy. The King of Prussia gave her the Gold Medal for Science. As she aged, no longer active in science but still symbolic of what women could achieve, the awards mounted up.[2]

After her death she became an icon, a symbol more than an actual person. She was a comet huntress, proof that women could pursue this area of science with success. When Margaretta Palmer was working on her doctoral thesis about a comet in 1847, she stated outright in her introduction that she had chosen comets because it was an area of astronomy, thanks to Caroline Herschel, in which women had made discoveries. Caroline Herschel's medal was put on display at her grand niece's college at Cambridge to show the young women studying there what they too might achieve.

Caroline Herschel's legacy continues to this day. After John's daughter-in-law published her memoirs in 1876 and then again after his youngest daughter, Constance, published an account of William and Caroline in the 1930s, biographies of this icon of feminine astronomy have abounded. With the advent of the internet and Google doodles, short, heroic biographies of Caroline Herschel have proliferated even

further. Yet, very few show the woman behind these great achievements who was seemingly at odds with the social conventions of her
time. Perhaps now that a more sympathetic story has been told, we
might start to look at her differently. For the sake of women struggling
to be heard and taken seriously in science, then as now, I hope so.

NOTES

Preface

1   Caroline Herschel to Margaret Brodie Herschel (her niece), Hanover, 24 September 1838, British Library Herschel archive – Eg. 3762 f.32–33.

2   The First 'Lady's Comet'

1   Alexander Aubert to Caroline Herschel, 7 August 1786. Reproduced in Constance Lubbock, *The Herschel Chronicle* (Cambridge: Cambridge University Press, 1933), p. 155.

2   Mrs V.D. Broughton (ed.), *C.L.H. Papendiek: Court and Private Life in the Time of Queen Charlotte being the Journals of Mrs Papendiek, Assistant-Keeper of the Wardrobe and Reader to Her Majesty*, 2 vols (London: Bentley & Son, 1887), p. 251.

3   See plate 1.

4   Caroline Herschel to Margaret Brodie Herschel. Reproduced in Lubbock, *The Herschel Chronicle*, p. 157.

3   William and Mary

1   See plate 2.

2   Caroline Herschel to John Herschel, 6 July 1840, British Library Herschel archive – Eg. 3762 f.59.

3   Broughton, *C.L.H. Papendiek*, p. 262.

4   See plate 3.

5   William Herschel to Alexander Herschel, 7 Feb 1788. Reproduced in Lubbock, *The Herschel Chronicle*, p. 178.

6   *Caroline Herschel's Autobiographies*, edited by Michael Hoskin (Cambridge: Science History Publications, 2003), p. 96.

4 Jérôme de Lalande

1 See plate 4.
2 Reproduced and translated in Isabelle Lemonon (translated by Laurent Damesin), 'Chapter 2: Gender and Space in Enlightenment Science: Madame Dupiery's Scientific Work and Network', in Donald Opitz, Staffan Bergwik, Brigitte van Tiggelen (eds), *Domesticity in the Making of Modern Science* (Basingstoke: Palgrave Macmillan, 2016).
3 William Herschel to Jérôme de Lalande, 5 September 1782, Royal Astronomical Society – W1/1 pp. 57–58.
4 Caroline Herschel to M. de Lalande, 12 September 1790, reproduced in Lubbock, *The Herschel Chronicle*, p. 252.
5 William Herschel to M. de Lalande 1788. Reproduced in Lubbock, *The Herschel Chronicle*, p. 198.
6 Caroline Herschel to Nevil Maskelyne, 22 December 1788, reproduced in Lubbock, *The Herschel Chronicle*, p. 245.

5 Astronomy and Engineering

1 See plate 5.
2 England, incidentally, had been run on a similar system, but after the Civil War it was simplified so the first two estates were represented by the House of Lords and the third by the House of Commons.
3 Peter Sabor and Lars E. Troide (eds), *Fanny Burney's Letters and Journals* (Penguin Books, 2001), p. 295.
4 See plate 6.
5 William Herschel to Joseph Banks, 29 August 1789, in Lubbock, *The Herschel Chronicle*, p. 164.
6 William Herschel to Joseph Banks, 21 October 1789, in Lubbock, *The Herschel Chronicle*, p. 165.
7 William Herschel to Joseph Banks, 4 September 1789, in Lubbock, *The Herschel Chronicle*, p. 164.
8 William Herschel, 'Account of the Discovery of a Sixth and Seventh Satellite of the Planet Saturn; with Remarks on the Construction of its Ring, its Atmosphere, its Rotation on an Axis, and its Spheriodical Figure', *Philosophical Transactions of the Royal Society*, 80 (1790).

6 Two More Comets

1 See plate 7.
2 Anyone who has ever seen the comedy television programme *Mock the Week* will be familiar with this line of reasoning.
3 From Sabor and Troide, *Fanny Burney's Letters and Journals*, p. 252.
4 Broughton, *C.L.H. Papendiek*.
5 Caroline Herschel to Alexander Aubert, 18 April 1790. Reproduced in Lubbock, *The Herschel Chronicle*, p. 248.
6 Caroline Herschel to Joseph Banks, 19 April 1790. Reproduced in Lubbock, *The Herschel Chronicle*, p. 249.

7   Joseph Banks to Caroline Herschel, 20 April 1790. Reproduced in Lubbock,
     The Herschel Chronicle, p. 250.
8   Nevil Maskelyne to Caroline Herschel, 22 April 1790. Reproduced in Lubbock,
     The Herschel Chronicle, p. 249.
9   Quotes from these paragraphs all compiled by Michael Hoskin in *The Herschel
     Partnership* (Cambridge: Science History Publications Ltd, 2003), p. 106; this
     quote is from Nevil Maskelyne to William Herschel, 16 January 1790.

7   Friends and Fans
1   *Caroline Herschel's Autobiographies*, p. 42.
2   Caroline Herschel, quoted in Lubbock, *The Herschel Chronicle*, p. 52.
3   Francis Wollaston to William Herschel, summer 1789, Royal Astronomical
     Society, Herschel Archive, RAS MS W.1/13.W.194.

8   Riots
1   Edmund Burke, *Reflections of the Revolution in France* (London: printed for J.
     Dodsley, 1791), p. 118.
2   Letters appended to some editions of Priestley's pamphlet, *An Authentic Account
     of the Dreadful Riots in Birmingham* (Birmingham, August 1791).

9   Order in the Skies
1   William Herschel to Caroline Herschel, 15 August 1802. Reproduced in
     Lubbock, *The Herschel Chronicle*, p. 312.
2   William Herschel, 'Miscellaneous Observations', *Philosophical Transactions of the
     Royal Society*, 82 (1792), p. 23.

10   Births and Deaths
1   Some sources give the date as 9 March.
2   Letter from Paul Adee to William Herschel, dated 7 March 1792, from the
     Herschel-Shorland family's private collection.
3   Quite plausibly this is Miss Lydia Rogers White, who features in Fanny
     Burney's royal court diaries as a well-known London hostess.
4   Mary Wollstonecraft, *Vindications of the Rights of Woman* (London: T.F. Unwin,
     1891), p. 32.
5   Ibid., p. 33.
6   Ibid., p. 34.
7   Ibid., p. 34.
8   F. Anne M.R. Jarvis, 'The Community of German Migrant Musicians in
     London *c.* 1750–*c.* 1850'. Masters degree in local and regional history, University
     of Cambridge, August 2003. Chapter 3: 'The Griesbach Family'. See also
     Appendix 1: 'Memoirs of George Griesbach' (see Maydwell.co.uk).
9   This is the date on his gravestone, though some historians have suggested the
     date was actually February 1793.
10   Found within the Herschel family's private collection, there is a photograph of
     Paul Adee in an envelope labelled 'catalogued by MFH'. MFH stands for Mira F.
     Hardcastle, daughter of John's daughter, Maria Sophia Herschel.

11 Home Life

1   Caroline Herschel, *Biographical Memorandums of my Nephew J. Herschel to the Best of My Recollections*, 27 May 1838. The original is at Harry Ransom Center, University of Texas, and a copy at the British Library, microfilm M.588(4).
2   Caroline Herschel to Margaret Brodie Herschel, 6 September 1833, from the British Library Herschel Archive, Eg.3761 ff.189–190.
3   'An Account of a Discovery of a Comet', in a letter from Miss Caroline Herschel to Joseph Planta, Esq., Secretary of the Royal Society. Read on 7 November 1793 and published in *Philosophical Transactions of the Royal Society*, 84 (1794).
4   William Herschel to Oberamtmann Schroeter, 20 August 1793. Reprinted in Lubbock, *The Herschel Chronicle*, p. 212.
5   Oberamtmann Schroeter to William Herschel, 29 November 1793. Translated from the German in Lubbock, *The Herschel Chronicle*, p. 213.
6   Professor Seyffer to Caroline Herschel in 1793. Reproduced in M.J. Herschel (ed.), *Memoir and Correspondence of Caroline Herschel* (London: Murray, 1876), pp. 92–93. NB: the memoirs give May as a suggested date for the letter; this, however, does not tally with his subsequent remarks about an eclipse, since the eclipse took place in September.
7   From M.J. Herschel, *Memoir and Correspondence of Caroline Herschel*, p. 142.

12 Solar Eclipse

1   Extract from Caroline Herschel's autobiography, as quoted in Lubbock, *The Herschel Chronicle*, p. 50.
2   William Herschel, 'Account of Some Particulars Observed During the Late Eclipse of the Sun', read 9 January 1794 and published in the *Philosophical Transactions of the Royal Society*, 84 (1794).

13 Originality by Stealth

1   See plate 8.
2   Charles Messier, in *Connaissance des Temps* (1800) – finally published in 1998.
3   Quoted in Simon Schaffer's 'Uranus and Herschel's Astronomy', *Journal for the History of Astronomy*, 12 (1981), p. 15.
4   Germaine Greer, *The Whole Woman* (London: Doubleday, 1999).
5   See plate 9.
6   See plate 10.

14 The Indefatigable Assistant

1   William Herschel, 'Description of a Forty-Foot Telescope', *Philosophical Transactions of the Royal Society of London*, 85 (1795), p. 349.
2   Ibid., p. 395.
3   Ibid., p. 396.
4   Ibid., p. 398.
5   1 May 1795, Caroline's Observing Journal, Royal Astronomical Society, Herschel Archive.

6   Caroline Herschel, 'Account of the Discovery of a New Comet in a Letter to Sir Joseph Banks', *Philosophical Transactions of the Royal Society of London*, 84 (1796), p. 131.

7   Ibid., p. 132.

15 Nevil Maskelyne

1   See Dava Sobel, *Longitude: The True Story of a Lone Genius who Solved the Greatest Scientific Problem of his Time* (New York: Walker, 1995), where Maskelyne is very much the 'baddie' to clockmaker John Harrison's hero.

2   Mary Croaken, 'Nevil Maskelyne and his Human Computers', in Rebekah Higgitt (ed.), *Maskelyne: Astronomer Royal* (London: Robert Hale, 2014).

3   From UCL's Legacies of British Slave-Ownership project.

4   See plate 11.

5   M.J. Herschel, *Memoir and Correspondence of Caroline Herschel*, Chapter 3.

16 The Other Brother

1   Anecdotes of John F.W. Herschel as noted down by James Stewart, September 1833, from the Herschel family private archive.

2   Alexander Herschel to William Herschel, 9 May 1785, National Maritime Museum, Herschel Collection.

3   Caroline Herschel to John Herschel, 18 April 1832, British Library, Herschel Archives, Eg. 3761 ff154–157.

17 New Beginnings

1   Caroline Herschel to Joseph Banks, 17 August 1797, Royal Astronomical Society Archive, RAS MSS Herschel CH 1/3.8.

2   Lubbock, *The Herschel Chronicle*, p. 254. Quoting her observing notebooks.

3   Caroline Herschel to Nevil Maskelyne, September 1798, reprinted in Lubbock, *The Herschel Chronicle*, p. 257.

Epilogue

1   Caroline Herschel to John Herschel, 26 December 1822, British Library, Herschel Archive, Eg. 3761 ff11–12.

2   See plate 12.

BIBLIOGRAPHY

Useful archival material for this book was found mainly in the British Library, Herschel Archive, Eg. 3761; the Royal Astronomical Society Herschel Archive, RAS MSS Herschel; the Royal Society Herschel Archive; the Herschel Collection within the Harry Ransom Centre, University of Texas; the Herschel Collection at the National Maritime Museum; and the family's own private library.

In 1912, John Louis Emil Dreyer brought together and published all of William Herschel's papers, those published by the Royal Society and earlier unpublished papers read to the Bath Philosophical Society. Although I have given only the *Philosophical Transactions of the Royal Society* references for the papers (now searchable online), these papers can also be found all together in J.L.E. Dreyer's *Collected Works of William Herschel* (1912).

Books mentioned or directly quoted in this book include:

Broughton, V.D. (ed.), *C.L.H. Papendiek: Court and Private Life in the time of Queen Charlotte, being the journals of Mrs Papendiek, Assistant-Keeper of the Wardrobe and Reader to Her Majesty*, 2 vols (London: Bentley & Son, 1887).

Burke, Edmund, *Reflections of the Revolution in France* (London: printed for J. Dodsley, 1791).

Greer, Germaine, *The Whole Woman* (London: Doubleday, 1999).

Herschel, M.J. (ed.), *Memoir and Correspondence of Caroline Herschel* (London: Murray, 1876).

Higgitt, Rebekah (ed.), *Maskelyne: Astronomer Royal* (London: Robert Hale, 2014).

Hoskin, Michael (ed.), *Caroline Herschel's Autobiographies* (Cambridge: Science History Publications, 2003).

— *The Herschel Partnership* (Cambridge: Science History Publications, 2003).

Jarvis, F. Anne M.R., 'The Community of German Migrant Musicians in London *c.* 1750–*c.* 1850', Masters degree in local and regional history, University of Cambridge, August 2003.

Lemonon, Isabelle (translated by Laurent Damesin), 'Chapter 2: Gender and Space in Enlightenment Science: Madame Dupiery's Scientific Work and Network' in Donald Opitz, Staffan Bergwik and Brigitte van Tiggelen (eds), *Domesticity in the Making of Modern Science* (Basingstoke: Palgrave Macmillan, 2016).

Lubbock, Constance, *The Herschel Chronicle* (Cambridge: Cambridge University Press, 1933).

Priestley, Joseph, *An Authentic Account of the Dreadful Riots in Birmingham* (Birmingham, August 1791).

Sabor, Peter, and Lars E. Troide (ed.), *Fanny Burney's Letters and Journals* (London: Penguin Books, 2001).

Schaffer, Simon, 'Uranus and Herschel's Astronomy', *Journal for the History of Astronomy*, 12 (1981), pp. 11–26.

Sobel, Dava, *Longitude: The True Story of a Lone Genius who Solved the Greatest Scientific Problem of his Time* (New York: Walker, 1995).

Wollstonecraft, Mary, *Vindications of the Rights of Woman* (London: T.F. Unwin, 1891).

Many more works besides this short list were of course used in the research for this book, and may be of interest as further reading. As a starting point to look further into the life of Caroline Herschel and the world in which she lived and worked, I would suggest (besides those offered above) the following titles:

Abir-Am, P.G., and D. Outram, *Uneasy Careers and Intimate Lives: Women in Science, 1789–1979* (New Brunswick, NJ: Rutgers University Press, 1987).

Brock, C., *The Comet Sweeper: Caroline Herschel's Astronomical Ambition* (London: Icon Books, 2007).

Fara, Patricia, *Pandora's Breeches: Women, Science and Power in the Enlightenment* (London: Pimlico, 2004).

Herschel, Caroline, *Catalogue of Stars: Taken from Mr Flamsteed's Observations* (London: Peter Elmsly, 1798).

Holmes, R., *The Age of Wonder* (London: HarperPress 2008).

—*The Romantic Poets and their Circle* (London: National Portrait Gallery, 2005).

Hoskin, Michael, *Caroline Herschel: Priestess of the New Heavens* (Sagamore Beach, MA: Science History Publications, 2013).

Hunter, L., and S. Hutton, *Women, Science and Medicine, 1500–1700: Mothers and Sisters of the Royal Society* (Stroud: Sutton, 1997) – especially Rob Iliffe and Frances Wilmoth's chapter, 'Mrs Flamsteed and Caroline Herschel'.

Ogilvie, M.B., 'Caroline Herschel's Contributions to Science', *Annals of Science*, 32 (1975), pp. 151–53.

Ogilvie, S.C., *A Bitter Living: Women, Markets, and Social Capital in Early Modern Germany* (Oxford: Oxford University Press, 2003).

Schiebinger, L.L., *The Mind Has No Sex?: Women in the Origins of Modern Science* (Boston, MA: Harvard University Press, 1989).

Uglow, Jenny, *The Lunar Men: The Friends Who Made the Future 1730–1810* (London: Faber & Faber, 2002).

Watts, Ruth, *Women in Science: A Social and Cultural History* (Abingdon: Routledge, 2007), p. 196.

Winterburn, Emily, 'Philomaths, Herschel, and the Myth of the Self-Taught Man', *Notes and Records of the Royal Society*, 68 (2014), pp. 207–25.

—'Learned Modesty and the First Lady's Comet: A Commentary on Caroline Herschel' (1787) '"An Account of a New Comet"', *Philosophical Transactions A*, 373.

—'Caroline Herschel: Agency and Self-Presentation', *Notes & Records of the Royal Society*, 69 (2015), pp. 69–83.

Zinsser, Judith, 'Mentors, the Marquise Du Châtelet and Historical Memory', *Notes and Records of the Royal Society*, 61 (2007), pp. 89–108.

ACKNOWLEDGEMENTS

Just as Caroline Herschel relied on her family, friends and professional associates in order to produce her best work, so did I rely on mine to research and write this book. I would like to thank, for example, Maria Blyzinsky, my predecessor as curator of astronomy at the National Maritime Museum in London, for first introducing me to the Herschel collection. Thanks go to Dr Kristen Lippincott and Dr Gloria Clifton for allowing and encouraging me to approach Imperial College with the possibility of using these collections as the basis for a PhD. And I would like to thank Professor Andy Warwick and Professor Rob Iliffe for the gamble they took in taking me on – a part-time student with a full-time job – and their patience as I very slowly worked on my thesis, taking two maternity breaks in the process. Thanks most definitely also go to my agents, Diane Banks and, more recently, Robyn Drury, for having faith in my ability to write and in the project itself; and to Sophie Bradshaw at The History Press for seeing in our proposal the makings of a publishable book. Thanks too to Martin Redfern at Diane Banks Associates and to Chrissy McMorris and the team at The History Press for their work seeing this project through to completion.

There are many archivists and librarians who helped me with my research for this book. The late Peter Hingley at the Royal Astronomical Society was always fantastically helpful and enthusiastic. The Royal Society archivists have always been delightful on my every visit. I would like to give particular thanks to the Herschels themselves, now the Herschel-Shorlands, who very kindly let me stay with them as I worked my way through their family archive in what was possibly the most productive week of my life. I have such fond memories of that week, not only of the treasures I discovered in that archive, but of the kindness of John and Esther Herschel-Shorland and their cups of tea and cosy chats over family history.

I have taken this work to so many conferences over the years that I could not possibly list them all, although I would like to thank everyone who gave me feedback and made this work progressively better. I would, however, like to mention just one conference, the American Astronomical Society Conference in Seattle, and thank Dr Woody Sullivan for making it possible for me to attend *and* be the historical section's keynote speaker. That was such a brilliant trip for so many reasons, partly academic, but also personal, giving me the confidence to throw myself fully back into research after motherhood.

My PhD examiners, Dr William Ashworth and Dr Patricia Fara, were fantastic and very kind. They helped enormously in teaching me how to turn my thesis into a book, as did my reviewer on *Dissertation Review*, Dr Barbara Becker. I would also like to thank Patricia Fara for living up to my slightly star-struck expectations and surpassing them in the tremendous amount of support she has given me, then and since.

I would like to thank my parents, Ange and Mike, for looking after my children in the early years of this project, and all the many pre-school outings they indulged in around Bloomsbury and South Kensington. I would like to thank my in-laws, Marlene and Alan, for all their help looking after my children up in Leeds, picking them up from school and making it fun so that they now complain if they are just coming straight home with me.

For similar reasons, I would like to thank my northern friends and fellow parents – especially Jane Wilson, Jo Weston, Shelley Hollingdrake and Sarah and Ed Conybeare – for all the many times they have stepped in, collected and cared for my children, and for their non-judgemental support and enthusiasm for this project, even when it must have seemed unlikely ever to get off the ground.

I would like to thank my children, Lottie and Sam, for not complaining or disturbing me too much as I disappeared upstairs to write on yet another weekend. I would like to thank you both for being suitably impressed at the idea of your mother as an actual real-life published author. And most of all, I would like to thank Bob, for everything – for being patient and supportive, for your unshakable conviction that I can write, for the beer and for your calmness every time I have panicked over IT.

INDEX

Note: *italicised* page references indicate illustrations